IS CHINA
AN EMPIRE?

IS CHINA
AN EMPIRE?

TOH Han Shih

World Scientific

EW JERSEY · LONDON · SINGAPORE · BEIJING · SHANGHAI · HONG KONG · TAIPEI · CHENNAI · TOKYO

Published by

World Scientific Publishing Co. Pte. Ltd.

5 Toh Tuck Link, Singapore 596224

USA office: 27 Warren Street, Suite 401-402, Hackensack, NJ 07601

UK office: 57 Shelton Street, Covent Garden, London WC2H 9HE

Library of Congress Cataloging-in-Publication Data

Names: Toh, Han Shih, author.

Title: Is China an empire? / Toh Han Shih.

Description: New Jersey : World Scientific, [2016] | Includes bibliographical references.

Identifiers: LCCN 2016028703| ISBN 9789814667418 | ISBN 9789814667425

Subjects: LCSH: China--Foreign economic relations. | China--Foreign relations--21st century. |
China--Economic policy--2000- | China--Politics and government--2002-

Classification: LCC HF1604 .T64 2016 | DDC 337.51--dc23

LC record available at https://lccn.loc.gov/2016028703

British Library Cataloguing-in-Publication Data

A catalogue record for this book is available from the British Library.

Desk Editors: Judy Yeo Jade Li/Dong Lixi

Printed in Singapore

Acknowledgements

I would like to thank Barry Sautman, Paul Hunneyball, Thum Ping Tjin and Diana Choyleva for useful discussions. I would also like to thank *South China Morning Post* for giving me the opportunity and privilege to report on Chinese trade and overseas investments during my stint in Hong Kong. It was during my time as a reporter with Hong Kong's leading English-language newspaper that I was inspired to write this book on such a topic.

Toh Han Shih
April 2016

Contents

ASIA, MIDDLE EAST AND RUSSIA

Chapter 1

Imperialists?

At a function room in a five-star hotel in Hong Kong, I asked Cao Yunde which Chinese state-owned enterprise (SOE) he used to work in. Smiling, he replied that it was not convenient to reveal it. This smacked of the opaque manner in which China was extending its huge influence into Cambodia.

Cao, a Chinese citizen who previously worked for an SOE, was the Chairman of Khmer Resources Investment, a Cambodian state-backed company.

The occasion was a press conference on 17 January 2013, which I attended as a reporter. At that press conference, Cao disclosed his company hoped to list on the Hong Kong Stock Exchange within a few years. At the time of the press conference, Khmer Resources had businesses in media, finance and mostly mining. It had a copper and gold mine in the Siem Reap Province, which was then acquired by a Chinese company, which Cao again refused to name.[1] Khmer Resources' shareholders included Chinese SOEs, Chinese listed companies and Chinese private firms, which Cao also declined to reveal, another sign of the opacity of Chinese investment in Cambodia.

---

[1] Toh Han Shih, *South China Morning Post*, "Cambodian miner Khmer Resources plans to tap Hong Kong market", 18 January 2013.

Although a Chinese national, Cao was an advisor to Chea Sim, the head of the ruling Cambodian People's Party, and held the rank of minister in the Cambodian government.

Cao's rank as advisor to a senior Cambodian leader bears partial similarities to the role of the French Resident General during French colonial rule of Cambodia. On 5 July 1863, King Norodom of Cambodia signed a treaty with France, allowing the French to establish a protectorate over his kingdom, where Cambodian kings would be the nominal rulers but real power lay with the French Resident General in Phnom Penh. The Cambodian king had feared the threat of his larger neighbours, Thailand and Vietnam, and was hoping for French protection. Cao's role is also partly similar to the residents of other European empires. For instance, when Indonesia was under Dutch colonial rule, actual power resided in the Dutch residents and governors, while the local sultans were ceremonial figureheads. Towards the end of the 19th century, the Sultan of Morocco, Moulay Abd el Aziz, was surrounded by British advisors including a military advisor and commander of the royal Moroccan army.[2] Of course, a crucial difference between Cao and the residents and advisors of the European empires is Cao wielded far less power than his earlier European counterparts. Nonetheless, it is safe to assume that Cao's position in Cambodia expanded Chinese influence in the Southeast Asian country.

The US also had advisors in Southeast Asia like the Chinese advisors in Cambodia. During the early 1960s, US President John Kennedy sent thousands of US "advisors" to South Vietnam to counter what the US saw as a Communist threat in Asia. This escalated to hundreds of thousands of US troops fighting a full-blown war against the Communists in Vietnam during the late 1960s under Kennedy's successor, US President Lyndon Johnson. During the Cold War, conventional US thinking saw the Communist bloc as a monolithic menace, with China supporting Communist insurgency in Southeast Asia. In turn, Chinese propaganda during the

---

[2] Frederick Quinn, *The French Overseas Empire*, Praeger, 2001.

Cold War branded the US as imperialists. Is it an ironic reversal now, that China is employing advisors in Cambodia as the French colonial rulers did in the 19th century and the US during the Vietnam War?

Are the Chinese behaving like the very imperialists whom they accused the US of being during the Vietnam War? By deploying advisors like Cao in Cambodia, is China behaving like bygone European empires which had extracted unequal treaties from China? Is the 21st century witnessing a new rivalry between two empires, China and the US?

The competition between China and the US over Cambodia in the 21st century is intense, similar to the European powers' scramble for resources in Africa and Asia from the 17th to 19th centuries. In July 2012, when then US Secretary of State Hillary Clinton visited Cambodia, she said Cambodia should not be "dependent on any one source of funding", an obvious reference to China.[3] Clinton was leading what was then the largest ever US business delegation to Cambodia seeking business opportunities in the Southeast Asian country. The Cambodian leaders did not heed Clinton's advice. In September 2012, Cambodian Prime Minister Hun Sen visited China, where he asked the Chinese government for loans to develop infrastructure in his country.[4] During his visit to China, Hun Sen signed four loan agreements totalling US$420 million.[5]

China values Cambodia's resources, just as the quest for resources, like spices and gold, was a driving force for European nations to first trade and then establish empires in Asia, Africa and Latin America from the 15th to 19th centuries. Cao was explicit about the rivalry of the great powers over Cambodia.

"Cambodia has abundant natural resources, such as gold, silver, iron, lead, zinc, copper, gems, coal, bauxite as well as petroleum. These

---

[3] Scott Stearns, *Voice of America*, "Clinton discusses investment, debt in Cambodia", 13 July 2012.
[4] *Xinhua*, "Roundup, Cambodian PM's visit aims to enhance ties with China", 3 September 2012.
[5] *China Economic Review*, "China grants ASEAN ally loans", 5 September 2012.

resources are paramount in arousing keen interest and intense competition among the world's great powers," Cao said.[6]

Khmer Resources discovered Asia's third largest bauxite mine in Cambodia, which contained more than 800 million tonnes of bauxite reserves with a value of more than US$100 billion, Cao added.

The Chinese infiltration of Cambodian economics and politics has resulted in substantial Chinese influence in the Southeast Asian nation. By 2013, China was the largest investor in Cambodia, having invested US$9.17 billion between 1994 and 2012.[7] Chinese loans to Cambodia stood at US$8 billion to US$9 billion, compared with Cambodia's GDP of US$14 billion in 2012, according to Singapore Foreign Minister K. Shanmugam at a forum in Singapore in November 2013.[8]

In 2013, China was already the biggest or second biggest trading partner of most Southeast Asian nations. By then, Asia was dependent on China for its prosperity and the reality of a China-dominated region was "already here", Shanmugam declared.

It would be an exaggeration to say Chinese advisors like Cao held as much power in Cambodia as the European colonial residents. It would also be off the mark to claim Cambodian Prime Minister Hun Sen was a powerless puppet like the Cambodian kings under French colonial rule. It would be safe to assume Hun Sen had at least as much independence, if not more, than South Vietnamese President Ngo Dinh Diem when there were US advisors in his country in the early 1960s. Nonetheless, Chinese influence in Cambodia is significant.

In return for its generous financing, China has gained sufficient influence over Cambodia to advance China's political interests.

---

[6] Toh Han Shih, *South China Morning Post*, "Cambodian miner Khmer Resources plans to tap Hong Kong market", 18 January 2013.
[7] Heng Pheakday, *East Asia Forum*, "Chinese investment and aid in Cambodia a controversial affair", 16 July 2013.
[8] Rachel Chang, *The Straits Times*, "ST Global Outlook Forum: 'China is already a superpower'", 2 December 2013.

Cambodia's decision to deport 20 ethnic Uyghur asylum seekers to China upon Beijing's request in 2009 is an example of this.[9] In 2012, Cambodia refrained from discussing the South China Sea disputes during the Association of Southeast Asian Nations (ASEAN) Summit, which resulted in the failure by ASEAN foreign ministers to issue a joint communiqué for the first time in ASEAN history.[10] The 10 members of the bloc failed to agree on how to respond to China's claims on parts of the South China Sea, which faced competing claims from ASEAN nations like the Philippines and Vietnam. The Philippines demanded a strongly-worded declaration of ASEAN's concerns, but Cambodia resisted any wording that would embarrass China. For this, the Chinese government thanked Cambodia for its role as chair during the July 2012 summit.[11] US State Secretary Clinton's call for ASEAN unity on the South China Sea dispute failed.

Although the Vietnam War ended in 1975, rivalry between the US and China in Southeast Asia has revived. In 2012, the US administration under President Barack Obama announced a "pivot" to Asia, which included increased US military presence in Asia.

During the Asia-Pacific Economic Cooperation (APEC) summit in Bali on 7 and 8 October 2013, Obama's pivot faltered and China was one-up on the US. Obama cancelled his attendance to deal with the US government shutdown caused by US government debt hitting its ceiling. It was the widely-held view among international media that Obama's no-show at APEC allowed Chinese President Xi Jinping to dominate the summit. Xi took advantage of Obama's absence to promote China's economic agenda among various APEC member states. In Bali, Xi held meetings with the leaders of countries including South Korea, Thailand, Australia and New Zealand, seeking to boost economic relations with these

---

[9] Heng Pheakday, *East Asia Forum*, "Chinese investment and aid in Cambodia a controversial affair", 16 July 2013.

[10] Ibid.

[11] *China Economic Review*, "China grants ASEAN ally loans", 5 September 2012.

nations. The photograph of APEC leaders in Bali was symbolic of China's central role and the marginalisation of the US. In the photograph, Xi took centre stage with his host, Indonesian President Susilo Bambang Yudhoyono, while US Secretary of State John Kerry, who stood in for Obama, was on the fringe in accordance with protocol due to his rank.

At that time, the US and China offered the region competing free trade pacts. At a China-ASEAN summit in Brunei in October 2013, Chinese Premier Li Keqiang expressed Beijing's desire to complete negotiations on a Regional Comprehensive Economic Partnership (RCEP) by 2015. The RCEP talks included ASEAN, China, Australia, India, Japan, New Zealand and South Korea. Meanwhile, Obama was offering his free trade pact, the Trans-Pacific Partnership (TPP). What is worth noting is that in 2013, China was not a member of TPP nor was the US a member of RCEP.

The rivalry between the US and China over Southeast Asia brings to mind the competition between the European empires of days gone by. From the 17th century till 1824, there was tension between the Dutch and British empires in the region encompassing Singapore, Malaysia and Indonesia. Anglo-Dutch rivalry over the spice trade boiled over to what is referred to as the "Amboyna Massacre" on the Indonesian island of Ambon in 1622. Several men, including employees of the British East India Company, were interrogated and tortured by agents of the Dutch East India Company. On 27 February 1623, 10 Englishmen, 10 Japanese and a Portuguese man were executed on the orders of the local Dutch Governor, Herman van Speult.[12]

On 28 January 1819, Stamford Raffles, an employee of the British East India Company and the founder of the British colony of Singapore, was anchored with a fleet of ships off Singapore. A party of locals from Singapore visited Raffles on his ship, and Raffles asked them if the Dutch had any authority over Singapore. After determining that the Dutch did not rule Singapore, Raffles

---

[12] D.K. Bassett, "The 'Amboyna Massacre' of 1623", *Journal of Southeast Asian History*, Volume 1, Number 2, September 1960.

signed a treaty with the local ruler, paving the way for British colonial rule in Singapore. By the early 19th century, the Dutch were too weak to challenge the British. The competing Dutch and British interests reached equilibrium in 1824, when both sides signed a treaty, where the British agreed to withdraw from Sumatra, Indonesia, while the Dutch agreed to quit India and Malaya.[13]

Competition between the US and China has another parallel in the tensions between the British and French over North Africa during the late 19th century, when French lobbyists increased their calls for the French conquest of Morocco.[14] Sultan Moulay Hassan, who ruled Morocco from 1873 to 1894, had run up large debts with the French banks.[15] Like the French banks which lent Morocco money, China, as part of its strategy in extending its global influence, has lent large sums of money through Chinese state banks to Cambodia and other developing countries in Southeast Asia, Africa and Latin America. During the late 19th century, France wanted to enter Morocco but faced possible conflict with Britain.[16] The two imperial powers reached a deal in 1904, where Britain ceded Morocco to France, while France allowed Egypt to come under the British Empire.[17]

The Chinese and US are competing not only in Southeast Asia but also in Africa, just as France, Britain, Belgium and Germany scrambled for markets or resources on the continent in the 19th century. China overtook the US as Africa's biggest trading partner in 2009.

Obama visited Senegal, South Africa and Tanzania in June 2012, on the heels of Xi's visit in March 2012 to Tanzania, South Africa and the Republic of Congo, where the Chinese President signed a series of deals.[18] In a bid to boost US influence

---

[13] Tarling, Nicholas, *Anglo-Dutch Rivalry in the Malay World 1780–1824*, Cambridge University Press/University of Queensland Press, 1962.
[14] Frederick Quinn, *The French Overseas Empire*, Praeger, 2001.
[15] Ibid.
[16] Ibid.
[17] Ibid.
[18] Toh Han Shih, *South China Morning Post*, "Experts differ on China's 'soft power' in Africa", 22 July 2013.

on the continent during his trip, Obama pledged US$7 billion to upgrade Africa's electricity infrastructure. But China's growing financial clout appeared to be holding sway over US influence. Around the time of Obama's visit, several African leaders rushed to China to sign deals worth billions of US dollars.[19]

When Nigerian President Goodluck Jonathan visited Beijing in July 2013, US$1.1 billion of loan deals were signed, including a US$500 million Chinese loan for the construction of four new international airports in Abuja, Lagos, Port Harcourt and Kano.[20] In June 2013, Sierra Leone President Ernest Koromo announced he had signed US$8 billion worth of infrastructure deals during his visit to China.[21]

In July 2011, UK Prime Minister David Cameron visited Africa to persuade African states to opt for the US and UK model of democratic capitalism, instead of the authoritarian state capitalism of China. Cameron was playing the role of a staunch US ally as part of the special relationship between the two English-speaking nations.

China is expanding its economic influence in Lusophone countries that previously belonged to the long-gone Portuguese empire which was the first global European maritime empire. The Lusophone nations in which China is economically active include Portugal, Brazil, Angola and Mozambique.

"If one travels around Angola, you repeatedly encounter signs stating China's role in building various infrastructure products. China's presence, initially discreet, is now felt very prominently. Lusophone Africa is incredibly important to China, driven by China's increasing energy and raw material requirements," said Hugo Williamson, the Managing Director of the Risk Resolution Group, an international risk consultancy.[22]

---

[19] Toh Han Shih, *South China Morning Post*, "African leaders prefer China's hard cash to US overtures", 18 July 2013.
[20] Ibid.
[21] Ibid.
[22] Toh Han Shih, *South China Morning Post*, "China's investment makes big imprint on Portuguese world", 31 January 2011.

China was an extremely important factor in the revival of the Brazilian economy from 2001 to 2010, Antonio Jose Rezende de Castro, the Brazilian Consul General in Hong Kong noted.[23] Since 2009, China has overtaken the US as Brazil's biggest trading partner.

In November 2010, five heads of Lusophone states and Chinese Prime Minister Wen Jiabao attended a meeting in Macau, underlining the importance China placed on Lusophone countries. The state-owned China Development Bank (CDB) pledged nearly US$1.5 billion in loans for Lusophone nations during the conference.[24] In 2011, 1,500 Chinese students were studying or going to Macau to study Portuguese, de Castro said. The students would be employed by the Chinese government in future dealings with Lusophone countries.

China is also making headway in Latin America. From 2001 to 2010, China's trade with Latin America jumped tenfold, making China the continent's second biggest trading partner by 2010 behind only the US.[25] China's acquisitions in Latin America more than tripled from less than US$4 billion in 2009 to more than US$12 billion in 2010, of which more than 90 percent was in the form of resources for export to China.[26]

Can it be said that the US and China are new empires competing for trade, resources and influence around the globe, like European empires in past centuries? Generally, both the Chinese and Americans do not like to see themselves as imperialists.

In China, the current Communist government and the previous Nationalist government encouraged the Chinese to see themselves as victims of imperialism. In the popular Chinese imagination, the "century of humiliation" lasted from the start of the First Opium War in 1839 till the 1949 founding of the People's Republic of China. During the century of humiliation, Chinese forces were

---

[23] Ibid.
[24] Ibid.
[25] Toh Han Shih, *South China Morning Post*, "China ties may be curse in disguise", 26 September 2011.
[26] Ibid.

defeated by the British Empire in the First Opium War, the British and French forces in the Second Opium War, the Japanese empire in late 19th century and finally invaded by Japanese forces between 1937 and 1945. With the founding of the People's Republic of China in 1949, Chairman Mao Zedong announced an end to the century of humiliation, declaring, "Nobody will bully us again." According to Mao's ideology, imperialists are enemies that must be opposed not only in China but around the world in "wars of liberation". In turn, US Cold War propaganda portrayed the Communist insurgency as Red imperialism.

Given the creation of the US with the expulsion of the British forces in 1776, empire is a naughty word for the Americans.

However, British historian Niall Ferguson, in two of his books, *Colossus: The Rise and Fall of the American Empire* and *Empire: How Britain Made the Modern World*, argued that the US is a *de facto* empire, despite its politically incorrect status in American eyes. In his book *Empire: How Britain Made the Modern World*, Ferguson writes, "And just like the British Empire before it, the American Empire unfailingly acts in the name of liberty, even when its own self-interest is manifestly uppermost."

The US has the world's most powerful navy with a global reach, just as the British Empire did in the 19th century. The US is the world's greatest military superpower and the world's biggest economy. The US operates a network of military bases and intelligence outposts around the globe, or alternately, works through its allies' military and intelligence facilities in Australia, New Zealand, Western Europe, Japan, South Korea and other countries. Even though the US normally does not invade or colonise other countries as the British Empire did, it possesses many of the characteristics of the British Empire. Hence, the US in the 20th and 21st centuries is the successor of the British Empire of the 19th century.

China under the emperors could be called an empire, based on linguistic arguments. In the English language, China before the Revolution of 1911 was referred to as an empire and its ruler was described as an emperor, not a king. The Chinese term for its traditional ruler was "huang" 皇, which is of a higher status than the

Chinese word for king, "wang" 王. Thus, it can be argued that the traditional Chinese ruler was an emperor, and by extension, China under dynastic rule was an empire.

The Chinese empire was a land-bound empire, controlling vast tracts of land, but China did not expand across the oceans unlike the French, Spanish, British, Dutch and Portuguese empires. Although Chinese communities have settled in various nations over the centuries, including South Africa, Indonesia, the Philippines and the US, no overseas Chinese empire or colony was created from these Chinese communities.

During the 15th century, Zheng He, a Chinese admiral in the Ming Dynasty navy, undertook seven voyages which traversed Southeast Asia, India, the Middle East and Africa. Zheng He's first voyage took place from 1405 to 1407, when he visited Malacca, Vietnam, Indonesia, Sri Lanka and India. The Portuguese made their first long-distance sea voyage later in 1419, when they reached the island of Madeira in the Atlantic Ocean.[27] Zheng He visited Malacca a century before the Portuguese captured it in 1511. The ships in Zheng He's expeditions dwarfed contemporary European ships and carried hundreds of well-armed soldiers. The presence of such a vast armada of huge ships carrying heavily-armed troops might have been intimidating for the kingdoms he visited, but these Chinese fleets never permanently conquered or colonised any place unlike the European maritime powers. Chinese officials like to point to Admiral Zheng He's voyages as an example of how China was not in the business of grabbing assets around the world, in implicit criticism of European imperialism.

While the sea voyages of Admiral Zheng He were but a fleeting phase in China's history, European nations embarked on a sustained maritime expansion from the 15th century, culminating in the establishment of European empires across the globe.

Portugal established the first European maritime empire in the 15th century, when it launched the first European long-distance sea

---

[27] A.J.R. Russell-Wood, *The Portuguese Empire 1415–1808: A World on the Move*, The Johns Hopkins University Press, 1998.

exploration and established outposts in Africa. Subsequently, Spain became another major maritime power in the 15th century, when it conquered Mexico and parts of Latin America as well as the Philippines. In the 18th century, France and Britain fought over North America and India, with Britain emerging triumphant. Britain was the undisputed master in the 19th century, ruling a global empire "upon which the sun never sets", as the well-known phrase goes. The Dutch had their empire in Indonesia, while the French had their empire in Indochina and North Africa, but British supremacy was unchallenged in the 19th century. The might of the British Empire rested upon its Royal Navy, by far the most powerful navy in the world in the 19th century. At the end of the Second World War, the US became the world's greatest superpower, challenged only by a hostile Soviet Union during the Cold War. Since the breakup of the Soviet Union in the early 1990s, the US, which commands the world's most powerful navy, was left standing as the lone superpower.

Like the European empires, the Chinese empire tried to expand through warfare and conquest. Throughout its history, the Chinese empire has attacked its neighbours with varying degrees of success and failure, such as the Mongols to the north and Vietnam to its south. As early as 111 BC, China, which was then ruled by Emperor Wu of the Han dynasty, accomplished its first successful conquest of Vietnam. During the 2nd century BC, Emperor Wu also sent various military expeditions into Mongolia, where they fought several battles with the nomadic horse-riding tribes called the Xiongnu. However, China has never deployed its navies to annex nations beyond its shores, which differentiates the ancient Chinese empire from the European maritime empires.

The Mongol empire, which successfully conquered many countries by land and unsuccessfully tried to invade some countries by sea, should not be identified with the Chinese empire. Rather, China was part of the Mongol empire in the 13th and 14th centuries. In 1276, the Chinese Emperor Zhao Xian of the southern Song Dynasty surrendered to the Mongol invaders, ceding control of the whole of China to the Mongols. In 1287, the Pagan kingdom of Burma fell to an invading army from China, which was not a Chinese army but a

Mongolian one. In the late 13th century, Kublai Khan, the ruler of China, launched armadas from China that invaded Japan and Indonesia, but failed. Again, it was a Mongol ruler, not a Han Chinese emperor, who launched the naval invasions.

The Chinese empire reached its greatest extent in history during the Qing Dynasty between 1644 and 1912. However, the Qing rulers were not Chinese but Manchus, a horse-riding tribe originating in northeast China that conquered the rest of China. During the 18th century, a Qing emperor, Qian Long, unsuccessfully tried to invade Burma and Vietnam.

Hence, it can be argued that when China was ruled by Han emperors, not foreign ones such as the Mongols and Manchus, the Chinese empire was often not very successful in conquering huge swathes of land and never conquered territories by sea. In various periods, Chinese emperors accepted tribute from other nations which they deemed as vassals, including Cambodia, Myanmar, Vietnam, Korea and Malacca. But the Chinese emperor did not directly control these countries.

Despite ruling over the greatest extent of territory in Chinese imperial history, the Qing Empire lacked the hunger for trade which drove European maritime powers like England, Spain, Portugal and Holland. In 1793, during British Ambassador Lord Macartney's trip to China seeking an expansion in trade with the Celestial Empire, Qing Emperor Qian Long rebuffed him with a letter that stated, "We possess all things. I set no value on objects strange or ingenious, and have no use for your country's manufactures."

Emperor Qian Long's refusal to open China to trade with Britain led to his empire's decline in terms of technology, military power and innovation, while Britain powered ahead with its industrial revolution. That was a key factor in the defeat of the Chinese empire in the First Opium War from 1839 to 1842, during the reign of Qian Long's grandson Dao Guang.

Today's China is no longer the self-sufficient empire largely shut off from international trade that it was during Qian Long's reign. China has a massive hunger for resources to feed its huge and booming economy, whether it is oil, iron ore, copper or food.

Chinese SOEs have been buying resources or acquiring resource-producing assets such as oil in Africa, farms in Australia and coal in Indonesia. China's drive for resources around the globe is similar to that of European empires.

China in the 21st century is getting more assertive at sea. China's creation of an Air Defence Identification Zone in November 2013 has generated fears of Chinese maritime ambitions among the Americans, South Koreans and Japanese. China declared that all foreign aircraft passing through that zone must notify and maintain contact with the Chinese authorities. The zone covered an area of sea off its east coast including the Japanese-controlled Senkaku Islands. These islands, called Diaoyudao by China, formed a tense flashpoint between China and Japan in 2013. In 2015, China reclaimed land to build a series of artificial islands in disputed waters in the South China Sea, which rattled Southeast Asian countries like the Philippines. Disputes over territory in the South China Sea had increased calls by many Asian nations in the region for US military presence in the region, US Defense Secretary Ash Carter noted on 1 November 2015.

Given China's increasing global economic influence and military assertiveness abroad, is China emerging as a *de facto* empire in the 21st century? Could the 21st century witness increasing rivalry between China and the US? How will relations between the two countries evolve in the 21st century?

Chapter 2

China's Global Economic Expansion

China in the 21st century bears partial similarities to the British Empire in the 19th century in certain respects.

At first glance, this may be hard to imagine. In the 19th century, Britannia ruled the waves, and as the saying goes, "the sun never sets on the British Empire" by virtue of its vast global reach. The British imposed their institutions in places like India, Hong Kong, Singapore and South Africa. If the natives did not like it, British warships could be summoned to conduct gunboat diplomacy. A possible gut reaction among some people might be, how could China be similar to the British Empire, which defeated the Chinese in two Opium Wars in the 19th century?

At least for the foreseeable future, Chinese armed forces in the 21st century cannot match the global reach and military supremacy of the Royal Navy in the 19th century. Although China is the most populous country, the geographical extent of China is limited, compared to the global span of the British Empire in the 19th century. China cannot and does not impose its institutions on the world. Chinese officials like to stress China will not force its will or institutions on other countries, having been a victim of imperialism in the past.

Nonetheless, China in the 21st century shares similarities with 19th century Britain in some important respects; in international trade, investment and infrastructure projects, especially railways.

China's predominance as the world's biggest trading power in the 21st century mirrors that of the British Empire in the 19th century. Historically, there has been a strong link between empire and trade. Trade was an important part of the Roman Empire, facilitated by its network of highways. The Mongol Empire of the 13th and 14th centuries established international trade on a level that probably had not been seen since the Roman Empire.[28] The Mongol Empire, the second largest empire in history behind the British Empire, established a land-based trading network spanning thousands of miles connecting Europe with China and Mongolia. From the 16th to 18th centuries, the Spanish empire ran a lucrative trade where silver was shipped from mines in South America to Spain, and goods were shipped between China and the Philippines and Mexico, when the latter two were part of the Spanish empire. Trade motivated the European maritime empires including the Portuguese, Spanish, British and Dutch to first explore lands beyond the oceans, which was followed by colonisation and empire.

Britain was the leading trading nation in the 19th century,[29] buying cotton from the US, wool from Australia, copper from Chile and wine from Portugal.[30] The US emerged as both the mightiest military power and pre-eminent trading power after World War II, as it spearheaded the creation of post-war global trade and financial architecture.[31] At the same time, the UK began to dismantle its empire.[32]

Following in the footsteps of the British Empire in the 19th century and the US in the 20th century, China has become the world's biggest trading nation in the 21st century. In 2013, China surpassed the US to become the world's biggest trading nation. US trade totalled US$3.82 trillion in 2013, according to the US Commerce Department. This was surpassed by the China Customs' report that

---

[28]Craughwell, Thomas, *The Rise and Fall of the Second Largest Empire in History: How Genghis Khan's Mongols Almost Conquered the World*, Fair Winds Press, 2010.
[29]*Bloomberg*, "China eclipses US as biggest trading nation", 13 February 2013.
[30]Hobsbawm, Eric, *Industry and Empire: The Birth of the Industrial Revolution*, The New Press, 1999.
[31]*Bloomberg*, "China eclipses US as biggest trading nation", 11 February 2013.
[32]Ibid.

put the value of Chinese trade at US$4.16 trillion in 2013. At a conference in Beijing in 2013, Chinese Foreign Minister Wang Yi said China was the biggest trading partner of 128 countries.

When Chinese paramount leader Deng Xiaoping launched reforms and opened the Chinese economy in 1978, the value of China's trade stood at US$20.6 billion. China ranked 32 among all nations and Chinese trade accounted for less than one percent of global trade.[33] In 2010, China's trade exceeded US$3 trillion, 143 times the level seen in 1978.[34] In 2011, China accounted for 10.4 percent and 9.1 percent of global exports and imports respectively, making it the world's largest commodity exporter and second largest commodity importer.[35] The value of China's trade rose nearly 40 times from US$111.68 billion in 1989 to US$4.16 trillion in 2013, according to official Chinese data.

China's exports since the late 20th century were largely driven by its manufacturing prowess, which created enormous demand for imports of commodities such as oil, natural gas and iron ore. China's thirst for oil to fuel its massive economy drove the country to surpass the US as the world's largest net oil importer in September 2013.[36] In 2012, China imported fuels and mining products worth US$533 billion, making it the second largest importer of these commodities in the world, according to the World Trade Organization (WTO). So great was the Chinese steel industry's demand for iron ore, that China imported 70 percent of its iron ore and accounted for the vast majority of global iron ore imports in 2014, according to the Metallurgical Mines' Association of China and KPMG.

The rise of British trade in the 19th century and the rise of Chinese trade in the 21st century have both been driven by industrialisation. Britain was the first country to industrialise in the movement called the Industrial Revolution. In the latter half of the

---

[33] Li Xiaojun, "China as a trading superpower" in Nicholas Kitchen (editor), "China's Geoeconomic Stratecy", *LSE IDEAS Special Report*, 2012.
[34] Ibid.
[35] Ibid.
[36] *Associated Press*, "China overtakes US to become world's biggest oil importer", 10 October 2013.

20th century and early in the 21st century, China was and is regarded as the workshop of the world, producing much of the world's clothes, shoes, toys and electronic goods. In 2012, China was the world's largest exporter of textiles, accounting for 33 percent of world exports, and the world's largest exporter of clothing, accounting for 38 percent of world exports, according to WTO. China is the world's biggest shoe producer, producing 7 billion shoes, accounting for 58 percent of global production in 2009.[37] In 2010, 80 percent of the world's toys were made in China, according to Euromonitor International. China's manufacturing production soared 107.9 percent from 2005 to 2010, according to the same organisation.

Not only is the country regarded as the world's factory, a region within China, the Pearl River Delta, in the southern Province of Guangdong, is popularly termed "the world's factory". Hong Kong industrialists played a major role in the delta's industrialisation, as they set up factories in the Pearl River Delta which is conveniently located within a few hours' drive from Hong Kong. With Hong Kong capital and expertise, the Pearl River Delta became the world's leading producer of light industrial goods, exporting products like clothes, shoes and toys through the ports of Shenzhen and Hong Kong to the rest of the world. In 2003, factories in the Pearl River Delta, many owned by Hong Kong businesses, accounted for 98 percent of China's export of watches, 73 percent of China's toy exports, 82 percent of China's shoe exports, one-third of China's clothing exports and 90 percent of China's exports of telephone sets.[38]

The Industrial Revolution caused Britain's share of global manufacturing to leap from 1.9 percent in 1750 to 22.9 percent in 1880.[39] Throughout most of the 19th century, Britain commanded the highest share of world manufacturing, until overtaken by the

---

[37] *IBIS World Industry Report*, "Global Footwear Manufacturing", 4 May 2010.

[38] Ip, Saimond, "Hong Kong and Pearl River Delta: the Road Ahead", *ACCA Annual Conference*, March 2003.

[39] Kennedy, Paul, *The Rise and Fall of the Great Powers*, Vintage, 1989.

US around 1900.[40] At that time, Britain accounted for 40 percent of the world's trade in manufactured goods.[41] Britain sucked in vast amounts of raw material and foodstuffs, while sending out vast amounts of textiles, iron products and other manufactured goods.[42] Around 1860, Britain produced 53 percent of the world's iron and consumed nearly half the world's cotton.[43]

The industrialisation of Britain in the 19th century and the industrialisation of China in the late 20th century accelerated the growth of their Gross Domestic Product (GDP). Britain's GDP rose from US$8.2 billion in 1830, when it had the third highest GDP in Europe, to US$16 billion in 1860, when it had the highest GDP in the world. And its GDP reached US$29.4 billion in 1890, when it maintained its top spot.[44] Britain's GDP per capita more than doubled from US$346 in 1830 to US$785 in 1890, in 1960 US dollars and prices, the highest in the world throughout that period.[45]

Similarly, China's GDP grew by leaps and bounds from US$296.15 billion in 1976, when its leader Mao Zedong died, to US$488.22 billion in 1992. It further expanded to reach US$1.2 trillion in 2000 and US$9.18 trillion in 2013. China's accelerating GDP was catching up with the slower growing GDP of the US which stood at US$15.68 trillion in 2013. In 2010, China overtook Japan as the world's second largest economy behind the US, a position Japan held for more than 40 years.

However, China's per capita GDP lags far behind the US and other developed countries even in 2012. China's per capita GDP in 2012 was US$6,091, well below the US per capita GDP of US$51,749 and the UK per capita GDP of US$39,503, according to the World Bank.

Economists disagree on when China will overtake the US to become the world's largest economy, but many agree this will happen in a matter of decades.

---

[40] Ibid.
[41] Ibid.
[42] Ibid.
[43] Ibid.
[44] Ibid.
[45] Ibid.

Robert Fogel, in his paper in *Foreign Policy* on 4 January 2010, forecasted that in 2040, China's GDP would reach US$123 trillion, triple the world's GDP in 2000. Fogel euphorically predicted by 2040 China's per capita GDP would hit US$85,000, more than double the forecast per capita GDP of the European Union (EU).

Although China will not overtake the US in per capita GDP by 2040, China will command 40 percent of the world's GDP by then, bigger than the US share of 14 percent and the EU share of 5 percent in 2010, Fogel predicted.

Even if we optimistically assume China has an annual GDP growth rate of 10 percent till 2040, this means China's GDP will reach US$93 trillion in 2040. This is short of Fogel's optimistic projection of US$123 trillion but a huge number nonetheless. Assuming an average US annual GDP growth rate of 2% from 2009 to 2040, which is roughly the historical US economic growth rate, US GDP will be approximately US$30 trillion in 2040. Based on these assumptions, China's GDP will be triple US GDP in 2040, in line with Fogel's forecast.

Another similarity between 19th century Britain and 21st century China is the fundamental change brought about by the industrialisation of both economies.

During the years approaching 2010, the Chinese government undertook a policy to raise factory workers' wages with the aim of driving low-cost, labour-intensive factories out of China to other countries where wages were lower, such as Cambodia and Bangladesh. In the years leading up to 2010, the Chinese government shifted its focus from producing huge quantities of cheap textiles, which were labour-intensive, to high-speed railway, which was capital-intensive. In late 2008, China launched a 4 trillion yuan (US$649 billion) stimulus package to counter the global financial crisis that flared up at that time. A major component of this stimulus package was the railway. Since China's first high-speed railway, the Beijing-Tianjin high-speed railway, started operation on 1 August 2008, China has embarked on a costly and ambitious programme of building thousands of kilometres of high-speed railway across the country. The Chinese government was estimated to have spent 4 trillion yuan on high-speed railway between 2011 and 2015, as reported by the *China Securities Journal*. By the end of 2013, China had the world's longest high-speed rail network at over 12,000 kilometres, accounting for most of the world's high-speed railway, according to Chinese state media.

Britain, during the Industrial Revolution of the 19th century, had undergone a similar transition.

The mechanised production of cotton marked the first phase of Britain's Industrial Revolution from 1780 to 1840, as related in *Industry and Empire: The Birth of the Industrial Revolution*, a book written by the late British Marxist historian Eric Hobsbawm. In the first half of the 19th century, cotton products accounted for half of all British exports, and textiles made Britain the world's factory. Armed with cheap textiles, British exports penetrated markets around the world.[46] During this period, cotton contributed more to Britain's accumulation of capital than any other industry, and the growth of Britain's chemical and engineering industries owned much to the cotton industry, according to Hobsbawm. Britain's predominance in textile exports in the first phase of its industrial revolution is reflected in China's position as the top manufacturer and exporter of clothing, textiles and other light industrial goods in the first phase of liberalisation and industrialisation reform.

By the mid-19th century, Britain's textile industry had matured, and the second phase of Britain's Industrial Revolution began, namely the rail industry, as Hobsbawm's book *Industry and Empire: The Birth of the Industrial Revolution* relates. The revolution in transportation in the form of railway and steamship opened new markets and expanded existing markets for Britain's exports. With the building of railways, originally a British technological innovation, around the world, vast new areas of the world became accessible.[47] Railway turned the British, hitherto a sea power, into a land and sea power.[48]

"Advancing cheap credit, building cheap transport, they drew a growing mass of producers in the Americas, Asia and Africa into their web," wrote John Darwin in his book *Unfinished Empire*.

---

[46]Darwin, John, *Unfinished Empire*, Allen Lane, 2012.
[47]Ibid.
[48]Ibid.

The progress of Britain's rail industry encountered bumps along the way. A speculative bubble, named the Railway Mania, arose in Britain in the 1840s, when railway shares rose to dizzying heights and then crashed, causing many British families to lose their savings. Yet Britain's titanic railway construction was the key to taking the country's industrialisation to a more mature phase, argued Hobsbawm in *Industry and Empire: The Birth of the Industrial Revolution*. "From the point of view of the entire British economy, they were, by accident rather than design, an admirable solution to the crisis of the first phase of British capitalism. Such a vast economic stimulus, coming at the very moment when the British economy was passing through its most catastrophic slump of the century [1841–1842], could hardly have been better timed."

This is similar to the Chinese government's 4 trillion yuan stimulus to counter the global financial crisis in late 2008, which staved off the worst effects of the global financial crisis for the Chinese economy.

Between 1830 and 1850, some 6 thousand miles of railway were laid in Britain at a cost of £240 million, an enormous sum of money in those days.[49] The capital cost per mile of rail in Britain was the world's most expensive during the 19th century, five times higher than in the US and seven times as high as in Sweden.[50] Many of the railways built in Britain made little economic sense, yielding modest profits or losing money.[51]

"Their sheer size dwarfed the most gigantic public works of the past," wrote Hobsbawm in *Industry and Empire: The Birth of the Industrial Revolution*.

This mirrors the complaints against the huge costs of high-speed rail in Hong Kong and mainland China. In 2010, Weng Zhensong, a Professor at the Economic and Planning Research Institute of the Ministry of Railways, warned that some rail projects in China were

---

[49] Hobsbawm, Eric, *Industry and Empire: The Birth of the Industrial Revolution*, The New Press, 1999.
[50] Ibid.
[51] Ibid.

having financing problems.[52] Economists such as those at Lombard Street Research, a UK economic think tank, have expressed fears that China's heavy spending on railway would incur huge debt, which would have negative consequences for its economy.

Uneconomical as it was, railways provided a long-lasting stimulus to the capital goods industries of Britain.[53] The huge expenditure required for Britain rail's construction transformed its capital markets, which offered financial products such as railway bonds.[54] The Railway Mania of the 1840s produced the stock exchanges of Manchester, Liverpool and Glasgow.[55]

Britain's rail boom resulted in the export of British capital. The improved sophistication of Britain's capital markets facilitated the mobilisation of large amounts of capital to fund massive projects and overseas investments.[56] Britain's booming textile industry and exports had accumulated much surplus capital that was seeking returns from investment.[57] Britain's rail construction spurred the growth of its heavy industries like steel and coal, which further accumulated capital.[58] The most obvious outlet then available for such surplus capital was investment abroad, and Britain was probably a net capital exporter at the end of the 19th century.[59] By 1870, £700 million of British capital was invested in other countries.[60] British capital was invested in overseas projects such as South American mines.[61]

Financed by exported British capital, Britain was responsible for a rail construction boom in Europe, the US and other parts of the world in the latter half of the 19th century, much of it supported by

---

[52] Toh Han Shih, *South China Morning Post*, "Rail woes persist despite spending", 29 January 2010.

[53] Hobsbawm, Eric, *Industry and Empire: The Birth of the Industrial Revolution*, The New Press, 1999.

[54] Ibid.

[55] Ibid.

[56] Ibid.

[57] Ibid.

[58] Ibid.

[59] Ibid.

[60] Ibid.

[61] Ibid.

British equipment and contractors.[62] From the 1840s to the 1880s, worldwide rail construction grew at an increasingly massive rate, with 100,000 miles of railway laid in continental Europe, 106,000 miles of track laid in the US and 20,000 miles in the rest of the world.[63] This rail build-out transformed countries like Germany and the US into major industrial economies and boosted international trade.[64]

Like 19th century Britain, China's industrialisation and massive railway development spurred the meteoric rise of Chinese foreign investment.

China's overseas direct investment (ODI) has grown tremendously since 2000, when its ODI was only US$1 billion, according to official Chinese data. From 2000 to 2008, China's ODI grew at a compound average growth rate of roughly 60 percent annually, according to the Chinese Ministry of Commerce. By 2014, China's ODI jumped to US$140 billion, according to that ministry. By the end of 2012, the stock of Chinese ODI had soared to US$531. 94 billion, the thirteenth largest in the world.[65] In 2012, China became the third largest source of ODI in the world.[66] By then, over 16,000 Chinese companies had created nearly 220,000 subsidiaries or other corporate structures in 179 countries or regions in the world.[67]

In 2012, China's ODI was 31 percent less than foreign direct investment (FDI) into China, according to official Chinese statistics. In 2014, China became a net capital exporter for the first time, with its ODI exceeding FDI into the country. Chinese ODI reached US$140 billion in 2014, more than the FDI of US$120 billion, according to the Chinese Ministry of Commerce. A Capital, a Sino-European investment firm, predicted that between 2013 and 2016, China would invest US$800 billion overseas.

A big chunk of overseas Chinese investments has gone into rail projects around the world, mirroring Britain's railway boom in the

---

[62] Ibid.
[63] Ibid.
[64] Ibid.
[65] *Asia Pacific Foundation of Canada* report, "China goes global 2013", November 2013.
[66] Ibid.
[67] Ibid.

19ᵗʰ century. Two Chinese SOEs, China Railway Group (CRG) and China Railway Construction Corp (CRCC) have become the world's biggest rail construction firms, laying thousands of kilometres of railway in Africa, the Middle East and Latin America. In 2013, the combined revenue of these two Chinese rail construction firms exceeded the 1 trillion yuan (US$162 billion) mark for the first time.

On 10 February 2009, CRCC signed a 6.65 billion Saudi riyal (US$1.77 billion) contract with the Saudi government to build an 18 kilometre light rail in the Muslim holy City of Mecca to transport Muslim pilgrims during the annual Haj pilgrimage.[68] As a sign of its importance, the agreement was penned in the presence of Chinese President Hu Jintao and Saudi King Abdullah bin Abdulaziz Al Saud. The Mecca light rail started operation in November 2010.

In August 2009, CRG announced it had won a US$7.5 billion contract to build a 471.5 km railway in Venezuela. On 9 January 2014, CRCC announced it had won a US$1.45 billion contract to build railway in Sudan.

During his visit to China in December 2013, UK Prime Minister David Cameron said Britain welcomed Chinese investment in the HS2 high-speed railway linking London to Birmingham, estimated to cost at least 40.6 billion pounds. History has come full circle for Britain, a pioneer in railway development and the first nation to build railways around the world.

Apart from railways, China is building other types of infrastructure around the world, including dams, ports, electric power facilities and roads. The value of international contracts won by Chinese firms in 2009 was 10 times more than 2000, according to the China International Contractors Association. By the end of September 2010, the cumulative total of international contracts won by Chinese firms was US$642 billion, according to the association.

China is providing billions of dollars of debt financing to African nations in state-supported deals where Chinese state-owned companies built infrastructure like railroads in return for African resources

---

[68]Toh Han Shih, *South China Morning Post*, "CRCC limits Mecca rail losses to 1.38b yuan", 24 January 2011.

like oil and metals to be shipped to resource-hungry China.[69] China's infrastructure investment in Africa in 2007 was more than the G8 countries combined, according to the Public Private Infrastructure Advisory Facility of the World Bank.

Angola is one of the African nations that have seen extensive Chinese-built infrastructure projects. In January 2010, Angola hosted Africa's flagship football tournament, the Africa Cup of Nations. In preparation for the games, China's Shanghai Urban Construction Group was awarded a U$600 million contract to build four 40,000-seat stadiums in four Angolan cities, namely Benguela, Cabinda, Luanda and Lubango.[70]

On 8 July 2013, China Harbour Engineering, a subsidiary of China Communications Construction, a Chinese state-owned infrastructure construction company, signed a US$700 million contract to build an airport in Khartoum, the capital of Sudan, with financing from the Export-Import (Exim) Bank of China.[71] In 2013, Sierra Leone President Ernest Koromo signed US$8 billion worth of infrastructure deals during his visit to China.[72]

Chinese infrastructure projects have also made inroads into Southeast Asia. For many years up till 2013, China was the biggest investor in Myanmar, Thurane Aung, a speaker at the Myanmar Urban Development Conference in Yangon that year noted.[73]

"China is the only country willing to invest massive amounts of money in infrastructure in Myanmar," said Nicholas You, Chairman of the Steering Committee of the World Urban Campaign, a UN initiative to improve the quality of the world's cities. "Chinese

---

[69] Toh Han Shih, *South China Morning Post*, "China's massive rail building mirrors Britain's push", 2 January 2010.

[70] Toh Han Shih, *South China Morning Post*, "China's investment makes big imprint on Portuguese world", Toh Han Shih, 31 January 2011.

[71] Toh Han Shih, *South China Morning Post*, "African leaders prefer China's hard cash to US overtures", 18 July 2013.

[72] Ibid.

[73] Toh Han Shih, *South China Morning Post*, "China to remain influential in Myanmar even as Western firms arrive", 13 May 2013.

companies will continue to make long-term investments in Myanmese infrastructure. They have the money."[74]

In Latin America, there has been a huge and rapid increase in Chinese dam projects.[75]

"China's involvement in hydropower development in Latin America has grown significantly since 2010. It's fair to say that Chinese dam-building companies are targeting the Latin American market," said Grace Mang, China Programme Director at International Rivers, a green non-governmental organisation (NGO) in the US.[76]

Prior to 2010, there were two reported Chinese hydropower projects in Latin America, Mang said. In January 2014, there were 22, of which three were completed, seven under construction and 12 on the drawing board, according to International Rivers.

As of the end of 2013, the three completed Chinese dams were in Belize and Ecuador with a total installed capacity of 47 megawatts (MW) and costing more than US$30 million. The seven being built in Latin America as of the end of 2013 had a total installed capacity of 2,087 MW and cost more than US$2.53 billion. The 12 hydropower projects being proposed as of the end of 2013 had a total installed capacity of 5,069 MW, and their total budget exceeded US$12.25 billion, according to International Rivers.

In 2013, Mexican President Enrique Pena Nieto announced a transport and communications infrastructure investment programme running from 2013 to 2018, under which the Mexican government would allocate US$300 billion for the construction of highways, railway, ports, airports and telecommunications infrastructure. Shortly thereafter, in January 2014, it was reported that Mexico was offering Chinese companies a share of the US$300 billion of infrastructure projects.[77]

---

[74] Ibid.

[75] Toh Han Shih, *South China Morning Post*, "Chinese dam builders rush to Latin America", 6 January 2014.

[76] Ibid.

[77] Toh Han Shih, *South China Morning Post*, "Mexico offers China US$300b in infrastructure deals", 11 September 2013.

"Mexico requires large investments in infrastructure, such as oil platforms, trains, ports, bridges and highways. China has premier quality in infrastructure and time-to-market delivery," said Fernando Moreno, Managing Director of Banco Interacciones, Mexico's largest infrastructure financing bank.[78]

Even the US is looking to China to build and invest in its infrastructure. A US Chamber of Commerce report in 2013 said the US faced a massive US$8 trillion infrastructure investment bill, and is courting Chinese investors to help foot such a huge bill.

"The US is poised to undertake the most significant expansion and modernisation of its infrastructure since the 1950s. The pressing need for capital to modernise US infrastructure is creating substantial new opportunities for Chinese investors," said the chamber in its report.

At a minimum, more than US$8 trillion of investment would be needed for transportation, energy and water infrastructure in the US until 2030, the chamber estimated. "In reality, a much higher amount of investment will likely be necessary. With a large and growing pool of capital, China is well positioned to participate in US infrastructure."

Chinese investment in the US soared from an annual average of less than US$1 billion before 2008 to over US$14 billion in 2013, according to the Rhodium Group, a US consultancy that studied Chinese investments in the US.

The rise of Chinese infrastructure construction companies to the top of the world stage has taken place within a decade. In 2012, *The Economist* ranked three Chinese state-owned firms as the world's three largest construction firms by revenue — China State Construction and Engineering, CRCC and CRG in descending order. Another Chinese state-owned company, China Communications Construction Corporation, China's biggest port builder, was ranked the world's fifth largest construction firm by *The Economist* in 2012. These four Chinese companies had total revenue of US$255.3 billion in 2012, more than the total revenue of the five non-Chinese construction

---

[78]Ibid.

firms in the top 10 list. In contrast, no Chinese company made it to *The Economist's* list of the world's 10 biggest construction firms in 2003. China's massive build-up of infrastructure at home and around the world was not without problems.

In 2010, CRCC announced it had suffered a net loss of 1.36 billion yuan in the third quarter of that year because of the Mecca light rail project. The loss was attributed to delays and cost overruns in the project. Another reason was political. A top Chinese leader, possibly at the cabinet level, had insisted to CRCC management that the light rail should be completed in time for the Muslim Haj pilgrimage in late 2010, resulting in increased costs, said a source acquainted with the project. China had a vested interest in maintaining good ties with Saudi Arabia, a major oil supplier to China. The project was taken off CRCC, which is listed on the Shanghai and Hong Kong stock exchanges, and transferred to its state-owned parent of the same name.

China's aggressive quest to rapidly roll out its high-speed railway came at a deadly price. On 23 July 2011, two high-speed trains collided near the city of Wenzhou in Zhejiang Province, China, killing 40 people and injuring at least 192 others. Commenting on the accident, the *People's Daily*, a leading Chinese newspaper often seen to be acting as the state's mouthpiece, said China did not need GDP growth smeared with blood.

In 2013, Li Changjin, then Chairman of CRG, admitted work had stalled on the US$7.5 billion Venezuelan railway that his company was building because the Venezuelan government had run out of money to pay for the project.[79] At that time, the Venezuelan government owed the Chinese company US$400 to US$500 million, he noted.

The problems encountered by Britain on its journey to become the world's rail power in the 19th century did not stop Britain from becoming the dominant military and economic power in that era. Naysayers may declare disaster for Chinese infrastructure

---

[79] Toh Han Shih, *South China Morning Post*, "China Railway project in Venezuela hits snag", 11 April 2013.

projects, citing the loss of life, massive debts and problems in overseas projects. However, as with Britain, such woes will not derail the rise of China as an economic superpower in the 21st century.

It may be asked, how could 21st century China be comparable with the 19th century British Empire just because they share similarities in trade and railway construction? It may be argued that even if China is the world's biggest trading nation and on its way to becoming the world's biggest economy, the Middle Kingdom lacks an essential ingredient of empire — military supremacy. After all, China in the 21st century is far from being the dominant military power that Britain was in the 19th century and the US since the end of World War II, and many analysts expect that it will remain the case for at least several decades.

Although China is not the military top dog, its ability to both build thousands of miles of railway and provide the billions of dollars needed to finance them is a killer combination that gives it geopolitical power far greater than simply trade and financial muscle. China's ability to build extensive infrastructure while providing vast amounts of easy financing for these projects gives the country enormous influence internationally, noted John Garver, Emeritus Professor at the Georgia Institute of Technology, US. Few countries, possibly no other country, can match China's ability to both build infrastructure and provide the huge financing for them, Garver explained at a seminar, "The Political Economy of China's Maritime Silk Road Initiative and South Asia", in Shanghai in November 2015. Although US, European and Japanese companies have large transportation and infrastructure companies, the US, Japan and European countries cannot match the massive amounts of Chinese money that fund infrastructure projects around the world, he pointed out. The US, Japanese and European banks are mostly not state-owned unlike their Chinese counterparts, and their shareholders would not normally allow them to give away billions of dollars of loans on easy terms. China's offer to fund costly infrastructure projects with generous financing makes it difficult for even poor countries to refuse such an offer.

Nonetheless, China is an example of a nation which need not be a military power to be an economic power. For years before it was overtaken by China in 2009, Germany was the world's biggest exporter. But Germany, restricted by the US, Britain and other victors in the Second World War, has not been allowed to become a military power in efforts to prevent the resurrection of the Nazi empire.

The rise of Germany and Japan as major trading nations since their defeat in the Second World War was partly due to the protection provided by the US which had defeated them in that war. Under Pax Americana established at the end of the Second World War, the US, as the dominant military power, provided the military umbrella that enabled much of the world, at least in the non-Communist bloc, to trade freely and securely. Similarly, the Royal Navy ensured Pax Britannica in the 19th century, which protected trade within the British Empire.

It makes sense that trade is secured by the military might of an empire. Under the Roman Empire, the Roman army maintained the security of trade along Roman highways. For the Mongol empire in the 13th and 14th centuries, Mongol horsemen and trading posts protected traders across the Eurasian steppes between Europe and China. At the height of the Spanish empire during the 16th and 17th centuries, Spanish warships escorted galleons carrying silver and gold from South America to Spain, protecting them from the English and other marauders.

Will China in the 21st century be like Germany and Japan, economic superpowers without military clout? Or will China be a full-fledged empire which will increasingly challenge the US on the world stage? To be able to better answer these questions, let us turn to Africa, a continent which has known imperialism all too well.

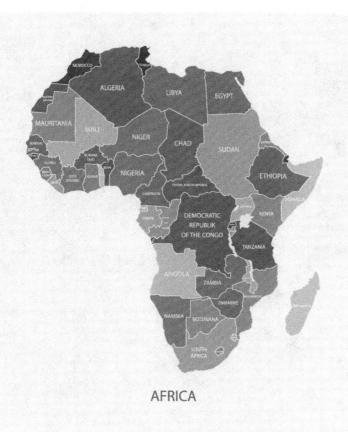

AFRICA

Chapter 3

China and Africa

3.1 Historical ties

The Chinese and Europeans have been familiar with Africa for centuries.

One of the earliest Chinese references to Africa is in a work titled *Youyang Zazu*, written by a Chinese scholar, Duan Chengshi, in the 9th century, which mentioned a land called Po-pa-li in modern Somalia on the east coast of Africa.[80]

The ancient Greeks and Romans had much intercourse with North Africa including Egypt through trade, settlement and military conquest. Both Chinese and Europeans launched major sea voyages to sub-Saharan Africa in the same century, the 15th century.

Of the seven voyages undertaken by the Chinese eunuch admiral Zheng He, the fourth, fifth, sixth and seventh voyages reached Mogadishu, the capital of modern Somalia, between 1413 and 1433.

Archaeologists have found Chinese porcelain made during the Tang Dynasty (618–907) in Kenyan villages, believed to have been brought over by Zheng He's fleet on their voyages during the 15th century.[81] On Lamu Island, off the Kenyan coast, local oral tradition

---

[80] Li Anshan, *A History of Overseas Chinese in Africa to 1911*, Diasporic Africa Press, 2012.
[81] *People's Daily*, "Children of the master voyager?", 3 November 2006.

maintains shipwrecked Chinese sailors, possibly part of Zheng He's fleet, washed up on the island. A young woman of Lamu Island, Mwamaka Sharifu, claimed to be a descendant of Chinese sailors who travelled with Zheng He.[82] Whether these claims of descent from Chinese sailors are true or not, the Chinese did not create colonies in Africa, unlike the Europeans.

The Portuguese were the first Europeans to create settlements in sub-Saharan Africa. Under Henry the Navigator, the Portuguese duke who was a pioneer in the age of European exploration, a Portuguese expedition reached Cape Blanco in Mauritania in West Africa in 1441. From 1482 to 1484, a voyage led by a Portuguese explorer, Diogo Cão, discovered Gabon, Congo and Angola.[83] The first European to reach the Cape of Good Hope on the southern tip of Africa was the Portuguese explorer Bartolomeu Dias in 1488. The discovery of the Cape of Good Hope opened a new European sea passage to China, India and Southeast Asia, which became an alternative route to the ancient land-based Silk Route. The discovery of the Cape of Good Hope paved the way for the European colonisation of Asia.

From the 15th to the 19th centuries, European occupation of Africa was confined to coastal areas for seaborne trade. In Angola, the Portuguese founded the Angolan capital of Luanda in 1575, which developed into a fort and then a city. By the end of the 16th century, the Portuguese controlled the coastal regions of Angola.

The most notorious items carried on European ships in the African trade were slaves. The transatlantic slave trade took place between the 16th and 19th century.

The Portuguese were the first to engage in the transatlantic slave trade, where slaves were transported on ships from Africa to the Americas. Others followed suit, including the British, French, Spanish, Dutch and Americans. In 1807, the British abolished the slave trade, followed by the Swedish in 1813, then the French and Dutch in 1814. In 1808, the British Royal Navy started to enforce the ban on the slave trade. America abolished slavery within its borders at the end of the American civil war in 1865.

---

[82] *China Daily*, "Is this young Kenyan Chinese descendant?", 11 July 2005.
[83] A.J.R. Russell-Wood, *The Portuguese Empire, 1415–1808: A World on the Move*, The Johns Hopkins University Press, 1998.

European occupation of Africa expanded greatly in the late 19th century. As late as the 1870s, European powers controlled only 10 percent of the African continent, all in coastal regions. By 1914, all of Africa except Ethiopia and Liberia were under European control. The French colonised more than 12 African nations, including Mauritania, Senegal, Ivory Coast and Mali in West Africa, Gabon, Congo-Brazzaville, Chad and Central African Republic in equatorial Africa, and Madagascar and Djibouti in east Africa. African states that were formerly part of the Italian empire include Ethiopia and Eritrea. African nations that were part of the German empire included Namibia, Togo and Rwanda. African states that once belonged to the British Empire included South Africa, Zimbabwe, Zambia, Kenya, Nigeria, Gambia and Sierra Leone. In Zimbabwe, colonialism began in the 1880s, when white colonists with Cecil Rhodes' British South Africa Company sought mining concessions there. Zimbabwe's former name was Rhodesia, as it was named after Rhodes. Lusophone African states that used to belong to the Portuguese empire included Angola, Mozambique and Guinea Bissau. The Democratic Republic of Congo, Rwanda and Burundi belonged to Belgium at one time or another. Even the Spanish had African colonies such as Equatorial Guinea.

The industrial revolution in Europe was a major driver of the European expansion into the heart of Africa. The industrial revolution of Europe enabled railway and roads to be built into the interior of Africa, and also created demand for African resources, which in turn spurred exploration and mining in the Dark Continent's interior. Likewise, China's industrial revolution is driving China's current economic expansion into Africa in its quest for resources and markets to sell Chinese manufactured goods to.

Commercial greed and territorial ambition fuelled rivalry among the European powers in "the Scramble for Africa". This culminated in Africa's partition at the Berlin Conference of 1884 and 1885, where the European powers struck an agreement on the rules of the game by which they would carve up Africa while minimising conflict among themselves. However, the Berlin Conference failed to prevent conflicts from breaking out between the European powers. Anglo-German rivalry spilled into war between German and British forces in east Africa during World War I.

After World War II, all African states gained independence from their European colonial masters, hastened by the "Winds of Change" speech made by British Prime Minister Harold Macmillan on 3 February 1960 in South Africa. His speech supported African nationalism and hinted that the British government would grant independence to most British African colonies, which occurred in the next few years. By 1960, most French African colonies were independent. During the 1970s, Portuguese colonies in Africa, such as Mozambique and Angola, gained independence.

Decolonisation in Africa was often affected by competition between the superpowers, the US and the Soviet Union. The Democratic Republic of Congo was an example of the African theatre of rivalry between the US and the Soviet Union during the Cold War. In 1965, a local army officer, Joseph-Desire Mobutu Sese Seko took power as President of Congo. Despite overseeing a one-party state with a notorious reputation for corruption, he received strong support from the US, which waned after the end of the Cold War in 1989. During the Cold War, the Soviet Union and China both supported the African drive against white-minority rule in various African states, in line with Communist ideology.[84] However, since the early 1960s, rivalry between the Chinese and the Russians in the Third World grew increasingly intense.[85]

During the 1960s, China offered economic, technical and military support to African countries and liberation movements in an effort to encourage wars of national liberation against African forces allied to the US and the Soviet Union.[86] During the Chinese Cultural Revolution in the 1960s, Chinese propaganda posters were created which featured heroic fighters in wars of liberation dressed like Chinese Red Guards, except the fighters were African.

In the early 1960s, the Soviet Union made efforts to gain influence in Africa, notably in Zaïre, Ghana, Guinea and Mali, but were

---

[84]Colin Legum, "The Soviet Union, China and the West in Southern Africa", *Foreign Affairs*, July 1976.

[85]Ibid.

[86]D.J. Muekalia, "Africa and China's strategic partnership", *African Security Review*, 13(1), pages 5–11, 2004.

clumsy in their dealings.[87] By 1973, Moscow had few worthwhile connections in black Africa, other than tiny Somalia and unstable Congo-Brazzaville.[88]

The Chinese, on the other hand, did better than the Russians in Africa, notably after their Cultural Revolution.[89] By avoiding blatant bids for political domination and tailoring their programmes to meet the particular requests of the Africans, China imparted a sense of both generosity and disinterest to its role which widened the Chinese sphere of influence in the continent.[90]

The Chinese had two particular successes.[91] The first was the expansion of China's friendship with Tanzania, fostered by the building of the Tazara Railway to Zambia. The Chinese government sponsored the construction of the 1,860 km Tazara Railway from the Tanzanian port of Dar es Salaam to the town of Kapiri Mposhi in Zambia, which was built between 1970 and 1975. China's second success was in winning the confidence of the major liberation movements in southern Africa to a greater extent than the Russians, despite Moscow's military and economic aid. With the exception of the African National Congress of South Africa, all the major liberation movements appeared to have found it easier to work with the Chinese than the Russians.[92] This was notably the case with the Front for the Liberation of Mozambique (FRELIMO), the Zimbabwe African National Union (ZANU) of Rhodesia, and SWAPO of Namibia.[93]

The Angolan War of Independence from1961 to 1974 provided an arena for the triangular rivalry among the Soviet Union, China and the US. The Soviet Union supported the Popular Movement for the Liberation of Angola (MPLA), which fought against the National Liberation Front of Angola, which was supported by

---

[87] Ibid.
[88] Ibid.
[89] Ibid.
[90] Ibid.
[91] Ibid.
[92] Ibid.
[93] Ibid.

the US, China and the government of Joseph-Desire Mobutu of the Democratic Republic of Congo, then called Zaire.

3.2 Sino-African ties after China's reform

China's economic reforms since the 1980s radically transformed economic relations between China and Africa. Since 2001, China's economic ties with Africa have expanded enormously. The rise of China as the world's factory in the 21st century created an enormous appetite for African resources as well as China's desire to sell its manufactured goods in Africa's markets. This is similar to the European quest for resources and markets that drove European colonisation of most of Africa in the late 19th century.

"African leaders have to realise we Africans are in a unique position we never enjoyed before," said Buddy Buruku, Policy Advisor at the African Centre for Economic Transformation, a policy institute based in Ghana.[94]

"Africa has an abundance of resources that China does not have much of. So Africa is the girl China has to court. There is a power we have as Africans we are not exercising. Realising that will make for a better [relationship] over time," she said.

In 2012, crude oil accounted for 70 percent of African exports to China, while raw materials made up another 15 percent and African manufactured goods only 8 percent.[95] As of 2014, one African country alone, Angola, competed with Saudi Arabia as the biggest oil exporter to China.

"China's desire to gain access to resources is well known, but almost equally important is its desire to tap Africa's billion-strong markets, which are consumers of cheap Chinese products," noted a report by Tom Cargill for Chatham House, a London think tank.

China's trade with Africa has made enormous strides, leaping from US$10.8 billion in 2001 to US$166.3 billion in 2011, according

---

[94]Toh Han Shih, *South China Morning Post*, "'Not everyone's a winner' in Africa's ties with China", 31 July 2012.
[95]Tom Cargill, *Chatham House Report*, "Our common strategic interests: Africa's role in the post-G8 World", June 2010.

to the Chinese Ministry of Commerce. In 2009, China overtook the US as Africa's biggest trading partner. In 2013, Sino-African trade surpassed US$200 billion, while China's investment in Africa rose 44 percent, Chinese President Xi Jinping told Senegalese President Macky Sall during the latter's visit to China in February 2014.

China has greatly expanded its presence in Africa, Richard di Bona, who runs a Hong Kong transport consultancy, noted. "Flying into Mauritius, it is not unusual to see large numbers of Chinese workers."[96]

By 2011, there were an estimated one million Chinese in Africa involved in a wide range of activities, including trading, investing, building, labouring and running micro-businesses, estimated the World Bank. Various studies and eyewitness accounts have described armies of Chinese workers living in military-style enclosed quarters, served with Chinese food and rarely mixing with locals, while working on the many Chinese-financed infrastructure projects throughout Africa.

China's financing investments in Africa rose from less than US$1 billion per annum before 2004 to US$7 billion in 2006 and US$4.5 billion in 2007, according to the World Bank.

A common model of Chinese investment in Africa is for Chinese companies to build infrastructure financed by Chinese banks, in return for African resources. The Chinese government finances infrastructure projects in Africa through loans by Chinese state banks like China Exim Bank, which requires at least half of all procurements to come from Chinese companies.[97] These loans were often repaid by oil or mining concessions, under an arrangement known as the Angolan model. By March 2006, China had become the biggest player in Angola's reconstruction after the end of its civil war in 2002.[98]

---

[96]Toh Han Shih, South China Morning Post, "Boom for contractors despite quality concerns", 13 July 2011.
[97]Toh Han Shih, South China Morning Post, "Chinese loans go a long way in Africa", 20 July 2009.
[98]Ibid.

Chinese infrastructure projects can be found in other African countries. The 18th African Union Summit was held in January 2012 at the Chinese-built African Union Conference Centre in Addis Ababa, Ethiopia. China paid for the US$200 million centre.[99]

An example of a Chinese infrastructure-for-resources deal in Africa is a deal struck by China Communications Construction. The Chinese state-owned infrastructure company announced in December 2011 that it signed a US$3 billion contract with African Minerals, a mining company headquartered in London, to build a port and railway in Sierra Leone to transport iron ore from the Tonkolili mine. The contract covers the second and third phases of the Tonkolili iron ore project, one of the most significant in West Africa.

Chinese construction firms have been able to win overseas contracts because they offer lower prices, backed by financial support from Chinese state banks — such as China Exim Bank — which offer loans on generous terms, claimed an international engineering executive who declined to be named.[100] The China International Contractors Association estimated that the value of Chinese construction projects in Africa jumped more than tenfold from US$1.81 billion in 2002 to US$19.75 billion in 2008.

Although there is disagreement on whether China is Africa's top investor, analysts agree on China's role as a major economic player on the continent.[101] There are different estimates of Chinese investments in Africa, but they point to a huge amount of Chinese financing of the continent.

Mergermarket, an international provider of data on mergers and acquisitions, ranked China first in investment in Africa in 2011 with a total of US$3.44 billion and at US$2.5 billion in 2012. However, UN data put China only fourth on the list for 2011, behind the United States, France and Malaysia.

---

[99]Toh Han Shih, *South China Morning Post*, "China treads lightly to improve image in Africa", 28 January 2012.

[100]Toh Han Shih, *South China Morning Post*, "Boom for contractors despite quality concerns", 13 July 2011.

[101]Toh Han Shih, *South China Morning Post*, "Rubbery numbers still add up to big role in Africa", 29 March 2013.

China's cumulative investment in Africa totalled US$40 billion in 2012, including US$14.7 billion of direct investment. And there are more than 2,000 Chinese-invested firms in Africa, Chinese Deputy Commerce Minister Gao Hucheng noted.

The Chinese government and Chinese state-owned banks are estimated to provide US$1 trillion of financing to Africa from 2013 to 2025, Zhao Changhui, the Chief Country Risk Analyst at China Exim Bank claimed.[102] China Exim Bank, a leading lender to overseas Chinese projects, will account for 70 to 80 percent of that US$1 trillion, which would include direct investments, soft loans and commercial loans, Zhao said.[103] China Exim Bank was looking to participate in infrastructure projects in Africa, including transnational highways, railways and airports, Zhao added. He estimated it would cost US$500 billion to build a continental rail network. China Exim Bank replied that Zhao's statements were his own views and did not represent the bank.

The Chinese and Australians are the leading dealmakers in Africa as of 2013, Anthony Desir, a Partner of Strategic African Mineral Investment Fund, an African resource consultancy, noted.[104] Desir estimated that the cumulative Chinese investment in sub-Saharan Africa totalled US$220 billion as of the first quarter of 2013.

Dane Chamorro, Asia Pacific Director of British consultancy Control Risks, said, "Even if China was not No. 1, the fact remains that for 2003 to 2013, it ranked near the top and has been willing to make investments in infrastructure in countries like the Democratic Republic of Congo that have trouble attracting investment."

A lack of transparency remained a big problem in getting exact figures for Chinese and non-Chinese investment in Africa, Lizzie Parsons, a senior advisor at British NGO Global Witness explained.[105]

---

[102]Toh Han Shih, *South China Morning Post*, "China to provide Africa with US$1tr financing", 18 November 2013.

[103]Ibid.

[104]Toh Han Shih, *South China Morning Post*, "Rubbery numbers still add up to big role in Africa", 29 March 2013.

[105]Ibid.

Chinese financing has brought benefits to Africa. It was partly thanks to Chinese investment that Africa registered 5.8 percent economic growth in 2007, its highest ever up till then, a World Bank report said.

After lifting millions out of poverty at home, China is helping to bring Africans out of poverty. The United Nations Development Programme had worked with China to reduce poverty in Africa at the Africa-China Poverty Reduction and Development Conference in November 2010 in Addis Ababa, Ethiopia.

"We are all drawn to an exchange of ideas with China because of the magnitude of its success in reducing poverty over the past three decades," said UNDP administrator Helen Clark at the conference.

China lifted more than 600 million of its people out of poverty between 1981 and 2005, according to the World Bank. In 1981, 84 percent of China's population was below the poverty line of US$1.25 a day, but that figure fell to 16 percent in 2005.

The extreme poverty rate in sub-Saharan Africa in the late 1990s was more than 58 percent, noted Clark, a former New Zealand Prime Minister. "Since then, rapid growth contributed to reducing the extreme poverty rate to 50 percent by 2005. A development breakthrough in Africa is within reach."

3.3 Problems in Sino-African relations

While China's huge and growing economic ties with Africa have generated benefits for both sides, they have also brought problems.

While Sino-African trade skyrocketed, it carried a trade imbalance in China's favour, which amounted to US$10 billion in 2010, prompting critics to say Sino-African trade was a one-way street in favour of China, which imported mainly oil and raw materials while exporting cheap manufactured goods in return.[106]

---

[106]Toh Han Shih, *South China Morning Post*, "China treads lightly to improve image in Africa", 28 January 2012.

"China's significant trade imbalance has been a major source of discomfort in Africa, causing political and social complications for China's investment across the continent," said Williamson.[107]

African unions have complained that cheap Chinese goods render locally produced goods uncompetitive, while African governments worry about the impact of cheap Chinese imports on local employment, Williamson noted. Unions are strong in many African nations because they were formed to oppose Western colonial masters, but they have switched their focus to Chinese firms, Williamson added.

Chinese employers had trouble dealing with African unions, Desir said.[108] "Chinese companies are threatened by the independence of African unions. Unions in China are directed by the state."

The South African government had warned the Chinese not to cause the South African textile industry to collapse from the flood of cheap Chinese textile exports, noted Roland Marchal, a research fellow at Sciences Po University in Paris, France.[109] As a result, the Chinese exported machines to Africa to equip local factories, he added.

In January 2012, Chinese Deputy Commerce Minister Gao declared China would redress its trade imbalance with Africa by opening its markets up to African goods, waiving customs duties on African products and encouraging Chinese firms to import more African products.[110] China would export higher-value products to Africa "to win the hearts of Africans to the made-in-China brand". In addition, China will increase its investments in African manufacturing and transfer technology and management skills to "change from made-in-China to made-in-Africa", Gao said.

---

[107] Ibid.

[108] Toh Han Shih and Jennifer Cheng, *South China Morning Post*, "China in Africa, no worse than others", 25 April 2012.

[109] Toh Han Shih, *South China Morning Post*, "China faces tougher deals in Africa", 7 October 2013.

[110] Toh Han Shih, *South China Morning Post*, "China treads lightly to improve image in Africa", 28 January 2012.

One African expert said mainland investment projects are viewed with a certain amount of caution and scepticism by labour unions in Africa.[111]

"African unions worry about Chinese investments because they are perceived to lead to mistreatment of local workers in some cases or because African workers are seen to lose jobs to Chinese," the expert said. "The irony is that lots of Chinese investments in Africa can lead to local unemployment because they bring in lots of Chinese workers. There are massive communities of Chinese workers springing up in Africa. Projects that used to employ lots of African workers now don't."

Although China is building billions of dollars of infrastructure in Africa, the problem was Western companies created jobs in Africa while the African perception was that Chinese companies brought their own workers to Africa, Marchal revealed.[112] Chamorro said there had been anti-China sentiment in African countries like Zambia, because of the Chinese workers brought in for large construction projects.[113]

Tensions between Chinese employers and African workers have erupted in violence. In October 2010, two Chinese supervisors shot 13 local workers during a labour dispute at the Chinese-owned Collum coal mine in Zambia, but none were killed. In April 2011, Zambian prosecutors dropped their case against the two Chinese supervisors.[114] The mine paid compensation to the 13 injured workers.[115]

At that time, then Zambian President Rupiah Banda was a supporter of Chinese investment, while the opposition leader Michael Sata had expressed anti-Chinese views.[116] China was then investing

---

[111] Ibid.
[112] Ibid.
[113] Toh Han Shih, *South China Moring Post*, "Rubbery numbers still add up to big role in Africa", 29 March 2013.
[114] Barry Bearak, *New York Times*, "Zambia drops case of shooting by Chinese mine bosses", 4 April 2011.
[115] Lewis Mwanangombe, *Associated Press*, "China's footprint grows in Zambia", 1 November 2013.
[116] Ibid.

more than US$1 billion per annum in Zambia, according to the Zambian government. After being elected Zambian President in September 2011, Sata changed his tune from anti-China to pro-China, and made a state visit to China in April 2013.[117]

Sata's earlier opposition to Chinese investments in his country was partly driven by allegations of labour abuses by Chinese companies.

Chinese-run copper mining companies in Zambia have routinely flouted labour laws designed to protect workers' safety and the right to organise, Human Rights Watch alleged in a report, "Zambia: workers detail abuse in Chinese-owned mines", on 3 November 2011. The report details persistent abuses in Chinese-run mines, including poor health and safety conditions, regular 12-hour and even 18-hour shifts involving arduous labour, and anti-union activities, in violation of Zambia's national laws and international labour standards.

A report by Johannesburg-based South Africa Resource Watch (SARW) in November 2012 alleged that Chinese companies engaged in widespread labour abuses in sub-Saharan Africa and subjected local employees in the mining industry to harsh and unfair working conditions.[118] The report, which investigated Chinese labour practices in Zimbabwe, Zambia, and the Democratic Republic of Congo alleged small Chinese mining companies were the chief culprits. According to the report, many Chinese firms did not observe minimum wage requirements.

However, China's track record on labour issues in Africa, flawed as it is, is no worse than those of Western powers. If the slavery, exploitation and racism of European colonial rule of Africa were included, it would be hard to dispute the fact that the European record is much worse than China's. A notorious example of European oppression in Africa is Belgian King Leopold II's rule over the Congo Free State (which includes today's Democratic Republic of Congo) from the late 19th century to early 20th century.

---

[117]Ibid.
[118]Marc Howe, "South African report highlights labor abuses in the Sub-Sahara", Mining.com, 9 November 2012.

Millions are estimated to have died, but as Leopold II's actions in the Congo Free State have been extensively documented in other works, they will not be repeated here. Even excluding slavery and European colonialism, the records of modern Western powers are not much better than that of the Chinese.

"What is wrong with the China-in-Africa discourse in Western media is that it focuses on Chinese investment as the bad apple," Yan Hairong, an Assistant Professor at The Hong Kong Polytechnic University who has researched China's involvement in Africa, said.[119]

"While Western interests frequently accuse Chinese companies of mistreating African workers, these criticisms are often voiced while standing on thin ice," said Williamson.[120]

It was true that in Zambia, workers in road construction projects managed by Chinese firms had complained of poor treatment and being fed very basic food, Williamson explained.[121] In Angola, "there have been examples of Chinese managers assaulted by African staff because of frustrations caused by mistreatment," Williamson said.

Yet African unions often complained about Western oil and mining companies as well, Williamson noted.

"Chinese companies are no worse than other companies," said Barry Sautman, a Professor at Hong Kong University of Science and Technology.[122]

Virtually all the major foreign-owned copper mines in Zambia, Africa's biggest copper producer, exploited workers and the environment, Sautman alleged.

A report by Human Rights Watch on Zambia singled out Chinese-owned mines — including the state-owned China Nonferrous Metals Mining Corporation (CNMC), one of the biggest

---

[119] Ibid.
[120] Ibid.
[121] Toh Han Shih and Jennifer Cheng, *South China Morning Post*, "China in Africa, no worse than others", 25 April 2012.
[122] Ibid.

copper producers in the world — of forcing workers to toil for long hours under dangerous conditions for meagre pay. The report alleged the Chinese-run copper mines fell short of common industry practices and paid Zambian workers much lower salaries than other international copper mining companies. CNMC has invested at least US$2 billion in Zambia.

Sautman and Yan conceded that Chinese-owned mines paid Zambian workers 20 to 30 percent less than other foreign-owned mines.[123] But workers at Chinese-owned mines were less skilled than those employed elsewhere, which partly explained the lower pay, Sautman argued. Yan pointed out that strikes had occurred at other foreign-owned copper mines in Zambia, besides those of CNMC.[124]

In reply to Sautman and Yan's criticisms, Matt Wells, Africa Researcher for Human Rights Watch, said, "We detail abuses by other multinationals. We do not imply these other companies have a perfect labour record. Our interviews showed CNMC, on average, had more severe problems in safety, anti-union activities and hours at work."[125]

The answer to the question of whether Chinese investors treat African employees worse than Western multinationals varied from industry to industry, Martyn Davies, Chief Executive Officer of Frontier Advisory, a South African consultancy, revealed.[126]

"There are instances where Chinese investors are not attuned to the local labour environment, and there are others where Chinese are no different to Western investors in the region," Davies said.

"The risk of corruption and bad practice exists for both Chinese and non-Chinese companies operating in the natural resource sectors," said Parsons of Global Witness.[127]

While Global Witness has expressed "serious concerns" over problematic Chinese businesses in Africa, for example, over the lack

---

[123] Ibid.
[124] Ibid.
[125] Ibid.
[126] Ibid.
[127] Ibid.

of transparency of China Sonangol, a joint venture between Angola's state oil company Sonangol and China-linked companies based in Hong Kong, Global Witness has also expressed concern that British energy giant BP won exploration rights in Angola after agreeing to make multimillion-dollar payments to obscure social projects controlled by Sonangol.

It is misleading to "compare the operations of a Chinese company to a Western one in Africa . . . What gives better insight is to compare how the Chinese companies operate in Africa versus how they operate at home," said Desir.[128] "They try to run their African operations the same way as in China. That is where things break down on both sides, because the cultural difference is so great."

Chinese companies tended to build grand infrastructure projects in capitals that pleased officials, but neglected the countryside, Desir pointed out.[129]

"China's strategy wins praise in African capitals. At the same time, it is losing hearts and minds in African rural areas, where the workers are. China is not neo-colonialist, but (Chinese) firms have moved into Africa too quickly to understand the complexities of tribal and regional politics. We are trying to convince our China clients that a flashy partnership between China and a government in Africa has little meaning to people who have to work in the mines or whose livelihoods are disrupted to satisfy China's growing resource needs," said Desir.

Then there are issues with the perceived quality of infrastructure projects built by Chinese companies in Africa.

In Angola, there are growing concerns about the quality of infrastructure built by Chinese construction companies since heavy rains in 2007 washed away many newly-constructed Chinese roads.[130] The Luanda General Hospital was closed because the building had developed cracks, forcing the evacuation of patients

---

[128] Ibid.
[129] Ibid.
[130] Toh Han Shih, *South China Morning Post*, "Boom for contractors despite quality concerns", 13 July 2011.

to tents, only four years after it was built by a Chinese state-owned firm, China Overseas Engineering Group Company, a wholly-owned subsidiary of China Railway Group.[131]

The quality of work done by Chinese construction companies in Africa is widely perceived to be inferior, according to a paper by Lucy Corkin, Christopher Burke and Martyn Davies from the Centre for Chinese Studies at Stellenbosch University, South Africa. The variation in quality largely depends on how well government authorities of various countries supervise these projects, according to Corkin, Burke and Davies.

In countries such as Sierra Leone and Angola where the government authorities lack the capacity or political will to enforce building codes, structures of sub-standard quality are more common than in countries where the authorities effectively enforce the law, the report by Corkin, Burke and Davies explained.

China's record of infrastructure projects in Africa is mixed, with some being better and some worse. The tale of two dams in Africa captures the differing sides of China's image as a major player in the development of hydropower around the world.[132]

The Gibe 3 Dam in Ethiopia built by Italian hydropower developer Salini Costruttori, had been criticised by international lobbyists opposed to what they said were the devastating environmental consequences it would create.[133] The Gibe 3 Dam, which was under construction as of 2013, had the financial support of Industrial and Commercial Bank of China (ICBC), one of the Big Four Chinese state-owned banks, and Dongfang Electric Corporation.[134] In May 2010, China and Ethiopia signed an agreement on the Gibe 3 Dam, which covered the supply of equipment by Dongfang, a SOE that is one of China's largest suppliers of power generation equipment. The contract covered in the May 2010

---

[131] Ibid.
[132] Toh Han Shih, *South China Morning Post*, "Ethiopia dam blot on China's record", 7 June 2010.
[133] Ibid.
[134] Ibid.

agreement had a value of US$495 million, with 85 percent to be financed by a loan from ICBC, according to Ethiopian media.

News that ICBC would finance the 1,870 megawatt (MW) Gibe 3, one of the largest hydropower projects in sub-Saharan Africa, dismayed Peter Bosshard, Policy Director of International Rivers, an international environmental NGO. "If ICBC funds the Gibe 3 Dam, this will be a serious setback for the efforts to make China's overseas dam building more sustainable," Bosshard said.[135]

"The Gibe 3 Dam is one of the most destructive infrastructure projects in recent years, and the World Bank and other international financial institutions have not approved funding for it," he added.

The dam threatened the livelihood of 500,000 indigenous people, because it could end the river's natural flood cycle and thus destroy harvests and grazing land, International Rivers explained.

ICBC's response was: "ICBC has long been attaching great importance to environmental protection, and will not finance projects that fail to reach environmental standards. We will keep a close watch on the progress and the environmental evaluation of the project."[136]

In contrast to the controversy surrounding Gibe 3, the Merowe Dam, another large African dam, has left a positive impression of China's track record on hydropower after an initial poor start, according to some observers.[137]

Since it was completed in 2008, the Merowe Dam has doubled the power generating capacity of Sudan. China Exim Bank, a leading Chinese state-owned lender to overseas Chinese projects, was the main foreign financier of the US$1.2 billion project with US$519 million of loans. A joint venture of two Chinese state-owned firms, Sinohydro and China International Water and Electric Corporation, built the dam's concrete body.

"Since 2003, China Exim Bank and Sinohydro have improved their environmental performance. China Exim Bank adopted an

---

[135] Ibid.
[136] Ibid.
[137] Ibid.

environmental policy in 2004 and a more detailed environmental guideline in 2007," Bosshard said.[138]

"In 2008, I met the Chinese Envoy to Sudan, Liu Guijin, in London," said Ali Askouri, President of the Leadership Office of Hamdab Dam's Affected People, a London-based NGO. Hamdab is the other name for the Merowe Dam.[139]

"I raised my concerns over the Merowe Dam with him, and he promised to look into the matter and work to improve the Chinese companies' performance in regard to the affected communities in Sudan. I have seen the Chinese seriously looking into improving their performance with local communities. The Chinese are now talking about getting with international bodies to improve the quality of their work to meet international environmental standards, and the affected communities," Askouri said.

In addition, there has been growing concern over the strings attached to the huge amount of Chinese money that poured into Africa.

Controversy has surrounded a US$9 billion agreement signed in 2008 between China and the Democratic Republic of Congo, where two Chinese state-owned firms, China Railway Group and Sinohydro, agreed to build railways and dams for the African country. Loans would come from China Exim Bank, and in return China would gain copper and cobalt mining rights in Congo. The arrangement rang warning bells at the International Monetary Fund (IMF), which believed it risked driving Congo's debts to dangerous levels.[140]

In 2009, then IMF Managing Director Dominique Strauss-Kahn said "the difficulty is that certain elements of the contract" would result in an increase in Congo's US$11 billion debt burden.[141] China's Ambassador to Congo, Wu Zexian, rejected criticism that the use of

---

[138] Ibid.
[139] Ibid.
[140] Toh Han Shih, *South China Morning Post*, "Chinese loans go a long way in Africa", 20 July 2009.
[141] Ibid.

Congo's mineral reserves as a guarantee for the infrastructure projects constituted external debt.[142]

"The Congo is in a very difficult situation and faces enormous challenges around poverty alleviation and development," said Martyn Davies. "The Chinese deal is certainly the best on the table, and no other foreign investor is able to match such a large financial package."[143]

"Those who oppose Chinese investment... All they need to do is to equal the help we are getting from China," the late Zambian President Levy Mwanawasa told a business forum in 2007. "We only turned to the East when you people in the West let us down. I know of no strings attached to Chinese investment."[144]

Zimbabwe is another example of an African country that preferred financing from China to multilateral institutions like the IMF and Western nations. In July 2009, the IMF told Zimbabwe it could not provide the country with more funds until it settled its debts of US$1 billion. Yet a few weeks earlier, Zimbabwe obtained a US$950 million loan from China, far more than the US$73 million of aid promised by the US.

"China's spending on Angolan infrastructure is in the billions of US dollars, while World Bank allocations to Angolan infrastructure are in the low hundred millions. Chinese loans are on better terms than those offered by the international financial institutions," said Tara O'Connor, Director of Africa Risk Consulting, a risk consultancy specialising in Africa.[145]

While the World Bank and the IMF are reluctant to fork out large long-term loans because Angola failed to raise transparency and governance standards, China has made available large sums of money, Lucy Corkin noted.[146] China Exim Bank extended US$12.5 billion more in loans to sub-Saharan Africa in the past decade than the World Bank, Fitch Ratings revealed. China Exim Bank lent US$67.2 billion to Africa between 2001 and 2010, compared with the World Bank's US$54.7 billion, according to Fitch Ratings.

---

[142] Ibid.
[143] Ibid.
[144] Ibid.
[145] Ibid.
[146] Ibid.

A representative from a non-government organisation working in Africa said: "If you get into bed with the IMF, they will force a globalisation agenda on you. China's principle of mutual respect of sovereignty is appealing. It is like borrowing from a commercial bank. As long as you repay the loan, they respect your privacy."[147]

"Many donor institutions are voicing concerns that any leverage they possess vis-à-vis African governments is rapidly being eroded by substantial concessional loans from China with few conditions," according to a report by the Centre for Chinese Studies, University of Stellenbosch, prepared for the Rockefeller Foundation, in 2007, titled "China's Engagement of Africa: Preliminary Scoping of African case studies".

Although some African leaders might prefer Chinese money to Western money, not everybody sees the huge investment and imports from China into Africa as an unmitigated benefit.

"Increasingly, China's role in Africa is contested, not by Westerners but Africans. Too often, descriptions of China-Africa relations assume Africans should be happy to get something from China. It is not the case," said Marchal.[148]

"How can you have an egalitarian discussion between two partners, when you have one big partner controlling the agenda and the Africans just coming to sign agreements? In a win–win [situation], bargaining should be equal. We have one big powerful nation [China] with a coherent policy and a clear vision about where it wants to go. In Africa, you have 54 countries with no coherent vision and sometimes unstable governments," said Hamadou Tidiane, a former Senegalese journalist and now Director General of a journalism school in Senegal.[149]

Tidiane was sceptical of the billions of dollars that China has offered Africa.[150] He said, "We don't eat growth rates. The ordinary

---

[147]Ibid.
[148]Toh Han Shih, *South China Morning Post*, "China faces tougher deals in Africa", 7 October 2013.
[149]Toh Han Shih, *South China Morning Post*, "'Not everyone's a winner' in China's ties with Africa", 31 July 2012.
[150]Ibid.

citizen cannot eat these numbers. They want good roads, good schools and good governance."

China tended to deal with individual African countries rather than the African Union, David Shinn, a former US diplomat in Africa, revealed in a report by British think tank Chatham House.

"Win–win so far has not been a reality, in part because the Chinese projects and their implementation leave a lot to be desired," said Howard French, Associate Professor at the Columbia University Graduate School of Journalism.[151]

The Chinese were better than their African partners at calculating the true costs of Sino-African projects, and the Africans could live to regret underpricing their assets that went into the projects, French pointed out.

He cited the example of a dam in Ghana built by Sinohydro, a Chinese state-owned dam construction firm that was paid largely in cocoa produced in the African state. This form of payment was risky because of cocoa price fluctuations, he noted.

However, African governments are driving harder bargains with China.

"There is push-back from many African countries," said Jean-Pierre Cabestan, the Head of Government and International Studies at Hong Kong Baptist University.[152]

Progress on some pending Sino-African deals had slowed, as the African side became more cautious about what terms they would accept from the Chinese, Desir pointed out.[153]

In September 2013, Addax Petroleum, a subsidiary of Chinese state-owned oil giant Sinopec, lost a ruling at an international tribunal in a legal dispute over an oilfield in Gabon that involved legal claims of more than US$1 billion.[154] The International Chamber of Commerce's arbitration court rejected Addax's bid to resume

---

[151] Ibid.

[152] Toh Han Shih, *South China Morning Post*, "China faces tougher deals in Africa", 7 October 2013.

[153] Ibid.

[154] Emma Farge, *Reuters*, "Sinopec's Addax loses court ruling on Gabon oil license-document", 13 September 2013.

operations at the oilfield and prevent the Gabon government from selling the licence to a third party. In January 2014, Addax signed a new agreement with the Gabon government for three new oilfields in the country, putting an end to the dispute.[155]

Some African ministers had complained about the lack of transparency and delays in contracts by Chinese companies, Marchal revealed. Although Chinese firms offer huge contracts liberally financed by Chinese banks, African officials said they had difficulty getting access to the fine print in the contract, he pointed out.[156]

Some Sino-African contracts have been reviewed to ensure better terms for the African parties, Parsons noted.[157]

"These factors have contributed to an adjustment in the dynamic relationship between African governments and Chinese companies," she added.

China's economic initiatives have not benefited ordinary Africans much, Desir explained. "In the beginning, the grand announcements of billion dollar deals were greeted with hope and excitement, but there have been so many unfulfilled promises of job creation or improved livelihood that China's goodwill is likely to be questioned whenever another large China deal is announced."[158]

Because many African nations are democracies, many African leaders need to deliver to their people, and hence ask better terms from China, Desir added.

Even when Chinese companies were not directly responsible for bad behaviour in Africa, they have been friendly with controversial African regimes accused of egregious abuses. One such Chinese-linked company is a mysterious firm based and registered in Hong Kong, China International Fund (CIF), whose ownership and operations were highly opaque.

"In Guinea, China International Fund signed a multibillion-dollar agreement with the military junta there in 2009, around the

---

[155] *International Oil Daily*, "Sinopec's Addax cuts deal in Gabon, ends dispute", 20 January 2014.
[156] Toh Han Shih, *South China Morning Post*, "China faces tougher deals in Africa", 7 October 2013.
[157] Ibid.
[158] Ibid.

time that its security forces massacred over 150 people and publicly raped many women. The company was effectively giving a lifeline to a regime ostracised by many countries," said Daniel Balint-Kurti, team leader at Global Witness.[159]

In December 2008, a military junta headed by Moussa Dadis Camara seized power in Guinea. In September 2009, the junta ordered troops to attack people protesting an attempt by Camara to become president. The soldiers went on a rampage of rape, mutilation and murder, according to media reports. The following month, US Secretary of State Hillary Clinton called on Guinea's military leaders to step down. At the same time, Guinea's Mines Minister, Mahmoud Thiam, announced CIF would invest US$7 billion in oil, gas, aviation, energy and infrastructure in Guinea, in return for becoming a strategic partner in all mining projects in the nation.

The real owner and mastermind of CIF and a group of related companies in Hong Kong, collectively called "the Queensway Group", is a mysterious businessman called Sam Pa.[160] Like a character out of a spy novel, Sam Pa went by many names including Xu Jinghua, Samo Hui and Antonio Famtosonghiu Sampo Menezes.[161] In 2012, a report of Global Witness, citing reliable sources within the Zimbabwean secret police, alleged Sam Pa appeared to have given as much as US$100 million to the Zimbabwean secret police, called the Central Intelligence Organisation.[162] In October 2015, Sam Pa was detained by Chinese authorities in a hotel in Beijing.[163] His detention was linked to Chinese state-owned oil giant Sinopec's oil projects in Angola.[164]

---

[159]Toh Han Shih, *South China Morning Post*, "African conflicts pressure China's neutrality", 3 August 2010.

[160]Yu Ning, Huang Kaixi, Yang Yanwen, *Caixin*, "Businessman linked to Sinopec's Angola deals said to face probe", 14 October 2015.

[161]Toh Han Shih, *South China Morning Post*, "HK advisor gave US$100m to Mugabe secret police", 5 August 2012.

[162]Ibid.

[163]Yu Ning, Huang Kaixi, Yang Yanwen, *Caixin*, "Businessman linked to Sinopec's Angola deals said to face probe", 14 October 2015.

[164]Ibid.

"In some cases, there are problems with a strict policy of non-interference," said Balint-Kurti.

"China will have to make a decision how to engage countries that are ill-governed," said Charles Stith, Director of the African Presidential Archives and Research Centre at Boston University.[165]

"The Chinese have traditionally taken the approach of non-intervention in their foreign policy. How you deal with regimes that oppress their people or don't fully develop their countries, has implications for long-term stability," said Stith, a former US Ambassador to Tanzania.[166]

"The problem for China is it prefers to cultivate relationships with African leaders who kowtow like deferential courtiers. When the people in these countries feel left out and vote out their disconnected leaders, what will China have?" asked Desir.[167]

African leaders, who were initially courted by China, were being removed or replaced through changes such as elections, Desir noted. "Losing partners in Africa is frustrating to Chinese state planners, because China's expensive *guanxi* (connections) evaporated when African government figures they cultivated no longer hold power."[168]

China paid a price when civil war broke out in Libya in 2011, resulting in the downfall and death of Libyan leader Muammar Gaddafi, with whom China had friendly relations. By early March 2011, China evacuated more than 35,000 of its nationals caught up in the North African country's violence.[169] This was one of the largest government-led evacuations of Chinese citizens from foreign soil in the history of China. Libya, Africa's third largest oil producer and fourth largest natural gas producer, had around 36,000 Chinese

---

[165]Toh Han Shih, *South China Morning Post*, "African conflicts pressure China's neutrality", 3 August 2010.
[166]Ibid.
[167]Toh Han Shih, *South China Morning Post*, "Rubbery numbers still add up to big role in Africa", 29 March 2013.
[168]Toh Han Shih, *South China Morning Post*, "China faces tougher deals in Africa", 7 October 2013.
[169]*Xinhua*, "35,860 Chinese evacuated from unrest-torn Libya", 3 March 2011.

working on 50 multimillion-dollar projects, mostly in oil, railways and telecommunications.[170]

A spokesman for the Chinese embassy in Tripoli, the Libyan capital, said Chinese nationals, mostly construction workers on railway, telecommunications and oil projects, and Chinese companies operating in Libya had been attacked by gun-wielding looters during the uprising against Gaddafi in February and March 2011. The Chinese Ministry of Commerce declared on its website that Chinese construction sites and camps in Libya had been "attacked and looted" in 2011. "China has suffered large-scale direct economic losses in Libya, including looted work sites, burned and destroyed vehicles and tools, smashed office equipment and stolen cash," it stated.

CRCC, a Chinese state-owned rail construction firm, had its assets in Libya looted, as "attackers wielded clubs and knives but carried no guns", CRCC Manager Yu Xingxi said. CRCC had suspended all its projects in Libya in 2011, Yu added."[171]

Since unrest in Libya broke out on 16 February 2011, CRCC said its project sites had been attacked, resulting in injuries to some employees and destruction of some equipment. All staff had been evacuated, the company added. CRCC had employed 3,573 people in three railway projects worth more than US$4 billion, the firm, which is listed in Hong Kong and Shanghai, added.

Another large Chinese state-owned infrastructure construction company, China State Construction Engineering Corporation, revealed its residential property construction projects in Libya, worth 17.6 billion yuan (US$2.85 billion), were under threat during the unrest in 2011.

"China needs to learn to heed global political risks. It is a very important lesson for the Chinese government to draw from," said Zheng Wei, Associate Professor and Director of the Department of Risk Management and Insurance with Peking University's School

---

[170]Ed Zhang and Toh Han Shih, *South China Morning Post*, "China pays for risky African ventures", 25 January 2011.
[171]Ibid.

of Economics. "Libya should be a wake-up call [for the Chinese government]," he added.[172]

"This is a risk that can take away all your potential gains, and knock down overnight all you have built [over years] — through a new government decree or simply a change of government," Zheng said.

South Sudan was another African nation where extensive Chinese investments were threatened by turmoil. China National Petroleum Corporation (CNPC), a Chinese state-owned oil giant, was the biggest equity partner in most of South Sudan's operational oilfields when civil war broke out in the country in December 2013. This resulted in hundreds of Chinese nationals and tens of thousands of refugees fleeing the conflict.[173]

"The conflict is a challenge to China's long-held policy of non-interference," said Parsons.[174]

"Chinese companies, notably CNPC, have invested in the country in recent years because of the oil fields there, [which are] some of the richest in the continent," added Parsons.

"China's investment into the Sudanese oil sector has rapidly descended into one of its most problematic investments in Africa. The conflict may result in a heightened sense of risk amongst Chinese state-owned enterprises investing in politically unstable parts of Africa," said Davies.[175]

3.4 Great power rivalry over Africa

Despite China's setbacks in some African countries like Libya, China is gaining influence on the continent. In contrast, the G8 group of advanced economies — France, Germany, Italy, Japan, Britain, Canada, Russia and the US — have been losing influence in Africa.

As a sign of the economic value African governments put on ties with China, several African leaders rushed to China to sign

---

[172] Ibid.
[173] Toh Han Shih, South China Morning Post, "South Sudan civil war still no deterrent to Chinese firms", 20 January 2014.
[174] Ibid.
[175] Ibid.

deals worth billions of US dollars in 2013.[176] In June 2013, Sierra Leone President Ernest Koromo announced he signed US$8 billion of infrastructure deals during his visit to China.[177] Nigerian President Goodluck Jonathan visited Beijing in July 2013, when US$1.1 billion of loan deals were signed, including a US$500 million Chinese loan for the construction of four new international airports in Abuja, Lagos, Harcourt and Kano.[178]

"China's assistance to and cooperation with Africa are changing the rules of the game and threaten to leave governments and organisations that do not act strategically by the wayside," stated a report by Swedish development organisation Diakonia and the European Network on Debt and Development.[179]

"The G8's influence in Africa is rapidly waning and being replaced by Chinese influence. The long-term consequences may be profound for the continent, resulting in not only an economic shift but also having political ramifications," said Davies.[180]

Failed promises, reduced foreign aid and disinvestment by traditional G8 investors in the past two years had hurt the standing of the group on the continent, Davies noted.

"The G8 nations have lost considerable commercial advantage in Africa over the past 20 years for several reasons, not all of which have to do with the formidable rise of China's global status," said Tara O'Connor.[181]

"G8 businesses have been ill-served by their media. G8 media organisations have peddled stereotypes and portrayed Africa as the hopeless continent, mired in war, famine and destruction, when the truth was the opposite," said O'Connor.

---

[176]Toh Han Shih and Adrian Wan, *South China Morning Post*, "African leaders prefer China's hard cash to US overtures", 18 July 2013.

[177]Ibid.

[178]Ibid.

[179]Penny Davies, Diakonia and the European Network on Debt and Development, "China and the end of poverty in Africa — towards mutual benefit?", August 2007.

[180]Ibid.

[181]Toh Han Shih, *South China Morning Post*, "Chinese loans go a long way in Africa", 20 July 2009.

"The overwhelmingly humanitarian interest of many Western countries has led to stereotyped perceptions of Africa in terms of only problems. These views are increasingly patronising, out of touch and a deterrent to serious business," stated a report by Tom Cargill for Chatham House, a London think tank.[182]

"The over-promising of what aid can deliver and the emphasis on aid to the exclusion of business have diminished the relevance of the G8 for Africa, mirroring the general shift in the global balance of power from West to East. The emerging economies of G20, including China, have brought entrepreneurialism, energy and recognition of mutual benefit that are increasingly attractive [to Africa]," wrote Cargill.

With the West and China courting Africa, Africans have the power to shop around for economic partnerships.

"What's unique is Africa for the first time has more than one suitor. That is where the power comes from. The last time Africa had the option of choosing between different partners was the cold war in the 1970s, when the Soviet Union and the West competed for influence in the continent," said Howard French.[183]

The US and China have competed for influence in Africa by offering economic goodies.

At the Forum on China-Africa Cooperation (FOCAC) summit in July 2012 in Beijing, China pledged US$20 billion in aid to various African projects across the continent, reinforcing Chinese key role in Africa's development aspirations. Hot on the heels of the China-Africa Summit, US State Secretary Hillary Clinton visited Africa in August 2012, which was viewed as a manifestation of US-China competition for influence in Africa.[184]

---

[182] Tom Cargill, *Chatham House Report*, "Our common strategic interests: Africa's role in the post-G8 world", June 2010.

[183] Toh Han Shih, *South China Morning Post*, "'Not everyone's a winner' in China's ties with Africa", 31 July 2012.

[184] Joel Ng, "Great Power Rivalry in Africa: Economic Engagement Holds Key", *Reliefweb*, 14 August 2012.

During a visit to Zambia in 2011, Clinton warned of a "new colonialism" in Africa, which was also viewed as an indirect reference to China.[185] During her subsequent African tour in August 2012, Clinton's speech in Senegal mentioned no names, but described America's partnership with Africa as one "that adds value rather than extracts it" — widely seen as a criticism of China's extraction of massive amounts of resources such as oil and minerals from Africa.[186]

During his state visit to Ethiopia in May 2014 as part of a 4-nation African tour, Chinese Prime Minister Li Keqiang said, "China will never pursue a colonial path like some countries did."[187]

Diakonia's report noted, "There is an underlying assumption that Western policy is essentially progressive and Chinese policy essentially negative. It is wrong to demonise Chinese policy ... and Western governments should practise what they preach."

3.5 Conclusion

China and the West do not have a sharp ideological divide over Africa, in comparison to the Cold War, which presented a stark choice between the Communism of the Soviet Union and the capitalism espoused by the US. There is ideological rivalry between China and the West over Africa, but not as harsh as the US-Soviet competition during the Cold War. Both China and the West offer capitalism with different ideological shades. China offers Africa economic aid and partnership, with state-owned firms playing a major role, under a policy of non-interference, which does not care whether an African nation is a democracy or not, and ignores human rights problems associated with a government. In contrast to China's state-led capitalism, the West promotes a liberal capitalism tied to democracy, freedom of expression and human rights.

---

[185] Ibid.

[186] Ibid.

[187] Zhang Pinghui, *South China Morning Post*, "Trade with Africa will double by 2020, Li Keqiang tells Ethiopia conference", 6 May 2014.

If Africa enjoys a substantial economic boost from its ties with China, African governments may prefer Chinese money to Western funds. In such a scenario, Western protests against the lack of democracy, freedom and human rights in Chinese capitalism may ring hollow, given that Africans can point to their slower progress before the Chinese stepped onto the continent in a big way, and Africans can argue that Western preaching of democracy and human rights has not translated into tangible progress for Africans.

But if China's investment and trade with Africa produces lop-sided economic growth accompanied by a widening wealth gap between elite and ordinary Africans, it can spark social unrest and the toppling of unpopular regimes. If this happens, it will be a historical irony, given that the Chinese Communist Party took power in 1949 with the collapse of the Nationalist Party, which was unpopular and corrupt. In such a scenario, Western liberal capitalism may appear more attractive to Africans than China's authoritarian capitalism. China can avoid this by creating projects that allow local Africans to gain good employment with decent wages and labour conditions, building infrastructure projects that benefit not just the elite but also the masses, and avoid colluding with and enriching unpopular African leaders through secretive and corrupt deals.

China and the West need not descend to all-out competition over Africa that plays out as a zero-sum game where one side gains at the expense of the other, although an element of competition is probably unavoidable. Africa's economic relations not only with China and the West, but also with other nations like Japan, can benefit all parties including Africans.

An example of both competition and cooperation between the US and China in Africa involves oil, a resource that is important to China.

"At the end of the day, market forces and bilateral relations will determine US and Chinese imports of African oil. You will see both cooperation and competition for resources in Africa between the

US and China. My hope and expectation is you will see more cooperation," said Stith.[188]

"It's no secret the US State Department tries to encourage the Chinese government to deal differently with countries where the leadership is guilty of gross violations of human rights. But the US takes a big picture in China's potential to positively effect change in Africa. The sum of China's role in the world is greater than the parts," Stith added.

"What that means is in any dynamic relationship, it's complicated and nuanced. While there may be agreements on some things in some parts of Africa, there may be disagreements on others," he said.

China's involvement in African projects has introduced competition, which has accelerated the execution of projects, notably in infrastructure, O'Connor noted.[189]

While Chinese firms may compete with other companies in the tendering of infrastructure projects, Chinese infrastructure projects in Africa can also complement those financed by other countries. In June 2013, US President Barack Obama announced his US\$7 billion Power Africa initiative to provide electricity to 20 million Africans. With China building railway and roads in Africa and Obama's Power Africa initiative, people and businesses, both African and foreign, can only benefit from the infrastructure provided by both the US and China. This will create a virtuous cycle where companies benefit from infrastructure like roads and electricity, which generate jobs and in turn raise the income of Africans. With rising income levels, Africa is becoming a growing consumer market in which China, US, Europe, Japan and other nations can sell their goods. China, a manufacturing powerhouse, will find a vast market in Africa to sell manufactured wares.

It is in the interest of China and the West to cooperate in contributing to Africa's prosperity, because a prosperous Africa will benefit

---

[188]Toh Han Shih, *South China Morning Post*, "African conflicts pressure China's neutrality", 3 August 2010.

[189]Toh Han Shih, *South China Morning Post*, "Africa looks to China as Western influence fades", 28 June 2010.

Africans, China, the West and other nations. Africa was identified as the world's poorest inhabited continent in March 2013, but most African nations will reach middle income status, defined as per capita income of US$1,000 per person per year, if Africa's GDP continues to grow at its current rate, according to the World Bank. In 2013, Africa's GDP growth was 5.6 percent, making it the world's fastest growing continent.

There are existing examples of cooperation between China and the West in Africa.

A Chinese state-owned company, China Three Gorges, and Energias de Portugal (EDP) planned to jointly invest US$2 billion in Africa between 2013 and 2020.[190] EDP was formerly a major Portuguese state-owned utility. The Portuguese government sold 21.35 percent of EDP to Three Gorges for 2.69 billion Euros in May 2012, making the Chinese state-owned firm the largest shareholder in EDP. The Portuguese government sold the stake as part of EU's conditions to resolve Portugal's debt problem.[191] This was the largest privatisation in Portuguese history and one of the biggest mergers and acquisitions in Europe in 2012.[192]

The Portuguese utility firm's board member Joao Marques da Cruz explained a good partner with financial muscle was important to EDP. "After the transaction, EDP got 1.8 billion Euros of loans from Chinese banks, which is obviously good," he said.

As part of the agreement, major Chinese banks including ICBC and Bank of China entered Portugal for the first time, Joao Soares da Silva, a managing partner of Morais Leitao, Galvao Teles, Soares da Silva & Associados, a Portuguese law firm that represented EDP in the deal noted.[193]

Both firms had entered into a strategic agreement to invest in projects around the world.[194] Three Gorges would invest in

---

[190]Toh Han Shih, *South China Morning Post*, "Three Gorges and EDP to pour US$2b into Africa", 15 November 2013.
[191]Ibid.
[192]Ibid.
[193]Ibid.
[194]Ibid.

Latin America and Africa, where EDP already had a presence, while the Portuguese firm would invest in Asia, including China. This deal enabled the Chinese state-owned firm to make inroads not only in Africa, but also Portugal and Latin America.

History has come full circle. Portugal was the first European nation to colonise sub-Saharan Africa, a few decades after the voyage of the Chinese admiral Zheng He to the continent in the early 15th century. Now China and Portugal are cooperating in Africa.

Chapter 4

African Perceptions of China

4.1 African voices

Some critics have alleged China's huge and fast growing economic presence in Africa is a form of neo-colonialism. Chinese officials have repeatedly denied this, saying China's economic ties with Africa were a win–win situation for both sides. Who is right? Is China a boon or bane for Africa? Surely African voices must be heard on such questions, since this concerns Africans.

At a talk at the Foreign Correspondents' Club in Hong Kong on 24 July 2012, Howard French of the Columbia University Graduate School of Journalism revealed that a major determinant of African perceptions of China is the interaction between Africans and Chinese living and working in Africa. French claimed it was "troubling" and "untrue" that negative reports on China in the Western media have caused Africans to have negative perceptions of China, troubling because it presumed Africans cannot think for themselves but must rely on the Western media. Many Africans do not read Western newspapers and thus Western media does not determine their perception of China, French pointed out.

Insight into African perspectives on China's impact on Africa can be gained from local newspaper reports. It is worth examining the reporting of China's economic impact on Africa in some of the leading English newspapers in five African nations, namely South Africa, Zimbabwe, Namibia, Zambia and Angola.

Although Africa has more than 50 countries, these five nations are a good representation of the continent. These five countries account for a substantial share of Africa's economy, which collectively stood at 28 percent in 2010. South Africa was the largest economy in Africa until it was overtaken by Nigeria in 2013. Zambia, Namibia, Angola and Zimbabwe have seen a significant surge of Chinese trade and investment in recent years.

These five African states practise different degrees of press freedom and encompass diverse political systems. Hence, they form a representative and diverse sample for studying the range of African newspaper coverage of China. South Africa has a high degree of democracy and press freedom while Namibia has one of the highest levels of press freedom in Africa. In contrast, Angola and Zimbabwe are regarded as less democratic, as their elections have been accused of not being totally free or fair, and both nations have some of the lowest degrees of press freedom in Africa. Meanwhile, Zambia's level of press freedom lies in between Namibia and Angola.

If relations between a government and China are friendly and the press is state-controlled, it would be reasonable to expect positive coverage of China in that nation's media. Conversely, if relations between a government and China are bad and the press is under the government's control, it would be reasonable to expect negative or hostile coverage of China. In a state with a high degree of press freedom, there would likely be greater diversity of views and more nuanced reporting on China. The less liberated the press, the more the press would express the ruling elite's view. The freer the press, the more likely the press would express the people's opinions.

4.2 South Africa

South Africa is one of the most important and richest countries in Africa, with a relatively free media.

In 2010, South Africa was the biggest economy among African nations, accounting for 21 percent of Africa's GDP, according to the

IMF. South Africa declined in rankings to become Africa's second biggest economy after being overtaken by Nigeria in 2013. South Africa's system of government is that of a parliamentary democracy and the courts are fairly independent. According to Reporters without Borders' Press Freedom Index of 2011–2012, South Africa ranked 42 out of 179 nations globally and was the 7th highest in Africa.

In 2011, South Africa was China's largest trading partner in Africa and the bilateral trade accounted for more than a quarter of Sino-African trade.[195] South African leaders place importance on economic relations with China. On the sidelines of the Nuclear Security Summit in Seoul, South Korea, in March 2012, South African President Jacob Zuma told Chinese President Hu Jintao that China was an "important potential partner" in South Africa's infrastructure plan to expand ports and railways, modernise roads and build dams, irrigation systems and power plants.[196]

Let us examine three South African English language newspapers, namely *Business Day*, *Mail & Guardian* and *the Times*, in their reporting of China.

4.2.1 *Business Day*

Business Day is South Africa's major business daily newspaper, owned by BDFM. BDFM is a joint venture between Avusa, a South African media firm listed on the Johannesburg Stock Exchange, and UK publisher Pearson, according to Avusa's website.

There are many articles on China, including the Chinese economy, China's economic dealings with other countries like the US and China's economic ties with South Africa. The large number of articles on China and the general attitude of these articles indicate the importance with which the paper views China.

My search of *Business Day*'s website found few articles strongly critical of China. I found some letters, articles and commentaries that criticised China in a measured and rational way.

---

[195] *All Africa Global Media*, "South Africa: Hu Jintao pays Zuma courtesy call", 26 March 2012.
[196] Ibid.

An editorial published on 26 March 2012, headlined "China's lessons go only so far", carried the secondary headline "South African voters will not sacrifice democracy for growth". The editorial criticised South African leaders' admiration of China's model of economic development, though it admits South Africa can learn positive lessons from China, such as China's high productivity and heavy infrastructure investment.

The editorial stated, "That is the essential flaw in the ANC's approach: it admires China's achievements, but does not appear to appreciate the fundamental differences between the two societies, nor the sacrifices that would have to be made if South Africa were to follow the same path. Political freedom is extremely limited in China. The key difference is that China is coming under popular pressure to democratise only after it has coerced its people to follow a particular path to growth; the ANC seems to want the horse to push the cart in that direction."

An opinion piece by Anthony Butler published on 30 March 2012 was critical of South African President Jacob Zuma for leaning towards China and opposing the West. This column by Butler, an academic at the University of Cape Town in South Africa, stated South Africa needs CRABS (Canada, Russia, Australia, Brazil and South Africa), as much as BRICS (Brazil, Russia, India, China and South Africa). Butler criticised the "naked enthusiasm" of South African leaders like President Jacob Zuma for BRICS, contending that BRICS makes Zuma look like "a serious statesman" and satisfies "deep seated anti-western and anti-US sentiment". BRICS marginalises Western democratic ideals, Butler argued.

An editorial headlined "Doing business in rogue states", published on 16 April 2012, was critical of China in a restrained manner. This article comments on South African telecommunications company MTN's business dealings in Iran, then regarded as a rogue state by the US. The article mentioned allegations that MTN worked with an Iranian company and Chinese technology firm Huawei Technologies to help Iranian intelligence services locate people through their cell phones, thus cracking down on dissent. This editorial takes a balanced approach towards China. The editorial states that although there are increased risks of doing business in emerging markets like Iran, it would be naive not to do so. The editorial argues, "As consumers we have all done business with China and many other states with dubious human rights track records merely by buying the goods they produce. Has this not been in the best interests of the Chinese people? Should South African businesses deal only with western-style democracies?" Yet the editorial stated the utilitarian argument is not entirely convincing and the sacrifice of activists' lives was unacceptable.

Some articles are sympathetic to China. For example, in the article headlined "West undermines Africa to thwart Chinese influence, says Thabo Mbeki" published on 28 May 2012, the headline and the statements by former South African President Thabo Mbeki are sympathetic to Africa and China while critical of the West. "His concern was that the West was worried China would secure Africa's resources for its own use and throw its weight around on the continent," the article reported.

Business Day acknowledges the growing economic interdependence between China and South Africa, and is generally positive towards Chinese investments in South Africa. However, editorials in *Business Day* do criticise China's lack of democracy and press freedom, and uphold South Africa's democracy and press freedom.

4.2.2 *Mail & Guardian*

The *Mail & Guardian* is a South African weekly newspaper published by M&G Media. In 2002, Zimbabwean publisher Trevor Ncube bought 87.5 percent of the newspaper and became its CEO. The *Mail & Guardian* newspaper and *Mail & Guardian Online* position themselves as South Africa's quality media, aimed at the intelligentsia interested in a critical approach to politics, arts and current affairs.

The articles in the *Mail & Guardian* showed a variety of attitudes towards China. Some were sympathetic towards China, while others cast China in a negative light, and some articles were mixed in their views of China, neither painting China as totally bad nor totally blameless.

Articles that were generally negative towards China include the following.

An article headlined "ANC ponders China policy" published on 29 November 2010 mentioned that the *Mail & Guardian* obtained a leaked document describing a trip by South African officials to China to learn the Chinese government's way of doing things. South Africa's ruling party, the African National Congress (ANC), was "deeply frustrated" with Chinese SOEs in South Africa, the article revealed. According to the leaked document, the Chinese Communist Party complained to the ANC delegation about the negative coverage by South African media of China's relationship with Africa. "The delegation agreed that China got a raw deal from the media, but the ANC leaders were adamant that China should not just cry on their shoulders, it should change the situation itself." This statement in the article testified to the *Mail & Guardian's* support for a free press and its refusal to obsequiously publish only positive reports on China.

The fact that the *Mail & Guardian* obtained a sensitive leaked document shows the courage of South African media in conducting investigative reporting on the South African government and China. The article said China-South Africa relations were "more complex than it looks". This article was critical of the ANC trying to learn from China, but did not vilify China in a sweeping, one-sided manner, instead it proposed the need for a critical attitude in examining what South Africa should and should not learn from China.

An article headlined "Ex-con is Khulubuse's links to Chinese deals" published on 7 January 2011 is an investigative exposé that alleged a South African-based Taiwanese man, Robert Huang Jen-chih, was a middleman in deals between Chinese companies and Khulubuse Zuma, a nephew of South African President Jacob Zuma. Although the article did not accuse Khulubuse Zuma of any wrongdoing, it describes in detail his dealings with a Chinese state-owned firm, Shandong Gold Group. The sceptical tone of the article indicates suspicion of the business transactions.

An article headlined "Zuma's confidante in Chinese purchase of Orkney" published on 6 August 2011 alleged Elias Khumalo, a close confidante of President Zuma, would benefit from the Chinese purchase of the Orkney gold mine in South Africa, which faced bankruptcy and had been managed by a politically-connected South African firm headed by former South African President Nelson Mandela's grandson Zondwa and President Zuma's nephew Khulubuse.

The fact that these two investigative reports on President Zuma's nephew were printed shows how free and fearless the South African press is, and shows it is not afraid to allege dubious dealings between Chinese companies and powerful, politically-connected South African figures.

An article headlined "Working for Chinese is hell on earth" published on 24 June 2011 reported that in Zimbabwe, workers were often "forced to work long hours for low pay" with inadequate protective clothing, but Zimbabwean officials turned a blind eye to their plight in order to protect the interests of officials who were benefitting from Chinese investment.

An article headlined "Africa gets a new angle on the Chinese take away" published on 14 April 2012 criticised the Chinese for ruining the wildlife of South Africa and Zimbabwe through the poaching of endangered species that are consumed by the Chinese. The article reported African villagers objected to Chinese miners stealing their dogs and eating them. Although it is a fact that Chinese eat dogs and a wide range of other animal species, this article may promote the stereotype of "Chinese eating anything".

In contrast to the articles above that were negative towards China, other articles were ambiguous in their attitude towards China, examples of which include the following.

An article headlined "Africans marvel, fret at China's hard workers" published on 21 August 2008 described how the influx of Chinese workers into Africa is generating a mixed reception of admiration and resentment among Africans.

An article headlined "Chinese wooing in Africa: Boom without democracy" published on 8 January 2011 declared, "China's initiative is yet another example of Beijing's offensive in Africa, a continent succumbing to China's wooing. Even the government of democratic South Africa is fascinated by the perspectives of growth and prosperity in China under an authoritarian regime. Just how fascinated the government of President Jacob Zuma, and especially his African National Congress (ANC) party, is by China's centralised planned economy and forced domestic peace can be read in the countless contacts and visits by high-ranking delegations to China."

Although the article cited problems such as poor working conditions in Chinese-owned factories in Africa, it reports on China's massive inroads into Africa in a factual manner.

The following articles are largely favourable towards China.

A commentary by Brendan O'Neill, headlined "Bring on the Chinese", published on 24 April 2008, lauded the huge growth of Chinese trade and investment in Africa, but was critical of Western NGOs.

"For more than a decade now, groups such as Oxfam have tried to convince us that poor Africa needs small-scale, sustainable development. In one fell swoop, the Chinese have nuked these rather patronising ideas by showing that it is possible to build massive infrastructure in poor Africa, and what's more, that Africans want this kind of investment. The spread of Chinese trading in Africa is causing a severe crisis of confidence among sustainable-minded Western charity and aid workers. Western observers should have more faith in poor Africans and their leaders. If Africans want to deal with Chinese investors who treat them as adults rather than as victims, good for them. It is time for Oxfam and others to cut the apron strings: Africans are grown-up enough to determine their own futures, and to decide who they want to work with," O'Neill wrote.

An article headlined "SA defends Chinese expansion in Africa" published on 25 August 2010 reported that the South African government defended China's investments in Africa, saying China was not pursuing a neo-colonialist policy and China's impact on Africa was positive. The article reported positive views on China by top South African officials like President Zuma and South African Trade Minister Rob Davies.

An article headlined "Far from home" published on 14 February 2011 portrayed the lives of various Chinese workers, executives and business people in Africa in a sympathetic light, describing how hard they worked and the challenges they faced in Africa. The article quotes Xu Hui, a Chinese businessman in Africa, defending China's record in Africa, "Western countries also buy oil and have mines around the world. People don't talk about 'grabbing', or 'new colonialism' there. So why is it different for Chinese? We are not sending our armies to places and saying: 'Now sell us this!'"

An article headlined "State of the Nation: Zuma adopts Chinese model" published on 3 February 2012 leads with the sentence "President Jacob Zuma is looking East for inspiration, as the ANC pushes for resource nationalism rather than a crude form of nationalism". The article is sympathetic to Zuma's interest in emulating the Chinese model. The article stated, "With the crisis of liberal capitalism in the developed world, *The Economist* magazine recently published a major analysis of state capitalism, which it said had helped grow emerging market giants such as China, but also posed serious risks."

An article headlined "Chinese myths shattered" published on 26 April 2012 quoted a report on Chinese traders in Africa by the Brenthurst Foundation, which provides advice and seminars on Africa's development. The article was nuanced and sympathetic towards the situation of Chinese traders in Africa. The harassment Chinese traders endured fed the mutual distrust and suspicion between the Chinese and Africans, the article stated. The report described the neglect Chinese traders felt at the hands of Chinese diplomats and officials, debunking the notion that "China operated as a remorseless monolith in Africa".

The widely used pejorative 'Fong Kong' to describe Chinese goods was increasingly used across Southern African countries, implying they were substandard replicas, said the report. But, the research said, the Chinese believed this resentment was a result of a lack of understanding, the article revealed.

The article clearly opposes negative stereotypes of the Chinese or perceptions of Chinese as an undifferentiated monolith. The article noted that legal problems faced by the Chinese traders forced them to disobey the law in South Africa. This shows the sentiment of the article to be sympathetic and understanding towards the plight of Chinese traders.

4.2.3 *The Times*

The Times of South Africa is a national daily newspaper published in Johannesburg.

Some articles in *The Times* are critical of China. For instance, an article published on 14 May 2012 was sympathetic towards the Dalai Lama, whom the Chinese government disapproves of. That article, headlined "China suffers from moral crisis, says Dalai Lama", led with the statement, "China is beset by a moral crisis, widespread corruption and lawlessness, leading millions of Chinese to seek solace in Buddhism, Tibet's exiled Buddhist leader, the Dalai Lama, said."

A blogpost on *The Times* website published on 5 September 2010 criticised the South African government for pleasing Beijing by boycotting the Dalai Lama. This article, headlined "Zuma's China policy: Is it good or bad for us?", did not call for an outright rejection of Chinese economic overtures in South Africa, but advocated a balanced approach in welcoming Chinese investments without submitting to Chinese influence. The blog article concludes, "South Africa has resisted tying its flag to the mast of any major power. This would be threatened if China aggressively enters the economy and offers to build cut-price infrastructure in exchange for greater global influence. South Africa's eager-to-please attitude which was displayed when the Dalai Lama's visit was prevented last year, is a sign of this sort of influence peddling. What South Africa has to accomplish is the very difficult balance between building better relations with China while retaining this country's corporate and social culture. To do anything less would be to place in jeopardy the matrix of values this country has been built on."

Some articles criticised South African leaders for their friendly relations with China.

For example, an article, published on 12 December 2011, quoted the South African Human Rights Commission saying, "The South African government's foreign policy is focused more on trading with China, and has failed to consider human rights." In addition, *The Times* cited commission spokesman Vincent Moaga in issuing the following statement, "When South Africa establishes trade and diplomatic relations with any country, it is absolutely imperative that human rights principles form one of the primary pillars of these relations." In the *Times* article, the commission criticised Chinese authorities for executing South African Janice Linden for drug smuggling.

It is difficult to conclusively determine if some *Times* articles pander to racist stereotypes of Chinese. For instance, an article published on 23 May 2012 said a Chinese immigrant beheaded and ate a fellow passenger on a bus in Canada, thinking he was attacking an alien. On the other hand, a *Times* article dated 18 May 2012 also paints a British citizen in lurid colours, with the headline "Thai police arrest Brit with roasted foetuses".

4.2.4 *Summary*

The three South African newspapers, namely *Business Day*, *Mail & Guardian* and *The Times*, carry many articles on China, which indicates the importance with which they regard China. The three South African newspapers carry articles exhibiting different attitudes towards China, some positive, some negative and some mixed. My search of the newspapers' websites, which is admittedly not exhaustive, did not result in finding any article that demonised China or depicted it as a villain and enemy, or play up prejudice that portrayed the China threat as "the Yellow Peril". I found the occasional article that may perhaps be perceived as pandering to racist stereotypes of the Chinese, but they are few and far between. On the contrary, the 26 April 2012 article in the *Mail & Guardian* headlined "Chinese myths shattered" was critical of the notion of "Fong Kong", a negative African stereotype of cheap, low-quality Chinese goods.

The South African media is not shy about exposing questionable business dealings between politically well-connected South African individuals and Chinese businesses. This is a sign of the relatively robust degree of press freedom in South Africa, and it is what good reporting should be. As mentioned above, the blogpost on *The Times'* website on 5 September 2010 expressed apprehension over the prospect of China "aggressively" entering the South African economy and called for South Africa not to overly depend on China. Nonetheless, my search did not find any South African newspaper article that accused China of neo-colonialism or imperialism in South Africa.

In general, the articles are thoughtful and balanced, even when they are critical of China. They neither uncritically laud everything China does in Africa nor launch into polemic attacks on China using hostile or racist terms.

4.3 Zimbabwe

For decades since gaining independence from white rule, Zimbabwe was dominated by one party accused of authoritarian tendencies, but after a power-sharing agreement came into force since 2008, the country is seeing more democracy and press freedom.

Zimbabwe is a republic headed by President Robert Mugabe from December 1987 till at least 2016. As of 2016, his party, the Zimbabwe African Union-Patriotic Front (ZANU) had been the ruling party since 1980 when it won a landslide victory in an election, which saw the black majority take over from white minority rule. Mugabe and ZANU won another election in 1990, but some observers alleged the elections were neither free nor fair. There were allegations of vote rigging, intimidation and fraud in the presidential elections of 2002[197] and parliamentary elections of 2005.[198] The general elections in March 2008 resulted in a run-off between Mugabe and Morgan Tsvangirai from the Movement for Democratic Change (MDC), an opposition party. Later in 2008, Mugabe and Tsvangirai agreed to a power-sharing agreement with Mugabe as President and Tsvangirai as the Prime Minister.

In 2001, the US imposed sanctions on Zimbabwe, citing the nation's poor human rights record, political intolerance and absence

---

[197] *Movement for Democratic Change report*, "Stolen — How the elections were rigged", 12 April 2005.

[198] *Independent Online Zimbabwe*, "Mugabe's former ally accuses him of foul play", 12 March 2005.

of the rule of law. In 2002, the EU imposed sanctions on Zimbabwe in response to violence in the presidential elections that year.

Mugabe has close relations with China that go back a long way. During the guerrilla war against white minority rule in the 1970s, China supported Mugabe's ZANU forces.[199] In 2008, China, in support of its ally, deployed its United Nations (UN) Security Council veto to block UN sanctions against Zimbabwe. China's growing economic ties with Zimbabwe are a valuable alternative economic support for the African nation which faced EU and US sanctions. In 2007, China became the biggest investor in Zimbabwe, with an investment portfolio exceeding US$600 million.[200] China's trade with Zimbabwe doubled from US$400 million in 2009 to US$800 million in 2011.[201]

According to Reporters without Borders' Press Freedom Index of 2011–2012, Zimbabwe ranked 117 out of 179 nations globally. As of 2015, the government banned many foreign broadcasting stations from Zimbabwe, including Sky News, Channel 4, American Broadcasting Company, Australian Broadcasting Corporation and Fox News. News agencies and newspapers from other Western countries and South Africa have also been banned in the country.

However, there has been measured relaxation of media restrictions in the country. In 2010, the Zimbabwe Media Commission was established by the coalition government, which allowed the publication of newspapers previously banned by Mugabe. In May 2010, the Commission licensed three new privately-owned newspapers, including the previously banned *Daily News*, for publication. Reporters Without Borders described these decisions as a "major advance".

4.3.1 *Financial Gazette*

The *Financial Gazette*, established in 1969, describes itself as "Southern Africa's leading business and political newspaper well

---

[199]Nathan Andrew and Robert S. Ross, *The Great Wall and the Empty Fortress: China's Search for Security*, W. W. Norton, 1998.

[200]*People's Daily*, "China ranks Zimbabwe's top investor: senior official", 24 April 2007.

[201]Rebecca Moyo, *The Zimbabwean*, "China and Zimbabwe trade doubled", 8 May 2012.

known for its in-depth and authoritative reportage that is anchored on providing timely, accurate, fair and balanced news". Its website states, "Owned by Zimbabwean investors, the weekly newspaper jealously guards its editorial independence and supports democratic and pluralistic politics and free market policies."

Some articles in the *Financial Gazette* refer to China as an "all weather friend" of Zimbabwe, suggesting the *Financial Gazette* is possibly friendly towards China.

An article headlined "PM goes zhing-zhong" published on 8 June 2012 reports that Prime Minister Morgan Tsvangirai, a member of MDC and a political rival of President Mugabe, was apparently shifting from an anti-China stance to a more friendly attitude towards China.

The article claimed, "The word 'zhing-zhong' is part of Zimbabwe's street lingo referring to cheap Chinese products that have flooded the local market. China and its nationals have also been disparaged by the Movement for Democratic Change (MDC) because of Beijing's closeness to ZANU. Rightly or wrongly, the Chinese were accused of siphoning Zimbabwe's scarce foreign currency earnings, dumping inferior products locally and exploiting locals they employ at a number of their companies dotted in and around the country. Since the formation of the MDC in 1999, Prime Minister Morgan Tsvangirai's party has had no qualms in disparaging the Chinese."

The article revealed it came as a surprise that Tsvangirai visited Beijing in May 2012, met Chinese Premier Wen Jiabao and urged Chinese businesses to invest in Zimbabwe. The article quotes analysts saying Tsvangirai had to visit China because of China's economic and political clout. The tone of the article suggested China is a powerful reality that could not be ignored.

A 26 July 2012 commentary headlined "Sino-Africa partnership: beneficial or exploitative" was balanced in its views on China's economic relations with Africa. The article argued that Africa could use China as a springboard for its growth, but warned the partnership carried significant risks, especially for Africa. The article said Africa risks being exploited by China and Africa must proactively ensure its interests are safeguarded to attain a win–win solution.

4.3.2 *The Zimbabwe Independent*

The Zimbabwe Independent is owned by AMH, "an independent media house free from political ties or outside influence", according to its website.

Browsing through the website of *The Zimbabwe Independent*, I found few articles favourable to China, but many negative articles on China with headlines like "Chinese mining uranium without licence" and "Outrage over brutal Chinese labour practices".

A 4 May 2012 commentary headlined "Candid comment: wily Chinese see opportunity in Zim malaise" portrayed China's investment in Zimbabwe in a negative light. The article noted, "This class from the lower echelons of Chinese society, come here as part of China's strategy to ease unemployment back home and create more revenue streams. Many arrived here to pick up the economic pieces during hyperinflation. They are not the dragons. They are more of the vultures that came to feast on our economic carrion."

The Zimbabwe Independent has conducted investigative reporting on the Marange diamond fields. It carried stories quoting a report titled "Financing a parallel government?" by Global Witness, a UK NGO. For instance, a 3 August 2012 article headlined "Securocrats use diamond firm as front" reported that Anjin, which was mining diamonds in the Marangee fields, was a joint venture between a Zimbabwean company Matt Bronze and a Chinese company Anhui Foreign Economic Construction Group. The article alleged Matt Bronze was a front company for the Zimbabwean Ministry of Defence, police and military, while Anhui Foreign Economic Construction Group was building a National Defence College in Zimbabwe, financed by China Exim Bank, a Chinese state-owned bank. This article indicated that *The Zimbabwe Independent* conducted investigative journalism into both the Zimbabwe establishment and Chinese interests in the African nation.

An opinion column headlined "China and recolonisation of Zim", published on 17 August 2012, portrayed Chinese as foreigners encroaching on Zimbabwe's economy. The article starts off, "Zimbabwe's heavily-indebted government appears to be selling the family silver to the Chinese in exchange for long-term loans. The advances, now totalling more than US$532 million in the last four years, have been secured in exchange for lucrative concessions in the tourism, agricultural and mining sectors."

The article concludes, "Economists say despite the Chinese loans appearing cheap and 'developmental', the country is sinking further into a debt trap which will manifest itself in the next five to six years when loan repayments become due. The Chinese have not only gained ground in tourism, but have also secured significant stakes in mining, agriculture and property sectors."

A 31 August 2012 article headlined "Zanu PF gets Chinese poll strategy" reported Zanu seeking advice from China in a manner that was critical of China. The article leads with, "In an unprecedented move to draw up strategies ahead of defining elections expected next year, Zanu PF has dispatched its provincial chairpersons to China where they would be coached by the Chinese Communist Party on political tactics to keep the former liberation movement in power. Political analysts said the trip by Zanu PF chairpersons suggested the party was keen on adopting elements of the one-party state approach prevailing in China where refined methods of suppression of freedom of expression and any form of dissent are used."

4.3.3 *The Herald*

The Herald is a government-owned daily newspaper in Zimbabwe. In 1981, Mugabe's government bought the newspaper. A search on the Herald's website found articles that were generally extremely pro-China.

A 20 September 2012 article headlined "Obama stalking Africa's resources" is not only pro-China but anti-US. The article declared, "Apparently, Africa is more scared of the US than ever before and is more worried about increasing US military presence and footprints in Africa. In fact, the US, has gone (into) overdrive to try and outwit China when it comes to Africa's resources, but the Chinese have a more effective non-military approach, that has left the US trailing behind, hence Washington has gone physical through a cocktail of sanctions in the case of Zimbabwe."

An article headlined "China ain't colonizing Zim" published on 1 October 2012 commented on a book titled "Win–win partnership? China, Southern Africa and the extractive industries". As its headline suggests, this article said China was not colonising Zimbabwe. The article stated, "The book adds to the growing criticism on China's investments in Zimbabwe. There have been some misplaced statements in the media and other social platforms which suggest that China is a new coloniser of Zimbabwe. China has been accused of expropriating Zimbabwe's resources. Accusations abound that the Sino-Zimbabwe relation is only beneficial to a small political elite. Such criticisms obviously come from people whose interests are threatened by the symbiotic relationship existing between Zimbabwe and China. Zimbabwe looked east after the West imposed illegal sanctions that were meant to bleed the economy and subsequently spark revolts. The sanctions are fast losing steam due to all-weather friends like China and Russia which have steadfastly stood by Zimbabwe. The West and their allies obviously cannot be excited by a relationship that impedes the intended objectives of their sanctions. The Sino-Zimbabwe relationship does not resemble colonialism. China's investment in Zimbabwe is based on win–win joint ventures that have benefited the country."

4.3.4 *Zimbabwe Guardian*

The *Zimbabwe Guardian* is an online news publication based in London, working with reporters based in Zimbabwe, according to its website. A search of the *Zimbabwe Guardian* website found articles generally favourable towards China, although there were a few articles casting China in a negative light. The manner in which

China is cast in a positive light in some articles is similar to that of the Chinese state media like *People's Daily*.

An example of a pro-China article is one headlined "China impressed by Zimbabwe's warmth", published on 9 November 2011. The article reported that visiting Vice Chairman of the Standing Committee of the National People's Congress of China, Zhou Tienong, was "impressed with the warmth and friendliness of Zimbabwean people."

An article headlined "Anjin Investments means serious business" published on 16 December 2011 cast the Sino-Zimbabwean joint venture in a positive light, in contrast to *the Zimbabwean Independent's* negative investigative reports on Anjin. The article quotes Anjin Director Munyaradzi Machacha as saying Anjin respected Zimbabwean labour laws.

An 18 February 2012 article headlined "Learn from the Chinese, urges Business Council of Zimbabwe" stated the Council Chairman David Govere was "hailing" the Chinese way of doing business and urging the Zimbabweans to learn from the Chinese.

"We have to behave like Chinese who can erect a big structure overnight and everyone should be involved in the movement so that we instil the sense of belonging," he said.

4.3.5 *The Zimbabwean*

This newspaper is based in the UK, where there is a high degree of press freedom and protection of freedom of expression. According to its website, this newspaper was founded by a group of Zimbabwean journalists.

Its website stated, "The paper has been a constant thorn in the side of the Zimbabwean authorities, who hijacked and burnt one of our delivery trucks full of newspapers in 2008 following the abortive Presidential run-off poll. Following that, the Mugabe regime imposed a punitive duty as a tariff barrier in order to kill the newspaper. We survived this, although with a drastically reduced print run, and it was finally lifted in August 2009. The hard copy is still printed outside Zimbabwe and trucked in to exploit a loophole in the draconian AIPPA legislation which requires all local newspapers to register with the government Media and Information Commission."

A search of the newspaper's website found most articles on China cast China in a negative light, sometimes even in their headlines. An article headlined "Chinese firms abusing workers: union", published on 19 November 2010, reported that the Zimbabwe Construction and Allied Trades Workers Union accused Chinese construction companies' staff of beating up and firing local workers at will. The article detailed the union's allegations without quoting any Chinese party to give the Chinese side of the story.

A 21 September 2011 article headlined "Chinese hike cyanide prices" reported that Chinese firms had "unilaterally" hiked the price of cyanide, an important chemical used in gold production. The article portrayed China's economic influence in Zimbabwe in a negative light. The article noted that local bosses had no choice but to depend on Chinese suppliers for cyanide, so the Chinese raised cyanide prices. The article declared, "Zimbabwe and China have signed what is known as the Favourable Nations Status which enables the Chinese to virtually "dump" products into the country without question. The ZIMRA (Zimbabwe Revenue Authority) Commissioner General, Gershom Pasi, confirmed that the Chinese were causing problems for his team based at border and entry points around Zimbabwe."

A reader's letter headlined "Chinese flood the market" on 3 July 2012 noted, "Our local manufacturers are running at a loss because the Chinese have flooded the market with cheap rubbish and we cannot compete with their prices. Our locally manufactured goods are of a high standard compared to the cheaper, low quality products dumped on us by the Chinese. The Chinese are given more 'rights' than us Zimbos and we are born and bred here."

In contrast to the above articles which were critical of China, an article on 25 November 2011 was relatively even-handed in its treatment of China. The article, headlined "ZBC's Chinese programming", reported that the state-run Zimbabwe Broadcasting Corporation would start airing programmes from the state-run China Central Television. The article quoted Zimbabwe Information Minister Webster Shamu calling China a "genuine brother". But the article also quoted Zimbabwe Deputy Information Minister Murisi Zvizvai of the opposition MDC party saying, "Zimbabweans want balanced reporting from ZBC, not Chinese programmes." The article quoted media studies lecturer Zenzele Ndebele of the National

University of Science and Technology in Bulawayo, saying the Chinese programming was only likely to appeal to core supporters of President Mugabe.

4.3.6 *Summary*

Among the Zimbabwean newspapers cited above, *The Herald* and *Zimbabwe Guardian* are strongly pro-China, while *The Zimbabwe Independent* and *The Zimbabwean* are strongly anti-China. It is not surprising that the Herald, owned by Mugabe's party, is strongly pro-China, given Mugabe's friendship with China. *The Zimbabwe Independent*, a privately owned newspaper that describes itself as independent, is generally critical of China. As mentioned above, a column in *The Zimbabwe Independent* on 17 August 2012 carried a headline that portrayed China as a neo-colonialist, namely "China and recolonisation of Zim". The column accused the Zimbabwean government of "selling the family silver to the Chinese." *The Zimbabwean*, based in the UK, a nation that protects press freedom, publishes articles critical of China. As indicated above, an article and a reader's letter in *The Zimbabwean* accused Chinese companies of flooding Zimbabwe with cheap Chinese goods. However, the *Zimbabwe Guardian*, an online newspaper similarly headquartered in the UK, is pro-China.

This diversity of views among Zimbabwean newspapers reflects the nature of Zimbabwean politics, where power is shared between two competing parties.

4.4 Namibia

Namibia gained independence from South Africa on 21 March 1990, following the decades-long Namibian War of Independence. This country has a multi-party democracy. Since independence, the ruling party has been the South West African People's Organization (Swapo), which was previously a liberation movement during the War of Independence.

Since the 1960s, during the Namibian War of Independence, China has provided various Namibian independence movements with moral and material support, according to China's Foreign Ministry. China and Namibia have developed close economic relations, with trade doubling between both countries between 2003 and 2006. During a February 2007 visit to the country, then Chinese President Hu Jintao pledged 1 billion yuan of concessional loans, US$100 million of preferential export buyer's credit, 30 million yuan of grants and 30 million yuan of interest-free loans to Namibia, according to China's Foreign Ministry.

In recent years, there has been a large influx of Chinese into Namibia. The number of Chinese shops quadrupled between 2004 and 2006.[202] Namibia's Ministry of Home Affairs had issued 20,000 work permits for Chinese citizens by 2006, which is significant for a country with a population of 2 million.[203]

Although Namibia's population is comparatively small, the country has a broad diversity of media, including two TV stations, 19 radio stations, 5 daily newspapers, several weeklies and special publications. According to Reporters without Borders' Press Freedom Index of 2011–2012, Namibia ranked 20 out of 179 nations globally, and had the second highest level of press freedom in Africa behind Cape Verde.

4.4.1 *The Namibian*

The Namibian is the largest newspaper in the country, constituted as a trust and established in 1985 with donor funding.[204] Its founder and former editor, Gwen Lister, declared *The Namibian* prides itself on its editorial independence.[205] In its early years, it was subject to firebombings, shootings and attacks for its articles that offended some quarters.[206]

---

[202] Christiane Doerner, *Atlantic-Community.org*, "Colonialism reloaded: China is conquering Namibia", 9 January 2009.
[203] Ibid.
[204] Gwen Lister, *The Namibian 25ᵗʰ Anniversary Commemoration Magazine*, 27 August 2010.
[205] Ibid.
[206] Ibid.

Prior to independence in 1990, *The Namibian* was generally supportive of Swapo. However, after independence and when Swapo became the ruling party, *The Namibian's* critical approach became a target of the Swapo government.[207] Between 5 December 2000 and 30 August 2011, government offices were banned from advertising in *The Namibian* and government funds were forbidden to be used to buy copies of *The Namibian*, according to the laudatory submission for the Hero of World Press Freedom Award to Lister.

In a foreword in the 15th anniversary magazine edition of *The Namibian* in August 2000, former UN Secretary General Kofi Annan declared *The Namibian* "had worked courageously in difficult and often dangerous conditions", and had contributed immeasurably to press freedom and nation building in Namibia. Annan wrote that *The Namibian* had maintained its integrity and independent stance throughout its existence. In a foreword in *The Namibian 25th Anniversary Commemoration Magazine* dated 27 August 2010, former South African archbishop Desmond Tutu commended *The Namibian* for "highlighting the brutality of apartheid" when Namibia was under South African rule and said *The Namibian* remained true to the ideals of telling the truth and press freedom.

Overall, *The Namibian's* coverage of China was balanced and fair. There were a significant number of articles with negative reporting and opinions of China, but there were also articles with positive reporting on China. Even the negative articles on China were generally sober and analytical, devoid of strident attacks. My search of *The Namibian's* website found no articles that demonised China or portrayed the Chinese in a racist manner.

A letter by John Sampson published on 20 July 2004 with the headline "In Defence of Chinese" noted there was "an upside and something good" about the growing number of Chinese in Namibia. The letter praised the Chinese work ethic and argued that cheap Chinese goods ensure poorer Namibians are able to afford them.

---

[207] Andreas Rothe, *Media system and news selection in Namibia*, Lit. Verlag Munster, page 29 to 32, 2011.

An article headlined "Concern over Chinese stripping all marine life", published on 6 January 2005, reported alarm over Chinese nationals in Namibia indiscriminately stripping the ocean of marine life. The article claimed the Chinese got away with their stripping because "everybody was scared to touch them".

An article headlined "Chinese demand fuels illegal ivory trade in Africa" published on 16 March 2005 reported that poachers are killing 6,000 to 12,000 elephants in Sudan each year to supply illegal ivory to meet growing Chinese demand. The article noted the Chinese government had stepped up efforts to ban illegal ivory imports, but Sudan authorities have done little to discourage the trade. The article placed part of the blame for the illegal ivory trade on the Sudanese army for its involvement in the transport of ivory. This article, though critical of Chinese parties, was balanced as it acknowledged Chinese government efforts to halt the illegal ivory imports.

A 22 June 2005 article headlined "Chinese chip in on State House" attested to the political clout of China in relation to the Namibian government but also took a suspicious, critical attitude towards the Chinese construction of the presidential residence in Namibia. The suspicion in the article is clearly visible in these sentences: "Minister of Works, Joel Kaapanda steered clear of mentioning any costs involved in the construction of the controversial State House. He said the new presidential residence was "still on the drawing board" and the cost would be covered by a "generous" grant from China. Under the Office of the President, N$90 million has been budgeted for construction this year, but Kaapanda provided no breakdown for how this money would be spent."

An 11 August 2006 article headlined "Govt should wise up to benefits of 'Chinese invasion'" was thoughtful, analytical, constructive and balanced. The article quoted Professor Gregor Dobler of the University of Basel saying the Namibian government should direct and police Chinese investments rather than just allow Chinese to run shops selling cheap goods in Namibia. He disagreed with "persistent rumours" that "the Chinese invasion" was a politically inspired policy aimed at world domination, saying that none of the shops relied explicitly on Beijing's support. Rumours of "more than 20,000 Chinese in Namibia" were exaggerated, with the real figure more likely to be less than 5,000, he noted. The article explained that the impact of the growing Chinese presence in Namibia was both positive and negative, posing "devastating competition" for local businesses while providing cheap goods that are affordable for the poorer sections of Namibian society.

Another letter also dated 28 November 2006 headlined "We need answers on Chinese influx" expressed scepticism over claims by Namibian Minister Joel Kaapanda that there were "not that many" Chinese working in Namibia. The letter questioned whether some of the Chinese workers in Namibia had legal work visas. The article said a large number of Namibian building companies were closing down due to the Chinese "infiltration". The article called on the Namibian government to "look after our own people first".

A letter by Mulife Muchali from Vancouver, Canada, published on 28 November 2006, headlined "Let's welcome the Chinese" argued that shunning the Chinese was counter-productive. The letter said Namibians must not be afraid of competing against "such a formidable and experienced people", but "embrace the people as our own brothers and sisters". The letter advocated the Ministry of Home Affairs process the applications of Chinese immigrants in Namibia "speedily" as part of globalisation.

An article headlined "Nam builders ramp up pressure on Govt over Chinese firms", published on 2 April 2007, quoted allegations by the Construction Industries Federation of Namibia regarding Chinese construction firms operating illegally in Namibia and appearing to "completely ignore" Namibian laws.

However, a 4 April 2007 article headlined "Chinese builders 'not only culprits'" quoted Namibian Labour Commissioner Bro-Matthew Shinguadja as reacting to allegations by the Construction Industries Federation of Namibia. Shinguadja explained that Chinese building contractors were not the only ones contravening laws and regulations, but subcontractors, all of whom are local, were the main culprits who did not comply with minimum wage and social security benefits.

A 22 June 2007 article headlined "Africa urged to be wise in dealing with China" quoted Ghana's Trade and Industry Minister Alan Kyerematen, who said Africa can learn from China's economic prowess and benefit from its relations with China, but should be cautious in its dealings with China and wary of China's intentions towards Africa.

4.4.2 *New Era*

The *New Era* is wholly owned by the Namibian government, according to its website.

Nearly all the articles found on the newspaper's website were positive on China, with virtually no article that was negative on China. A rare exception is an article published on 28 June 2012 headlined "Chinese economy in SADC, a growing concern". The article suggested Chinese economic activity in the Southern African Development Community (SADC) has sparked growing concern regarding unethical business behaviour.

A 23 November 2004 article headlined "China's activity in Africa — sparks interest but not concern" mentioned some concerns over China's growing economic role in Africa. The article pointed out "crumbling sports stadiums" in many African capitals and the fact that China's outreach in Africa is "raising some eyebrows in some Western capitals". Nonetheless, the article is positive in its take on China, describing the Chinese as "capitalists, not colonialists". The article quoted US Ambassador Jendayi Frazer as having said China "is not a threat to us".

On the other hand, there were many articles with friendly headlines on China, for example, a 26 October 2004 article with the headline "China a true African friend", another article with the headline "Namibia welcomes Chinese investors" published on 6 March 20, a 24 July 2012 article with the headline "President praises Chinese generosity", and an article with the headline "Much to learn from the Chinese" published on 21 November 2012.

An article published on 22 May 2012 with the headline "Cultural similarities between China and Africa" described the nature of

African culture as monolithic as supposedly was Chinese culture. The article claimed, "Peoples of African descent are linked by shared values that are fundamental features of African identity and culture. These include hospitality, friendliness, consensus and (the) common framework-seeking principle, ubuntu, and the emphasis on community rather than on the individual." The article added that "Chinese culture, the centre of Asian cultures, typically stands for collectivism, similar to African communalism".

One wonders whether other Asians would agree with the notion that Chinese culture stands at the centre of Asian cultures. Given that *the New Era* is owned by the Namibian government, such an article suggests the Namibian government may look to the Chinese authoritarian form of government, with no democracy and press freedom, as a role model. This article raises questions of whether the culture of Africa, a continent with many countries, can be described as monolithic and whether African culture favours the collective over the individual.

An article headlined "Sino-African relations are historical", published on 3 August 2012, noted that Sino-African relations are increasingly portrayed by the West as neo-colonialism on the part of China. The article claimed that "at close scrutiny", it seems "the other way around". The article noted, "Propaganda is used to systematically implant the notion of an enemy (China) in the minds of the local population. As far as propaganda, psychological control and the motivation of American politics of predominance and the creation of enemy stereotypes are concerned, the US power elites have surpassed all previous records."

Ironically, the effusive praise for China's impact on Africa and criticism of the West in this article of 3 August 2012 showed *the New Era* was also indulging in propaganda. While the article on 3 August 2012 criticised the West for creating stereotypes of China, the article of 22 May 2012 raised the question of whether it was creating stereotypes of African and Chinese cultures.

A 13 November 2012 article headlined "Africa must look East for its solutions" praised China in gushing tones: "China's historic achievements have arrested international attention. European scholars and politicians, including former US Foreign Secretary Henry Kissinger, point out that China's peaceful development has demolished dominant Western theory that the 'Western Mode' is the only social and economic development mode." The article said Westernisation has failed Africa. "Taking China as a good example, Africa will find out her own way to tackle her own problems," the article declared.

The articles above indicate that *the New Era*, and the Namibian government which owns it, are critical of Western democracy and prefer the Chinese authoritarian form of government.

4.4.3 *Summary*

The *New Era*, a newspaper wholly owned by the Namibian government, casts China in an extremely positive light, and the style of its articles on China is similar to Chinese state propaganda. In contrast, *The Namibian*, which has a reputation for independence and opposing the establishment, is balanced in its reporting on China, with both positive and negative viewpoints expressed. Even an independent newspaper like *The Namibian* is not hostile towards China in an extreme or one-sided way.

4.5 Zambia

Since Zambia gained independence from Britain on 24 October 1964, it had been a one-party state till 1991. From 1991 to September 2011, the ruling party was the Movement for Multi-party Democracy (MMD). In September 2011, a former opposition politician, Michael Sata, who belonged to the Patriotic Front (PF) party, was elected as the Zambian President. While in opposition, Sata often criticised Chinese companies in Zambia, accusing them of using "slave labour" and complaining that they employed Chinese workers at the expense of Zambians.[208] After becoming president, he told Chinese

---

[208] Andrew England, *Financial Times*, "Sata gives Chinese investors guarded welcome", 26 September 2011.

companies that they were welcome to invest in his state, but they had to obey local laws.[209]

China is an important investor in Zambia, Africa's biggest copper producer, and Chinese firms are estimated to have invested more than US$2 billion in the country.[210] There have been tensions between Chinese and Zambians, with Zambian miners killing a Chinese supervisor and injuring another in a pay dispute at the Collum coal mine in 2012[211] and two Chinese supervisors accused of shooting 13 Zambian miners at the same coal mine in 2010.[212]

According to Reporters without Borders' Press Freedom Index of 2011–2012, Zambia ranked 86 out of 179 nations globally.

4.5.1 *The Times of Zambia*

The Times of Zambia is owned by the Zambian government.

There is little news on Chinese business activities in Zambia in this newspaper, which is unusual considering the important role of China in Zambia's economy. An article headlined "Ghana detains 90 Chinese for illegal mining", published on 14 October 2012, is sympathetic to the Chinese side. The article noted, "China is eager to be seen as capable of maintaining the security and rights of its citizens abroad."

4.5.2 *The Zambian Post*

The Zambian Post is an independent Zambian newspaper and one of the most highly-circulated newspapers in the country. *The Zambian Post* has been involved in wrangles with the Zambian government. In 2001, its editor Fred M'membe was arrested for calling then

---

[209] Ibid.
[210] Ibid.
[211] *The Guardian*, "Zambian miners kill Chinese supervisor and injure another in pay dispute", 5 August 2012.
[212] Barry Bearak, *New York Times*, "Zambia drops case of shooting by mine bosses", 4 April 2011.

Zambian President Frederick Chiluba a thief.[213] M'membe was again arrested in 2005 for writing an editorial critical of then Zambian President Levy Patrick Mwanawasa, according to a report on Freedom House's website in 2007.

Compared to *The Times of Zambia*, which has few articles on Chinese businesses in Zambia, *The Zambian Post* carries many articles on this issue, some of which are negative towards China.

A commentary by Tommie Hamaluba headlined "Sata on Chinese investment", published on 26 December 2009 when Sata was in opposition, supported Sata's criticism of Chinese investment in Zambia.

A 28 January 2011 letter to the editor headlined "Be wary of China" expressed deep worries about "the gradual invasion of Africa by China". The letter declared, "Not that I'm xenophobic, but we need to protect our resources against plunder through neo-colonialism, which Kwame Nkrumah said is the last stage of imperialism (and is worse than colonialism). It's heartbreaking when one hears the bad treatment the Chinese are giving to our African brothers working in Chinese-run industries."

One example of negative reports on Chinese business activities in Zambia is a 23 July 2011 article headlined "Court fines Chinese company for tax evasion". The article reports that chief resident magistrate Joshua Banda fined a Lusaka-based Chinese company K3 million (US$564) after convicting it for making false tax returns for wheat supplies worth over K400 million (US$75,214). (K is the Zambian currency Kwacha).

Another example of negative reporting on China is an article headlined "ACC to sign MoU with Auditor General's office" published on 13 February 2012. It mentioned a Chinese company, Jiangsu Wujin Corporation, was awarded a contract to upgrade urban roads in Zambia at a cost of over K117 billion (US$22 million) and the Chinese company submitted a fake security bond and obtained a K5 billion advance payment on the project.

---

[213]Derek Ingram, "Commonwealth update", *The Round Table*, volume 367, page 585–611.

Some articles appear to defend the Chinese, but contain elements that put China in a negative or ambiguous light. One example is an article headlined "ZFE justifies Chinese locking up workers" which was published on 23 July 2011. The article focused on the Zambian Federation of Employers' (ZFE) defence of Chinese labour practices. However, the headline and the content of the article made ZFE and Chinese employers look ludicrous. The article quoted ZFE Executive Director Harrington Chibanda as saying, "The Chinese culture entails every minute counts in the line of production and we have not taken this seriously as Zambians. The locking up of workers is for productivity levels as opposed to violation of human rights." Such a quote may play up to negative stereotypes of Chinese employers as behaving in an inhumane manner in the pursuit of productivity and profits.

Another article quoted a source defending Zambian President Michael Sata, saying he was still tough on the allegedly exploitative behaviour of Chinese investors, but other sources in that article were critical of both Sata and the Chinese. The 1 March 2012 article headlined "PF stance on exploitative Chinese hasn't changed, says Kabimba" quoted Wynter Kabimba, Secretary General of the ruling PF, as saying his party has not changed its "tough stance" on exploitative Chinese investors. Kabimba, who was later appointed by Zambian President Michael Sata as the nation's Justice Minister in September 2012, declared Chinese firms in Zambia must comply with Zambian law and must not pay Zambian workers "slave wages". While in opposition, Sata had campaigned heavily on the platform that he would punish Chinese investors who abused Zambians. The article noted, "However, analysts have observed that President Sata's stance has since changed, going by his constant praise of Chinese investors. Some analysts even fear that the PF government could go the MMD way in selling Zambian workers to exploitative investors."

However, there were also articles that put China in a positive light.

A 27 July 2010 article headlined "Bingguo urges Africa to reject opposition to relations with China" quoted Chinese State Councillor Dai Bingguo urging African nations to reject opposition to friendly ties with China. The article quoted Dai extensively and largely gave the Chinese side of the story, which portrayed China as being beneficial to Africa.

An article headlined "Zhou happy with govt policies towards China", published on 7 December 2012, gave the Chinese point of view on Sino-Zambian relations. The article quoted Chinese Ambassador to Zambia, Zhou Yuxiao, as saying, "When the PF was in opposition, it made strong efforts to demonise China ... but I am happy that the China-Zambia cooperations (sic) have grown from strength to strength."

4.5.3 *Zambian Watchdog*

The *Zambian Watchdog* describes itself as "Zambia's leading investigative 24-hour breaking news newspaper" with the motto "for uncensored news and views on Zambia". The newspaper was forced into exile in 2009 and has ended its print version and has only an online version. Its journalists operate undercover and anonymously in Zambia.

Among the three Zambian newspapers examined, the *Zambian Watchdog* is the most negative towards China and had some articles with strong anti-China headlines. Examples of negative headlines include "Why are Chinese companies allowed to bring prisoners to work in Zambia?" (11 January 2013), "China-Jiangxi's Zambian 'slaves' in Chinsali down tools" (3 January 2013) and "Chinese investor slices ear of his Zambian 'slave', bribes police" (20 October 2012). The word 'slaves' has sensitive connotations for Africans, given the history of slavery in Africa.

An article headlined "Another minister in China to admire buildings and thank China", published on 29 May 2012, mocked the Zambian government, President Sata and China. The article said, "In what has now become a fashion for a Zambian minister to visit and thank China every week, Defence Minister Geoffrey Mwamba is in Shanghai. In exchange, Chinese nationals have been coming into Zambia in plane-loads and taking up simple jobs that can be done by Zambians. While in opposition, the PF government condemned the influx of Chinese nationals into Zambia and current president Michael Sata even threatened to expel the Chinese if he became president. But once in power, one of the first actions Sata took was to have lunch with Chinese investors and invite more to come."

A commentary headlined "Sata needs basic integrity", published on 14 October 2012, was also critical of Sata and China. The commentary noted, "Sata promised to rein in the Chinese in the Zambian industry. He accused their firms of discriminating against Zambian workers on the mines. He denounced them for operating mines with sub-standard safety measures and for housing Zambian workers in 'ghetto' compounds. Sata further condemned them that they refused to employ Zambians instead were transporting workers from China even for manual labour jobs. These problems are still there even today! His U-turn on his positions casts serious doubt on his integrity."

A 17 December 2012 article headlined "Kabimba accused of financially benefiting from PF women tailoring project" reported that senior members of the ruling PF party accused Secretary General Wynter Kabimba of gaining financially from a programme funded by the Chinese government.

The article headlined "China-Jiangxi's Zambian 'slaves' down tools", published on 3 January 2013, reported that construction at a government office stalled after local workers downed tools. The article listed a litany of the workers' complaints, including beatings by employers. It played up the workers' complaints without giving any defence on the part of the Chinese parties.

However, positive articles on China were also found in the *Zambian Watchdog*.

A 2 July 2012 column by Dambisa Moyo supported China against the US. The article noted that in June 2011, US Secretary of State Hillary Rodham Clinton gave a speech warning of a "new colonialism" threatening Africa, implicitly referring to China without naming the country. Moyo said, "Despite all the scaremongering, China's motives for investing in Africa are actually quite pure." The column added, "Moreover, the evidence does not support a claim that Africans themselves feel exploited." The article argued, "The fact that so many African governments can stay in power by relying on foreign aid that has few strings attached, instead of revenues from their own populations, allows corrupt politicians to remain in charge. Thankfully, the decrease in the flow of Western aid since the 2008 financial crisis offers a chance to remedy this structural failure so that, like others in the world, Africans can finally hold their governments accountable."

What the column failed to address was whether the generous loans and aid provided by China to African governments with little or no strings attached, irrespective of their human rights record, was propping up unpopular repressive regimes.

An article headlined "Give Sata a chance — China", published on 1 October 2012, was favourable to both China and Sata. The article noted that Chinese Ambassador to Zambia Zhou Yuxiao was confident President Sata would "spur Zambia to prosperity". The article said, "Relations between Zambia and China have remarkably improved since President Sata extended a hand of friendship when he assumed office after a rough pre-election start."

A commentary headlined "Why Chinese Envoy Zhou Yuxiao is right", published on 16 October 2012, took a positive but nuanced view of China. It noted that the Zambian government and multinationals must shoulder much of the blame for problems in Zambia's mining sector. The article admitted that China should not be entirely blamed for the problems in Zambia's mining sector. The article cited Zambia's "appalling labour laws" and explained that Zambia's poor governance has provided fertile ground for corruption in the nation's mining sector.

In early August 2012, Zambian miners killed a Chinese supervisor and seriously wounded another in a pay dispute at the Collum coal mine. The coverage of this issue in the *Zambian Watchdog* was mixed.

An article headlined "Nine arrested in death of Chinese supervisor", published on 6 August 2012, took an unfriendly stance on China and President Sata. This is evident in the opening sentences, "Desperate not to lose Chinese money over the death of a China man at Collum Coal Mine in Sinazongwe, the Zambian (sic) government through its police have arrested seven people. This is the same Collum mine where Chinese managers fired on rioting workers two years ago. The Chinese managers were charged with attempted murder, but the charges were dropped. Maybe miners this time were ready for their bosses. And Labour Minister Fackson Shamenda has profusely apologised to Beijing for the death of 50-year-old Wu Shengzai, a supervisor at the coal mine."

The article continued, "Police immediately picked up two miners in connection with the riot and seven more people were arrested by police last night bringing the number to nine."

On the other hand, there were articles on this incident that were sympathetic to China.

In an article headlined "MMD condemns killing of Chinese manager but blames PF decree of minimum wage" published on 7 August 2012, the opposition party, Movement for Multi-party Democracy (MMD) expressed condolences to the bereaved family and the Chinese government, and called for perpetrators to be "severely punished". In that article, MMD President Nevers Mumba blamed the ruling Patriotic Front (PF) party for creating a "volatile environment between employers and employees".

A 7 August 2012 article headlined "China's Ambassador to Zambia warns of deteriorating relations" quoted Beijing's Ambassador to Zambia Zhou Yuxiao saying relations between China and Zambia may be at risk due to the killing. The article gives Zhou's point of view. Zhou said this was a "very serious tragedy" because it will create fear among Chinese investors in Zambia and called for the punishment of guilty parties.

An article headlined "Zambia still safe, secure investment destination, Sakeni assures Chinese community", published on 7 August 2012, quoted Zambian chief government spokesman Kennedy Sakeni saying Zambia is still safe for Chinese investment.

4.5.4 *Summary*

It is noteworthy that *The Times of Zambia*, which is owned by the Zambian government, has little coverage of the substantial Chinese business activities in Zambia. A likely reason is the change in Sata's attitude towards China, from a critical position before becoming president to a friendly stance after becoming president. Perhaps Sata's U-turn is an embarrassment for this government-owned newspaper. On the other hand, *The Zambian Post* and *Zambian Watchdog*, which are not owned by the Zambian government, carry more articles on Chinese business activities in Zambia, including negative articles. The *Zambian Watchdog*, whose print operations are banned by the Zambian government, is the most negative among the three towards China. Nonetheless, both the *Zambian Watchdog* and *The Zambian Post* do carry positive articles on China.

4.6 Angola

Angola gained independence from Portugal in November 1975, when the People's Movement for the Liberation of Angola (MPLA) became the ruling party. A few months later, Angola descended into a state of civil war with MPLA fighting the National Front for the Liberation of Angola (FNLA) and the National Union for the Total Independence of Angola (UNITA). MPLA was backed by the Soviet Union, while UNITA and FNLA received military aid from the US and South Africa.

Initially after independence in 1975, Angola was a one-party Marxist-Leninist state ruled by the MPLA. In 1992, the civil war was temporarily halted and elections were held. MPLA won a majority in the parliamentary elections while MPLA's candidate for President, Jose Eduardo dos Santos, won the first round of the presidential election against Jonas Savimbi of UNITA. The second round was never held. Opposition parties alleged the elections were fraudulent. Savimbi withdrew from the election, and civil war resumed. In 2002, Savimbi was killed in a battle with MPLA troops, and shortly after that, a ceasefire was reached. UNITA gave up armed struggle and assumed the role of the main opposition party while MPLA remained the ruling party.

China is Angola's most important economic partner. The single most significant commodity in the Sino-Angolan economic relationship has been crude oil. According to the Economist Intelligence

Unit (EIU), crude oil composed over 95 percent of Angola's exports as of 2010. China accounted for the biggest share of Angolan exports in 2010 at 43.8 percent in 2010, according to EIU. In 2011, Angola was the second largest supplier of oil to China behind Saudi Arabia.[214]

Angola scored poorly on the 2008 Ibrahim Index of African Governance, according to the Mo Ibrahim Foundation, an organisation that promotes governance in Africa. It ranked 44 out of 48 sub-Saharan African countries, scoring particularly badly in the categories of Participation and Human Rights, Sustainable Economic Opportunity and Human Development.

According to the Reporters without Borders' Press Freedom Index of 2011–2012, Angola ranked 132 out of 179 nations globally, one of the lowest in Africa. Angola's media is mainly controlled by the ruling MPLA.[215]

4.6.1 *Angola Press Agency (ANGOP)*

Angola Press Agency (ANGOP) is the official Angola news agency. ANGOP was previously allied with the Telegraph Agency of the Soviet Union (TASS), the official news agency of the former Soviet Union.

For articles dealing with Sino-Angolan relations, the only articles found were those that cast Sino-Angolan relations in a positive light. An article headlined "Ambassador to China thanks for year personality award" dated 18 March 2013 reported that Angolan Ambassador to China Garcia Bires received a Personality of the Year award from a group of Chinese media. The report reported the event in glowing tones, "Garcia Bires was awarded the title for his great diplomatic knowledge and poetic and romantic temperament.... He said he accepted the award with great esteem, on behalf of the Angolan government... The diplomat added that he

---

[214] EIA, *Eurasia Review*, "Angola Energy Profile: Second largest oil producer in Sub-Saharan Africa behind Nigeria — Analysis", 4 January 2013.
[215] Celia W. Dugger, *New York Times*, "Angola's New Constitution Consolidates President's Power", 21 January 2010.

was receiving the award on behalf of the people of Angola and for the friendship and solidarity existing between Angola and China."

Outside Angola, there were some reports that put China in a less favourable light. Some ANGOP articles on Chinese activities in other African states were not favourable to China.

An article headlined "CPJ asks Congo to release imprisoned journalist", published on 17 February 2013, reported that an African media advocacy group, the Committee to Protect Journalists (CPJ), called on the Congolese government to release an editor sentenced to six months in prison on defamation charges. Joachim Diana Gikupa, editor of a daily newspaper La Colombe, had written a report alleging a Chinese company, which managed a Congolese hospital, had sold expired medicine.

A 21 February 2013 article headlined "Zambia seizes control of Chinese state-owned mine amid safety fears" reported that the Zambian government took over a Chinese-owned coal mine in Zambia and revoked its licence due to safety lapses. The article quoted Zambian Mining Minister Yamfwa Mukanga saying the mine had a poor safety, health and environmental record.

One might think the state news agency of Angola, a nation with friendly ties to China, would always contain positive articles on China. Interestingly, some articles on China's domestic issues did not put the Chinese government in a positive light.

An article headlined "Dalai Lama presses China to investigate Tibetan self-immolations", dated 13 November 2012, quoted the Dalai Lama urging the Chinese government to investigate Tibetans' protests against the Chinese government through the act of immolation. Although the article cited the Chinese government's view that Tibet was a part of China and the Dalai Lama was interfering in China's domestic affairs, the article gave prominent coverage to the Dalai Lama's point of view. Given that the Chinese government expresses displeasure with countries that cultivate friendly ties with the Dalai Lama, it is significant that the ANGOP ran this article.

A 28 December 2012 article headlined "China: China tightening controls on Internet" painted China's leaders in an unfavourable light for controlling the Internet.

An article headlined "In China, public anger over secrecy on environment", published on 10 March 2013, reported that Chinese microbloggers, Chinese state media and the National People's Congress expressed disquiet over the scarcity of information on environmental issues in China, and were critical of the Chinese government over issues surrounding the poor quality of air and water in China. The article described the National People's Congress as "the largely rubber stamp parliament" of China.

An article headlined "Democratic hopes dashed for Hong Kong 2017 election", published on 28 March 2013, appeared to sympathise with Hong Kongers' aspirations for democracy. The first sentence went, "Hopes that Hong Kong's 2017 election will be genuinely democratic have been dashed after a senior Chinese leader said, regardless of the vote, Beijing will have the final say on who is appointed Hong Kong's next leader." The article quoted Albert Ho, a pro-democracy lawmaker of Hong Kong's Democratic Party, describing the Chinese government's move as a "pre-emptive strike" to contain Hong Kongers' expectations of universal suffrage.

4.6.2 *Summary*

ANGOP was highly positive on articles that dealt with relations between China and Angola. However, on issues not related to Angola, ANGOP carried many articles that were critical of China. Given that ANGOP is the state news agency in a country with low press freedom, the likely reason ANGOP is positive on China-Angolan relations is the wish to place the Angolan government in a good light rather than a desire to please China. The fact that ANGOP carried articles that are negative on China in matters not concerning Angola shows it is not afraid of displeasing China.

4.7 Conclusion

Looking at the English-language press in these five African states, it is clear that even the most independent newspapers do not demonise China. For instance, *The Namibian*, a newspaper with a reputation for standing up to the establishment in the face of fierce opposition, is balanced in its reporting on China.

Some newspapers that are relatively free of government censorship published both positive and negative articles on China. For example in Zambia, *The Zambian Post* and the *Zambian Watchdog*, which are not owned by the Zambian government, carried both negative and positive articles on China. In a country where no single party is dominant, such as Zimbabwe, different newspapers offer a diverse range of views on China. Among the Zimbabwean newspapers, *The Herald*, which is owned by Zimbabwean President Mugabe's party, and the *Zimbabwe Guardian* are strongly pro-China, while *The Zimbabwe Independent* and *The Zimbabwean* are anti-China.

This shows that wherever there is a liberated press regime in Africa, China is unlikely to suffer unfair stereotypes or racist portrayal in the media. If there are negative articles on China, they will be counter-balanced by positive articles.

Unsurprisingly, government-owned newspapers, such as *The Herald* of Zimbabwe and *New Era* of Namibia, were positive in their coverage of China and were sometimes reminiscent of Chinese state media in their propagandistic style. They echo their government's friendly relations with China. But in the case of the Angolan state news agency, ANGOP, it tends to support the local government rather than China. ANGOP seems to have praised China only when it was praising its own government, but was not shy of criticising China when the Angolan government was not involved.

The friendly attitude towards China in state-owned media should not be seen as an unequivocal benefit to Beijing. If relations between China and an African government should deteriorate, the local state media can be expected to turn against China. If that happens, it is quite likely the local state media's negative reporting on China will not be objective, but by comparison, independent media will be more balanced and fair in reporting on China.

Hence, a free and independent African media will benefit China and foster healthier relations between China and Africa, even if it carries articles critical of China. The Chinese government need not fear a free African press.

This survey of English-language media in five African nations has shown that African media have criticised Chinese individuals and companies for corruption or bad behaviour; a few Zimbabwean news articles were found to accuse China of neo-colonialism or portray China as an economic threat, and some South African and Zambian media articles have criticised their governments for being too friendly with China, but most articles have not portrayed China as an evil empire out to exploit Africa.

Although China gets its share of criticism in the African media, apart from a few exceptions, the African press did not see China as a neo-imperialist nor did they paint the Chinese in racist colours. So, to the question of whether the African media perceives China as imperialist or neo-colonialist, the answer is mostly "no". Against accusations that China is a neo-imperialist in Africa, African media generally have sided with the Chinese government's stance that China has no imperialist designs on the continent. Both the state-owned and relatively freer media have not depicted China as imperialist. State-controlled media tends to reflect the views of the government, while the more independent media generally reflects more the view of the people. Although this analysis has looked at only English-language media in five countries, it can fairly be said that both African governments and African peoples do not perceive China as imperialist.

SOUTH AMERICA

Chapter 5

Cracking the Monroe Doctrine

On 22 July 2014, Chinese President Xi Jinping met retired Cuban Communist leader Fidel Castro, on his visit to Cuba.

During Xi's visit to Cuba, 29 agreements were signed, Chinese state media reported. Among the deals, China Exim Bank offered Cuba a 730 million yuan (US$115 million) loan for Santiago Port, Cuba's second largest port. Meanwhile, China Minmetals Corporation, a Chinese state-owned firm, would spend US$600 million to buy Cuban nickel ore. This was part of Xi's tour of four Latin American countries, namely Brazil, Argentina, Venezuela and Cuba, where he witnessed billions of dollars of deals signed.

China-Caribbean ties have strengthened since the mid-2000s and would likely continue to expand under President Xi, who has emphasised relations with the region more than his predecessors, a report dated 16 May 2014 by the US-China Economic and Security Review Commission (USCC), a US government body that advises the US Congress on Sino-US relations, stated.

Xi extended his good wishes to Castro for his upcoming 88th birthday, while Castro said Russia and China were "two countries called to lead a new world that will allow the survival of humanity", according to media reports.

More than 50 years before Xi's meeting with Castro, the survival of humanity was at stake during the Cuban Missile Crisis, when the US and the Soviet Union confronted each other eyeball-to-eyeball amidst the prospect of nuclear war. Castro was the Cuban leader during those tense times.

In 1959, Castro, a Communist leader, came to power in an armed revolt that overthrew the right wing Cuban dictator Fulgencio Batista. The US government distrusted Castro due to his cosy relationship with Nikita Khrushchev, the Soviet leader. On 17 April 1961, under the orders of US President John Kennedy, 1,400 Cuban exiles from the southern US state of Florida launched an invasion at the Bay of Pigs in Cuba. Castro's army crushed the invasion on 19 April 1961. Shortly afterwards, President Kennedy's predecessor, Dwight Eisenhower, told Kennedy that "the failure of the Bay of Pigs will embolden the Soviets to do something that they would otherwise not do".[216]

In 1962, the Soviets built nuclear missile sites in Cuba targeting the US. In October 1962, US spy planes discovered Soviet missiles in Cuba. Subsequently, US President Kennedy imposed a naval blockade around Cuba and US forces worldwide were placed on heightened alert.

On 22 October 1962, President Kennedy warned in a speech, "It shall be the policy of this nation to regard any nuclear missile launched from Cuba against any nation in the Western Hemisphere as an attack by the Soviet Union on the United States, requiring a full retaliatory response upon the Soviet Union."

On 24 October 1962, the Soviet news agency TASS broadcast a telegram from Khrushchev to Kennedy, in which the Soviet leader warned that what he described as the Americans' "outright piracy" would lead to war.

On 25 October 1962, the Chinese state newspaper *People's Daily* declared, "650 million Chinese men and women were standing by the Cuban people."

With mutual warnings of war issued between US and Soviet leaders, the world seemed to be on the brink of nuclear Armageddon.

---

[216] Kenneth Michael Absher, *Mind-Sets and Missiles: A First Hand Account of the Cuban Missile Crisis*, Strategic Studies Institute, US Army War College, 2009.

However, the US undertook secret negotiations with the Soviet Union. On 27 October 1962, Kennedy secretly agreed to remove all US missiles in southern Italy and Turkey, in exchange for the Soviet Union removing all missiles in Cuba. The world breathed easier when the two superpowers stepped back from the brink of nuclear war.

What prompted the US to come that close to World War III with the Soviet Union over this small Caribbean island nation? Part of the answer is found in the Monroe Doctrine.

On 19 April 1961, amid Cold War tensions between the US and communist Cuba, a *New York Times* article explained, "The United States Government's determination to halt Communist subversion in Latin America, and Cuba in particular, has its roots in the Monroe Doctrine. President James Monroe announced in 1823 that the United States would consider any attempt by European powers to extend their 'system' to this hemisphere 'as dangerous to our peace and safety.' The President's unilateral statement gained increasing acceptance as the United States grew stronger, and in the last century has served as a basic precept in this country's hemispheric policies. In the Eighteen Twenties, as now, both Cuba and Russia figured in the formation of the United States' policy toward Latin America."

The *New York Times* article continued, "Monroe's policy came to be considered a permanent 'doctrine' at the turn of the century. Secretary of State Richard Olney referred to it in 1895 when he declared that the United States was practically sovereign on this continent. In that same year, a rebel Cuban junta, directed by Thomas Estrada Palma, an exile in New York, received United States' sympathy in its efforts to incite a revolt against the Spanish in Cuba. In 1898, the doctrine was invoked as one of the justifications for the Spanish-American war and the United States' occupation of Cuba, following the blowing up of the battleship Maine in Havana Harbor. The occupation lasted until 1902, when the Republic of Cuba was formed."

The Monroe Doctrine eventually became a longstanding tenet of US foreign policy.[217] The three main concepts in the doctrine

---

[217] *Office of the Historian, US Department of State, https: history.state.gov.*

were separate spheres of influence for the Americas and Europe, non-colonisation, and non-intervention.[218] Monroe's administration warned European powers against interfering in the affairs of Latin American states.[219] While the Americans generally objected to European colonies in the New World, they wished to increase US influence and trading ties throughout the region to their south. And European mercantilism posed the greatest obstacle to US economic expansion.[220] In particular, the Americans feared Spain and France might reassert colonial influence over the Latin American peoples who had just overthrown European rule.[221]

Apart from Cuba, another small Central American country, Nicaragua, fell under the shadow of the Monroe Doctrine. US forces intervened in and occupied Nicaragua at various times from 1909 to 1933. In 1909, the US provided political support to conservative forces rebelling against Nicaraguan President Jose Santos Zelaya. On 18 November 1909, US warships were sent to Nicaragua after revolutionaries were executed on the orders of Zelaya, who resigned later that year. US Marines occupied Nicaragua from 1912 to 1933, except for a nine-month interval starting in 1925.[222]

From 1927 until 1933, a rebel Nicaraguan general, Augusto César Sandino, led a guerrilla war first against the Nicaraguan government and then against the US Marines.[223] After US forces withdrew from Nicaragua in January 1933, Sandino reached an amnesty agreement with the Nicaraguan government. In 1934, Sandino was assassinated by soldiers of the US-backed General Anastasio Somoza Garcia, who ruled Nicaragua from 1936 till his own assassination in 1956. The Somoza family, supported by the US, continued to rule Nicaragua till 1979.

Sandino's memory lived on in his country. In 1979, a rebel force called the Sandinista National Liberation Front, named after

---

[218] Ibid.
[219] Ibid.
[220] Ibid.
[221] Ibid.
[222] *Socialist Worker*, "US violence for a century: Nicaragua: 1912–1933".
[223] D. Vukelich, "A disaster foretold", *The Advocacy Project*.

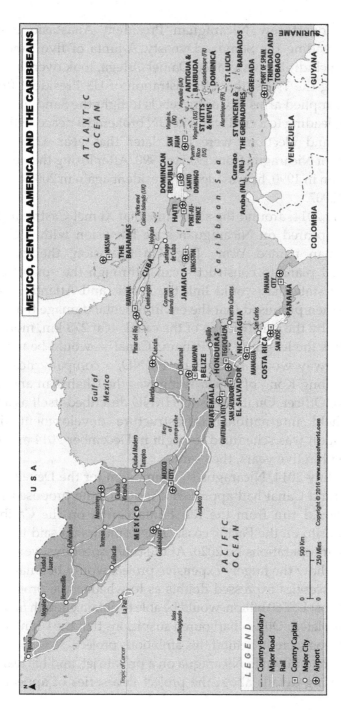

Source: Maps of World

Sandino, overthrew Nicaraguan President Anastasio Somoza Debayle, ending the Somoza Dynasty. A junta of five Sandinista leaders, including a man called Daniel Ortega, took over the country. During the 1980s, the administration of US President Ronald Reagan supplied arms to Contra rebels to fight the Sandinista government, leading to a civil war. The UN brokered a peace settlement in 1990, and elections were held later that year. Ortega was President of Nicaragua from 1985 to 1990. After losing the presidential election in 1990, he was elected president again in 2006 and took office in 2007.

In July 2014, around the same time that Xi met Castro in Cuba, Ortega appeared on Nicaraguan state television with a Chinese businessman named Wang Jing. On television, the two men announced plans to construct a canal through the small Central American state that would link the Pacific and Atlantic Oceans. The two men promised that the environmental damage that might be caused by the construction of the canal — at 278 km, more than three times the length of the Panama Canal — would be minimal. The waterway would be built by HKND, a company headquartered in Hong Kong of which Wang was the Chairman and Chief Executive Officer. On its website, HKND described itself as a "privately held international infrastructure development firm". Construction was scheduled to begin in December 2014 and completed within five years, they said.

On 7 July 2014, Nicaragua's Commission for the Development of the Grand Canal had approved a route for the proposed canal, which would run from the Río Punta Gorda on the Caribbean Coast to Brito on the Pacific coast. The Commission said the canal would start operations by 2020. At the time, questions were raised regarding how the hugely expensive project would be financed.

Some sceptics expressed doubts as to whether the project, estimated to cost US$60 billion, would be able to obtain enough financing to be completed. Others harboured suspicions that the Chinese government was secretly behind this ambitious project.

Wang had flown to Nicaragua on a private jet, and his team has been offering details about the project in a series of appearances that were live-streamed on the Internet from Nicaraguan state television.[224] The 41-year-old Chinese businessman told Nicaraguan university students that the project would bring "radical change" to Nicaragua, the Western Hemisphere's second poorest nation, and spread wealth "to the whole country."[225]

This Chinese businessman, Wang, took over the construction of the Nicaraguan canal from an earlier aborted project undertaken by a US businessman in the 19th century. In 1825, the government of the Federal Republic of Central America, which included Nicaragua, considered building a canal through Nicaragua. Throughout the 19th century, the local government held negotiations with US officials on this proposed canal. On 25 August 1849, the Nicaraguan government signed a contract with Cornelius Vanderbilt, an American tycoon. The contract granted his Accessory Transit Company the exclusive right to construct the Nicaragua canal within 12 years. However, civil war and an invasion by a US adventurer, William Walker, prevented the canal from being completed. The US abandoned plans to construct a waterway in Nicaragua in the early 20th century after the US government had purchased the French interest in the Panama Canal.

China has succeeded in Latin America (including the Caribbean and Central America) where the Soviet Union had failed. China has broken through the Monroe Doctrine to expand its influence among the southern neighbours of the US. What the Soviet Union failed to do with its nuclear missiles in Cuba, China succeeded with its generous investment, financing and trade deals in Latin America.

China's engagement with the Caribbean is primarily economic in nature, while Beijing also seeks to expand its political links with Caribbean countries, the 16 May 2014 USCC report on "China's expanding and evolving engagement with the Caribbean" noted. Political concerns — namely competition with Taiwan for diplomatic recognition — also drove Beijing's involvement in the region, the

---

[224]Tim Johnson, *McClatchy DC*, "Financing still a mystery as Nicaragua unveils details of giant canal", 9 July 2014.
[225]Ibid.

USCC report stated. As of 2014, Beijing maintained economic and political relations with the five Caribbean states that still recognized Taiwan (Haiti, the Dominican Republic, Saint Kitts and Nevis, Saint Lucia, and Saint Vincent and the Grenadines), the USCC report added.

"In general, Caribbean countries — at the official and grassroots levels — tend to view China favourably. Exceptions include displeasure at the local level with imported Chinese labourers and other problems associated with the influx of Chinese into local communities and markets," the USCC report declared.

Part of the reason for China's success in wooing Latin America is Beijing's provision of an economic alternative to some nations that had strained economic ties with the US.

When Xi toured Latin America in July 2014, Argentinian President Christina Fernandez de Kirchner might have felt the Chinese leader could not have visited her country at a more opportune time. Xi's visit to Argentina came at a time when Kirchner had less than two weeks to resolve a dispute over her country's unpaid debts or see her country default for a second time in 13 years.[226] A US judge, Thomas Griesa, had barred Argentina from paying its bonds unless it also paid some hedge funds that had sued to collect Argentinian debt.[227] Argentina had until 30 July 2014 to make US$539 million in interest payments to investors or the country would be declared to be in default.[228]

Unable to raise money by selling bonds abroad, Argentina was struggling to find alternative sources of funding. During Xi's visit to Argentina, the two governments approved 20 agreements, including a 70 billion yuan (US$11 billion) currency swap between the two countries' central banks. China also agreed to lend Argentina US$2.1 billion to buy railroad equipment and finance the construction of dams in southern Argentina to the tune of US$4.7 billion.

---

[226]Ken Parks, *Wall Street Journal*, "Argentina-China deals reflect Asian country's growing influence", 20 July 2014.
[227]Ibid.
[228]Ibid.

Notwithstanding the goodies Xi brought, the Argentinian government defaulted on its US$1.5 billion debt to creditors, including some US vulture funds on 1 August 2014, after failing in its negotiations with creditors on the previous day. However, the Argentine government denied it was in default.

In August 2014, Argentina filed a lawsuit against the US at the International Court of Justice in The Hague, the principal judicial arm of the UN, accusing the US of violating Argentinian sovereignty.[229] Argentina claimed the US "committed violations of Argentine sovereignty and immunities and other related violations as a result of judicial decisions adopted by US tribunals concerning the restructuring of the Argentine public debt", according to the filing.

Xi's Latin American tour in July 2014 included another country with strained ties with the US: Venezuela. In February 2014, Venezuela expelled several US diplomats, accusing them of aiding opposition protests, and the US responded a few days later by expelling some Venezuelan diplomats, according to news reports. In May 2014, US Congress passed the Venezuelan Human Rights and Democracy Protection Act that would impose economic sanctions on Venezuelan officials involved in mistreating protestors.

China offered an alternative to Venezuela, which was deemed a pariah state by the US, by increasing trade with Venezuela after the US banned arms sales to that country in 2006 over a supposed lack of commitment to counterterrorism efforts.[230] During Xi's visit to Venezuela in July 2014, Venezuela signed 38 agreements worth US$18 billion with China, in the presence of Venezuelan President Nicolas Maduro and Xi in Caracas, the Venezuelan capital. One of the deals included China providing an additional US$4 billion to the Joint Chinese-Venezuelan Fund, which financed

---

[229] Andrew Trotman, *Daily Telegraph,* "Argentina files legal proceedings with UN against Obama government", 7 August 2014.
[230] Kamilla Lahrichi, *Asia Sentinel,* "China's growing military sway in Latin America", 4 August 2014.

infrastructure and development projects in the Latin American country.[231]

In contrast to Xi's visit to Caracas in 2014, angry crowds attacked and nearly overturned the car of US Vice President Richard Nixon in the Venezuelan capital during his goodwill tour of Latin America in 1958, a reflection of the anger felt by some Venezuelans towards US policy.

The Joint Chinese-Venezuelan Fund helped to keep afloat the Venezuelan economy, which was in deep trouble. In the middle of October 2014, there were widespread reports in the international media that Venezuela might default due to falling oil prices. In an interview with Venezuelan newspaper *El Universal*, Vice-President for Economic Affairs Rodolfo Marco Torres said the country would not be affected by the fall in oil prices, thanks partly to the Joint Chinese-Venezuelan Fund.

Since 2006, Chinese banks have pledged US$50 billion in loans to Venezuela, mainly in the energy sector, according to the Economist Intelligence Unit.

"China cannot allow Venezuela to collapse. It will be a huge loss to China," said Paulina Garzón, Director of the China-Latin America Sustainable Investments Initiative at the American University College of Law.[232]

From 2010 to 2014, Venezuela was among the 10 biggest oil exporters to China, according to various studies. She noted 50 percent of Chinese loans to Latin America went to Venezuela, which is estimated to have the world's biggest oil reserves.[233]

Another Latin American country that was economically resuscitated by China was Ecuador. Chinese banks rescued the Ecuadorian economy in 2009, after the country defaulted on its loans in 2008, Garzón noted. At that time, it was almost impossible for Ecuador to obtain a loan in the international market, she stated.

---

[231] Toh Han Shih, *South China Morning Post*, "Beijing seen as lifeline to Latin American economies", 20 November 2014.
[232] Ibid.
[233] Ibid.

"Chinese loans to Ecuador reached about US$10 billion last year. Chinese investments in sectors like mining, oil and infrastructure helped the country recover its financial credibility," said Garzón.

In 2013, China provided 61 percent of Ecuador's financing needs, in return for nearly 90 percent of the South American country's oil, a report from Amazon Watch, a US NGO, revealed.[234] The rise in Ecuador's debt held by China, which exceeded US$7 billion in 2014, had sparked concerns over an erosion of Ecuador's sovereignty, the Economist Intelligence Unit reported.

From 2005 to 2014, China has provided more than US$100 billion in loan financing to Latin American countries and firms, Inter-American Dialogue, a US think tank, estimated. Between 2005 and the end of 2013, total financing in Latin America from China's two major state-owned policy lenders alone, the China Development Bank and China Exim Bank, amounted to US$102.2 billion, according to the China-Latin America Finance Database. Chinese loans to Latin America were growing faster than their Western counterparts, an Inter-American Dialogue paper stated.[235] Before 2008, China's annual lending to the region never exceeded US$1 billion.[236] In 2010, such commitments rose to a record high of US$35.6 billion, more than those of the World Bank, Inter-American Development Bank and US Export-Import Bank combined, and was US$29.1 billion in 2013, according to the China-Latin America Finance Database.

The financial dependence of some Latin American countries on China in the 21st century finds a precedent in the financial dependence of Latin America on the British Empire in the early 20th century. Going back to the early 20th century on this issue, Vladimir Lenin, in his book, "Imperialism: The Highest Stage of Capitalism", quoted the writings of Gerhart von Schulze-Gaevernitz, a German professor of political science: "South America, and especially Argentina, is so dependent financially on London that it ought to be described as almost a British commercial colony."

---

[234] Amazon Watch, "Amazon in Focus", Fall 2014.
[235] Kevin P. Gallagher, Amos Irwin, Katherine Koleski, Inter-American Dialogue Paper, "The New Banks in Town: Chinese Finance in Latin America", March 2012.
[236] Ibid.

It is still uncertain whether the financial dependence on China will be so strong as to drive any Latin American nation to be a semi-colony of China. What is certain is China has reduced Latin America's economic dependence on the US. However, the lack of transparency of Chinese loans in Latin America has left some analysts uneasy.[237]

"China's deals are driving the destruction of the Amazon rainforest, rolling back indigenous peoples' rights and undermining Ecuador's sovereignty and democracy. These deals are also increasing our dependence on Amazonian oil when we should be keeping it in the ground to combat climate change," said Adam Zuckerman, an environmental and human rights campaigner at Amazon Watch.[238]

During Xi's visit in July 2014 to Brasilia, the Brazilian capital, to attend a BRICS (Brazil, Russia, India, China, South Africa) summit, BRICS nations agreed to set up a new US$100 billion development bank, to be based in Shanghai, that would fund infrastructure projects, offering developing nations an alternative source of financing to Western-dominated financial institutions.

Xi's visit to Brazil also witnessed the establishment of two Chinese-backed investment funds offering a total of US$25 billion to Latin American and Caribbean nations, as well as the launch of a US$10 billion credit line by the state-owned Bank of China for the Community of Latin American and Caribbean States (in Spanish: Comunidad de Estados Latinoamericanos y Caribeños, or CELAC).

With China offering such strong economic sweeteners, the Brazilian government has not always acceded to US requests regarding China. In February 2011, during a trip to Brazil, US Secretary of the Treasury Timothy Geithner urged Brazil to do more to lobby China to revalue the Chinese currency, according to media reports. However, in an interview published in the *South China Morning Post* on 11 April 2011, Brazilian Deputy Minister of Development, Industry and Foreign

---

[237] Toh Han Shih, *South China Morning Post*, "Beijing seen as lifeline to Latin America economies", 20 November 2014.
[238] Ibid.

Trade, Alessandro Teixeira declared Brazil would not join the US in pressuring China to revalue the yuan.

"My government is not in commercial war with China and will not try to push China to change its policies. Brazil will not ask China to revalue the yuan," Teixeira said.

In Beijing that week, Brazil and China signed at least 10 cooperation agreements during the visit of a 350-strong Brazilian delegation led by Brazilian President Dilma Rousseff.

"We don't take this as a triangular relation. We're not married to any single economy," Teixeira added.

In 2009, China overtook the US as Brazil's biggest trading partner.

The history of Chinese trade with Latin America goes back centuries. During the 16th century, in a matter of years after the Spanish empire was initially established in Latin America and the Philippines, Spanish colonies in Mexico and the Philippines started trading with the Chinese empire during the Ming Dynasty. The trade involved Spanish galleons sailing between Guangzhou, Manila and Acapulco. From Guangzhou, Chinese silk and porcelain were exported to Acapulco in return for Mexican silver.

Fast forward to 2014 and China has become South America's second-largest trading partner behind the US. China's trade with Latin America grew fivefold from US$49 billion in 2005 to US$255.5 billion in 2012, according to the IMF. By 2014, China was already the biggest trading partner of Brazil, Chile and Peru.[239]

A UN study in 2014 predicted Latin America's trade with China would surpass the continent's trade with Europe by 2016. Some estimates forecast that by 2020, China would overtake the US as Latin America's largest trade partner, according to an article by Peter Hakim and Margaret Myers in *China Policy Review*, a magazine of the State Council.

China's huge trade with Latin America was unbalanced, bringing some negative side effects.

In 2011, most Chinese exports to Latin America were manufactured goods, while less than 20 percent of Latin American exports to

---

[239]Toh Han Shih, *South China Morning Post*, "China's trade with Latin America set to outpace the EU within two years", 17 March 2014.

China were manufactured goods, according to the UN. In 2009, more than 80 percent of Latin American exports to China came from a handful of commodities, namely iron, soya beans, crude oil and copper, according to a report by Kevin Gallagher published by the Centre for Latin American Studies at the University of California, Berkeley.[240]

With the influx of cheap Chinese manufactured goods, Brazil lost 700,000 manufacturing jobs and US$10 billion in income in 2010, Foreign Policy in Focus, a US think tank, estimated. Some 60 percent of Latin American anti-dumping complaints targeted China, mainly related to manufactured products including textiles and footwear, a joint report by the Woodrow Wilson International Centre for Scholars, Institute of the Americas, and the Chinese Academy of Social Sciences concluded.[241]

Chinese investments in South America have also been growing rapidly.

China's acquisitions in Latin America jumped from less than US$4 billion in 2009 to more than US$12 billion in 2012, of which more than 90 percent was resources for export to China, wrote Gallagher. Major Chinese deals in Latin America included the 2010 buyout by Chinese state-owned oil giant Sinopec of the Brazilian arm of Spanish oil major Repsol for US$7.1 billion, and a 2010 agreement that Brazil oil major Petrobras would supply oil to China for 10 years in return for a US$10 billion loan from China Development Bank.[242] In 2010, Venezuela, the largest oil producing nation in Latin America, signed a similar agreement to supply China with 200,000 barrels of oil per day for 10 years in return for US$20 billion worth of loans, while Ecuador gained a US$1 billion loan from China to finance oil and infrastructure projects.[243]

---

[240]Gallagher, Kevin P., *Berkeley Review of Latin American Studies*, "China discovers Latin America", Fall 2010.

[241] *Woodrow Wilson International Centre for Scholars, Institute of the Americas, Chinese Academy of Social Sciences*, "China, Latin America and the United States: The New Triangle", January 2011.

[242]Toh Han Shih, *South China Morning Post*, "China ties may be curse in disguise", 26 September 2011.

[243]Ibid.

There has been a huge increase in Chinese hydropower projects in Latin America, which has expanded China's geopolitical clout in the continent, but also drawn allegations of poor corporate social responsibility.[244] Prior to 2010, International Rivers, a US green NGO, was aware of only two Chinese hydropower projects in Latin America. In January 2014, there were 22, of which, three were completed, seven under construction and 12 on the drawing board.[245]

The three completed Chinese dams are in Belize and Ecuador with a total installed capacity of 47 MW and costing more than US$30 million. The seven being built in 2014 had a total installed capacity of 2,087 MW and cost more than US$2.53 billion. These seven were in Costa Rica, Ecuador and Honduras. This included the US$1.7 billion Coca Codo Sinclair dam in Ecuador built by Sinohydro, a Shanghai-listed state-owned dam builder, and financed by China Exim Bank.

The 12 proposed hydropower projects as of 2014 were in Ecuador, Guyana, Honduras, Peru and Argentina, with a total installed capacity of 5,069 MW. Their total budget, which included funding from Latin American sources, was more than US$12.25 billion.[246] These included two dams in Argentina to be built by Shanghai-listed China Gezhouba and Argentine firms with a total value of US$4 billion, with financing from two Chinese state-owned banks, China Development Bank and Bank of Communications.[247]

Patricia Adams, Executive Director of Probe International, a Canadian NGO, noted that China was expanding its dam-building into Latin America partly for geopolitical reasons.[248] For example, Chinese state-owned firms had replaced those from Taiwan to build three dams in Honduras, which recognised Taiwan instead of China, Adams revealed.[249]

---

[244] Toh Han Shih, *South China Morning Post*, "Chinese dam builders rush to Latin America", 6 January 2014.
[245] Ibid.
[246] Ibid.
[247] Ibid.
[248] Ibid.
[249] Ibid.

China's huge dam construction and investment in Latin America has not been unambiguously positive for the region or totally welcome by the locals.

"At first glance, China's agreements with Ecuador and Venezuela appear mutually beneficial," said Margaret Myers, Director of the China and Latin America Programme at the Inter-American Dialogue, a US centre for policy analysis.[250]

"But the extent to which they will benefit Ecuador and Venezuela is less certain. In the absence of institutional controls and macroeconomic foresight, oil-tied investments in Ecuador and Venezuela are unlikely to generate long-term, sustainable growth. Chinese investment in Latin America continues to promote growth, but long-term success will require strong institutions and responsible policy formulation," she said.

Myers' sentiment was echoed in the Woodrow Wilson report, which cautioned that the inexperience of Chinese companies in labour relations, environmental concerns and relations with local communities had caused local friction.

"There is great resistance to dam-building in Latin America and special worry about Chinese dams because of the opaque nature of China's decision-making and poor quality in these dams. The construction industry is more plagued by corruption than any other and China's dam-building industry is well known for corruption," said Adams.[251]

In November 2012, local workers at Sinohydro's Coca Codo Sinclair dam project complained at a meeting with Ecuador's Minister of Labour Relations, Francisco Vacas and members of the Ecuadorian National Assembly that they had not received all their wages and had been subject to physical and verbal abuse and sexual harassment, local media reported. A Sinohydro spokesman said the Latin American press report was inaccurate, and Vacas

---

[250]Toh Han Shih, *South China Morning Post*, "China ties may be curse in disguise", 26 September 2011.
[251]Toh Han Shih, *South China Morning Post*, "Chinese dam builders rush to Latin America", 6 January 2014.

affirmed the company's compliance with Ecuadorian labour regulations on November 26 2012.[252]

"Strong local opposition has contributed to the view that while Latin America is a market with a lot of opportunities, it is also a very difficult market because Chinese companies are not familiar with local issues," Mang of International Rivers said.[253]

Apart from dams, there has been local opposition to other Chinese projects in Latin America.

In 2010, the government of Rio Negro Province in Argentina signed a deal to lease 320,000 hectares of farmland to Heilongjiang Beidahuang Nongken Group, one of China's largest rice millers and soya bean processors. Under the pact, the group planned to invest US$1.45 billion to grow soya beans, wheat and other agricultural products on the land for 20 years, according to the Americas Programme of the Centre for International Policy, a US think tank. The deal, which was made public only after it was signed, generated enormous national opposition.[254] As a result, in February 2011, Argentinian President Kirchner announced restrictions on the acquisition of land by foreigners.

In March 2014, the state-owned Aluminum Corporation of China (Chalco) announced it had to partially halt operations at its US$3.4 billion Toromocho copper mine in Peru under orders from the country's environmental watchdog over environmental concerns. The Peruvian environmental agency found Chalco had been dumping waste in local lakes.

Even if there was some local opposition to Chinese ventures in Latin America, this has not prompted the US to side with Latin American grievances against Chinese interests. In contrast, during the Cold War, US propaganda played up the suffering of those under Communist rule, with the aim of winning support for the US against the Red menace. Generally, the US has not seriously objected to the huge and growing Chinese economic clout in Latin America.

---

[252] Ibid.

[253] Ibid.

[254] Toh Han Shih, *South China Morning Post*, "China ties may be curse in disguise", 26 September 2011.

In the following statement in the USCC report of 16 May 2014, the USCC, a US Congressional advisory body, said China's growing economic links with the Caribbean has created beneficial opportunities for the US, but warned that the US risked losing influence in the region.

"Indeed, there are many opportunities for the United States to benefit from China's economic engagement in the region, particularly its investments in and financing of port infrastructure and shipping and its involvement in humanitarian aid and disaster relief efforts. These opportunities notwithstanding, US policymakers should closely monitor China's growing involvement in the Caribbean. Beijing likely judges it has an opportunity to fill a vacuum caused by a decrease in US and European trade, investment, and other business ties following the global economic crisis (in 2008). In Caribbean countries, the narrative that the US has neglected the region while China has embraced it is pervasive. Although this message is misleading (current US trade and diplomatic ties with the region are more robust than those of China), its persistence could limit the effectiveness of US policy in the Caribbean," said the USCC report.

Although the USCC report adopted a cautionary stance towards China, its attitude was far milder than that displayed in the Kennedy administration's rush to block Soviet advances in Cuba during the Cuban Missile Crisis.

Apart from trade and investment, China has supplied weapons to Latin America. The arms supplied by the Chinese to Latin America have not roused strong opposition from the US. Latin American governments have welcomed the limited Chinese military deals.

For instance, in October 2011, Argentina announced an agreement with the China National Aero-Technology Import & Export Corporation to produce the CZ-W11 ultra-light helicopter.[255]

"The advance of relations between Argentina and China somehow breaks away from [Argentina's] international relations of the 1980s when we always depended on the United States. In the case of

---

[255] Gabriel Marcella, "China's military activity in Latin America", *American Quarterly*, Winter 2012.

China, the bilateral defense relation is indicative of a strong strategic relation, which has to do with very strong political and commercial ties," said Roberto De Luise, Undersecretary of International Affairs of Defense in Argentina's Ministry of Defense.[256]

"US officials are not publicly concerned about China's military activities. Frank Mora, Deputy Assistant Secretary of Defense for Western Hemisphere Affairs, stated in 2009 that while the US stands for transparency, China's arms and technology transfers are standard in the international community, and some of the equipment can help Latin American governments improve security and counter drug trafficking," wrote Gabriel Marcella in an article, "China's military activity in Latin America" in *Americas Quarterly*, Winter 2012.

A spokesman at the US embassy in Argentina stated the official US position, "The United States welcomes the emergence of a peaceful, stable, and prosperous China that plays a responsible role in world affairs. We encourage China to develop mutually beneficial relations throughout Latin America that uphold international trade and investment standards of transparency and good governance while also respecting local regulations."[257]

Even a military cooperation agreement between China and Argentina in 2015 did not appear to worry the US too much.

At the conclusion of a state visit to China by Argentine President Cristina Fernández de Kirchner on 5 February 2015, the governments of China and Argentina released a joint communiqué announcing prospective military sales and defense cooperation agreements. If finalised, these agreements would raise China's arms sales to Argentina to a level far higher than anything in the past, and possibly create inroads for further sales of Chinese arms to other Latin American nations, a USCC report of 5 November 2015 titled "China's military agreements with Argentina: a potential new phase in China-Latin American defense relations", stated.

---

[256]Kamilla Lahrichi, *Asia Sentinel*, "China's growing sway in Latin America", 4 August 2014.
[257]Ibid.

Under these agreements, for the first time, Argentina would consider buying Chinese military jets. China would also sell corvettes and armoured personnel carriers to Argentina. Both countries announced a satellite tracking and control station in the Argentine Province of Neuquen would be built and operated by a subsidiary of the Chinese People's Liberation Army.

"These developments would mark an expansion of China's broader defense engagement with Latin America that would carry several implications for the United States. First, US arms suppliers would likely see continued market share reduction," the USCC report of 5 November 2015 noted.

"Second, the United States may face a new regional security hazard, albeit harmless in the absence of an external conflict. Third, regional actors might use Chinese arms in ways unfavorable to US interests," USCC added.

However, the USCC report concluded, "Despite the rapid growth and proximity of China's defense engagements, they present no direct security threat to the United States, and China's statements, interests, and actions can be monitored to ensure regional hazards remain inactive going forward."

China's increasing arms sales to Latin America has not sparked a confrontation between China and the US, in contrast to the Soviet Union's placement of missiles in Cuba, which brought the Soviet Union and US to the brink of a nuclear world war. While the US might be warily monitoring China's increasing influence in Latin America, Washington has not objected to China's growing economic linkages and arms sales to this region. As earlier mentioned in this chapter, the Monroe Doctrine was partly driven by US fears that European powers might reassert colonial influence over Latin America. The fact that the US has not objected to China's growing presence in Latin America indicates Washington does not see China as a new empire in this continent. The history of relations between the US and its southern neighbours have not always been harmonious. If American, Chinese and Latin American actors cooperate wisely, China might even improve Latin America's relations with the US.

Chapter 6

Southeast Asia: Playing Both Sides

By virtue of its location at the crossroads of India and China, Southeast Asia has historically absorbed the peoples and influences of both major civilisations. For centuries, Indians and Chinese migrated to Southeast Asia, bringing their cultures and religions with them. Southeast Asia absorbed Indian architecture, Hinduism and Buddhism from India, while Vietnam adopted Confucianism and Chinese architecture from China. Chinese migration to Southeast Asia resulted in one country, Singapore, having a Chinese majority while other countries in the region including Indonesia, Malaysia and Thailand have Chinese minority populations that play influential roles in their economies.

From the 16th century onwards, various European powers and the US established their empires in different parts of Southeast Asia.

In what is present day Malaysia, the Portuguese conquered Malacca in 1511 while the Dutch seized Malacca from the Portuguese in 1641. In 1786, The British East India Company leased Penang Island from the Sultan of what is today the Malaysian state of Kedah. From that year till the early 20th century, the British progressively gained control of the whole of Malaya.

The Spanish colonised and conquered the Philippines beginning in the 16th century. In 1898, Spain lost the Spanish-American War and as a result, ceded the Philippines to the US. Local Filipinos declared the First Philippine Republic in the same year, but the US would have none of it. The Philippine-American War broke out from 1898 to 1902, ending with the US as the victor in control of the Philippines.

From the late 16th century till the early 20th century, the Dutch first traded in Indonesia, and subsequently gained parts of Indonesia in a piecemeal process. During the 19th century, the British colonised Singapore and conquered Burma, now referred to as Myanmar, in two Anglo-Burmese wars. Also in the 19th century, the French colonised Laos, Cambodia and Vietnam.

After the end of World War II, all these Southeast Asian nations gained independence at various points of time from the late 1940s till the 1960s.

Since the latter half of the 20th century, this region has come under the influence of two modern superpowers, China and the US, just as it was influenced by the two great Asian civilizations of India and China in ancient times. Southeast Asia has been trying to maintain a triangular relationship with the two superpowers, which is as tricky as a woman maintaining a delicate balance in managing two competing suitors.

6.1 Myanmar

On 19 November 2012, US President Obama and Burmese democracy icon Aung San Suu Kyi stood side by side at a press conference in her home in Yangon, Myanmar or Rangoon, Burma as it was formerly called. Obama embraced and kissed the 67-year old woman on the cheek, which was widely photographed and reported around the world. Perhaps Obama, a Nobel Peace prize winner, was just showing his appreciation for his fellow Nobel Peace laureate's decades-long fight for democracy, which put her under house arrest on and off over a 21-year period from 20 July 1989 to 12 November 2010.

Nearly two years later, on 13 November 2014, again at a press conference in Suu Kyi's home in Yangon, she warmly embraced Obama. Obama expressed support for her, voicing opposition to a

Myanmar constitutional rule that prevented the pro-democracy icon from becoming president of the Southeast Asian state. Obama publicly gave a blunt assessment of shortcomings in Myanmar's reforms and democratisation.

Obama was visiting Myanmar to attend an ASEAN (Association of Southeast Asian Nations) Summit in 2014, which also saw the presence of Chinese Prime Minister Li Keqiang. At that summit, Premier Li witnessed the signing of US$8 billion of deals between China and Myanmar, as China and the US competed for influence

US President Barack Obama and Aung San Suu Kyi in Yangon, Myanmar, in November 2012

Source: VCG

over Myanmar. Premier Li chose not to meet Suu Kyi, but hob-nobbed with Myanmar President Thein Sein.

A military junta had ruled Myanmar for decades and kept Suu Kyi under house arrest between 1989 and 2010. Pro-democracy protests flared up in the country in 1988, which was suppressed by the military, consequently killing many protestors. The brutal crackdown prompted the US and EU to slap sanctions on Myanmar. In 1990, the military government held free elections for the first time in three decades, with Suu Kyi's party, the National League for Democracy (NLD), winning most of the seats and the popular vote. The military junta refused to acknowledge the election and continued to rule the country.[258] For her stance on democracy in defiance of the junta, Suu Kyi, the daughter of a revolutionary and the father of modern Burma, Aung San, won the 1991 Nobel Peace Prize while under house arrest.

However, Suu Kyi has also made friendly overtures to China. At the invitation of the Chinese government, she visited China from 10 June to 14 June 2015, at the invitation of the Chinese government. On 11 June 2015, she met Chinese President Xi Jinping at the Great Hall of the People in Beijing, Chinese state media reported. The Chinese President did not hug and kiss Suu Kyi like Obama, but smiled and shook her hand, as shown in photos in Chinese state media.

The "traditional friendship between China and Myanmar" has not changed for 65 years since the establishment of diplomatic relations in 1950, Chinese state media quoted Xi saying. "China always looks at the China-Myanmar relationship from a strategic and long-term perspective. We hope and believe Myanmar will maintain a consistent stance on the China-Myanmar relationship and be committed to advancing friendly ties, no matter how its domestic situation changes."

In an interview with the *South China Morning Post* in January 2013, Suu Kyi said the US should not be considered as a challenge to Myanmar's long relationship with China. Asked by the Hong Kong newspaper for her comments on Myanmar's resurgent ties with the US, Suu Kyi replied, "I don't think it needs to be an exclusive

---

[258] Ibid.

relationship. It doesn't mean we have to be friends either with the US or China. We need to be friends of both. China is a neighbour and the US is a very, very powerful nation that is eager to help with emerging democracy."[259]

In March 2013, Suu Kyi visited the controversial US$1 billion Letpaudang mine, the largest copper mine in Myanmar which was a joint venture between the Burmese military and China North Industries Corporation, a Chinese state-owned arms manufacturer.[260] Although local villagers had campaigned against the project, AFP quoted her telling villagers, "If we stop this project, it will not benefit local people or the country. We have to get along with the neighbouring country whether we like it or not."

Suu Kyi's call for her country to have friendly relations with both the US and China typifies the predicament of Southeast Asia, where most nations have tried to maintain a delicate ménage a trois with both China and the US.

Since Suu Kyi's final release on 13 November 2010, the Myanmar military government has been trying to break the embrace of China, then the biggest investor in the country, and has started flirting with the US and other nations. In November 2010, days after the Myanmar military leaders released Suu Kyi, Myanmar Prime Minister Thein Sein was in the Cambodian capital of Phnom Penh courting investment from Vietnam, Cambodia, Thailand and Laos.

Since Thein Sein became Myanmar President on 30 March 2011, he instituted reforms which led to the lifting of most EU and US sanctions against his country. In November 2012, the US government lifted restrictions on imports of most products from Myanmar. In April 2013, the EU removed most sanctions on imports from Myanmar, in recognition of the country's political liberalisation. One source of motivation for the Myanmese government's reforms

---

[259] George Chen, *South China Morning Post*, "US and China both have roles to play: Suu Kyi", 28 January 2013.

[260] Andrew Buncombe, *Independent*, "Aung San Suu Kyi urges support for controversial Chinese-backed copper mine", 13 March 2013.

is that it does not want to rely too much on China, Salil Tripathi, Policy Director at the Institute for Human Rights and Business in Britain, noted.[261]

Myanmar's dependence on China had caused discomfort among its leaders, given the two nations' complex relationship. Beijing has been a supporter of the government but has also backed Kachin rebels along the Sino-Myanmese border, Williamson pointed out.[262]

On 30 September 2011, Thein Sein suspended the US$3.6 billion Myitsone dam project, whose main investor was China Power Investment Corporation, a Chinese state-owned power conglomerate. Located in northern Myanmar near the Chinese border, the dam was to become the world's 15th largest hydropower project with an installed capacity of 6,000 MW.[263]

"There have always been tensions between the Burmese and Chinese governments, and this issue brought these to the surface," said Sean Turnell, an Associate Professor at Macquarie University in Australia.[264]

Around the time Thein Sein announced the suspension of the Myitsone dam, Myanmar had been reaching out to the US, India and Thailand. On the same day the dam was suspended, in a rare visit to Washington, Myanmar Foreign Minister Wunna Maung Lwin held a "productive" meeting with Derek Mitchell, the new US policy coordinator for Myanmar, and other US officials, the US State Department revealed.[265] This followed Mitchell's visit to Myanmar earlier that September. Also in September 2011, Myanmar and India agreed to double their trade to US$3 billion by 2015, according to *The Hindu newspaper*.[266] On 5 October 2011, Thai Prime

[261] Toh Han Shih, *South China Morning Post*, "China to remain influential in Myanmar even as Western firms arrive", 13 May 2013.

[262] Ibid.

[263] Toh Han Shih, *South China Morning Post*, "Dam postponement seen as rebuke to Beijing", 10 October 2011.

[264] Ibid.

[265] Ibid.

[266] *The Hindu*, "India, Myanmar to double bilateral trade to $3 billion", 27 September 2011.

Minister Yingluck Shinawatra visited Myanmar to bolster ties. During the visit, contracts to build a road and a bridge were signed between both nations and Yingluck pushed for Thai investment in other port and road projects in Myanmar.

"Even though the Myanmar government welcomes big invest-ments from China, these investments are sometimes perceived with suspicion," said Pavin Chachavalpongpun, a Researcher at the Institute of Southeast Asian Studies in Singapore.[267]

"China controls big businesses in Myanmar, especially in the northern states. Than Shwe is keen to lessen the Chinese influence by inviting new players like India and European countries to invest [there]," he said.

Myanmar's military junta mostly welcomes Chinese invest-ment, Turnell noted. "But they do have mixed feelings. They need the money, but are very sensitive to China's dominance of Myanmar's economy."[268]

Many of Myanmar's military leaders had fought against the communist party in the country — seen as a proxy for their counterparts in China — in past decades, Turnell added. "There are ancient fears within Burmese society that China will over-whelm them. The one claim to legitimacy that Myanmar's generals have is the protection of national sovereignty. This claim will be in doubt if people fear the country is being sold out to China."

Exacerbating the mistrust is that many ordinary Burmese are angry that land, forests, gas and gems were sold at knock-down prices to China, Turnell revealed.

"In the past, Chinese companies played a big role in Yangon. In the future, all countries will play a big role, because we want all countries to share in the investment," said Toe Aung, Deputy Head of City Planning and Land Administration at the Yangon City

---

[267] Toh Han Shih, *South China Morning Post*, "China's uphill battle to invest in Myanmar", 3 January 2011.
[268] Ibid.

Development Committee, during a conference in Yangon in May 2013.[269]

"Yes, China used to be the dominant investor, but its relative importance will shrink," said Thurane Aung, Director of Dagon International, a Myanmese conglomerate, at that conference.[270]

Myanmar's cooling attitude towards China and increasing warmth towards other countries has accelerated since then. Of the 36 oil-and-gas blocks Myanmar awarded to 47 companies of various nationalities since October 2013, none was given to a single Chinese firm.[271] The winning firms came from countries like the US, UK, Holland, Russia, Thailand and Brunei. Yet, prior to 2013, Chinese companies had dominated Myanmar's oil-and-gas sector.[272] As of July 2014, the Myanmese government had awarded two new telecoms licences to Telenor of Norway and Ooredoo of Qatar, but none to any Chinese firm.[273]

However, Nicholas You, Chairman of the Steering Committee of the World Urban Campaign, a UN initiative to improve the quality of the world's cities, said: "US and European firms are not investing in US and Europe. You don't expect them to invest in Myanmar."[274]

"China is the only country willing to invest massive amounts of money in infrastructure in Myanmar," You said. "Chinese companies will continue to make long-term investments in Myanmese infrastructure. They have the money."

China will remain a major investor in Myanmar, Tripathi said. "There is the competitive advantage of geographical proximity and

---

[269] Toh Han Shih, *South China Morning Post*, "China to remain influential in Myanmar even as Western firms arrive", 13 May 2013.
[270] Ibid.
[271] Toh Han Shih, *South China Morning Post*, "China's rivals catching up in investment race in Myanmar", 21 July 2014.
[272] Ibid.
[273] Ibid.
[274] Toh Han Shih, *South China Morning Post*, "China to remain influential in Myanmar even as Western firms arrive", 13 May 2013.

familiarity with the market. But over time, China's share will drop."[275]

6.2 Indonesia

Indonesia's flamboyant and colourful first President, Sukarno, flirted with the Communist bloc (including China) and the US, in ways far more intimate than that between Obama and Suu Kyi. In a BBC television documentary I watched, a former US CIA spy recounted Sukarno's visit to the US in the 1950s.

"He had to have a date every night," the former CIA agent recalled.

During the 1950s, the CIA made an explicit video of a man looking like Sukarno making love to a woman, in an effort to blackmail or embarrass the Indonesian leader, whom the US government felt uncomfortable with for getting too close to the Communist bloc, as related by BBC. The attempt backfired. When the video was publicised, it made Sukarno even more popular with his people, because in the eyes of many Indonesians, the video testified to the virility and sexual success of their leader, the former CIA operative said.

When Sukarno visited Moscow in the 1960s, the KGB sought to take advantage of his fabled sexual appetite, by sending a batch of glamorous young women posing as airhostesses to his hotel.[276] When the Russians later confronted him with a film of the encounter, Sukarno was apparently delighted. Legend has it that he even asked for extra copies.[277]

The reason both the CIA and KGB tried to trap Sukarno in sex scandals was his reputation of having a legendary sexual appetite for women. From the 1920s to the 1960s, he had at least 10 wives.

---

[275] Ibid.
[276] Tim Lister, *CNN*, "Sex and espionage: a long and sordid history", 18 April 2012 http://security.blogs.cnn.com/2012/04/18/sex-and-espionage-a-long-and-sordid-history/
[277] Ibid.

His presidential palaces were decorated with paintings of voluptuous naked women. He even complained in his autobiography that whenever he saw a skirt, people would accuse him of getting sex crazed.

Sukarno continually accused foreign powers of trying to blackmail him by playing up his image as a rampant womaniser. This is revealed in declassified US government documents of the Office of the Historian at the US State Department. The following phone conversation was recorded between US President Lyndon Baines Johnson and his Special Assistant for National Security Affairs McGeorge Bundy on 1 May 1964:

> *President Lyndon Baines Johnson (LBJ) [reading a newspaper account]: "Sukarno says he'll issue orders for action Sunday to a million Indonesians who volunteered to aid his efforts to crush Malaysia."*

> *McGeorge Bundy: You'll be glad to know he's not coming to the US right now.*

> *LBJ [paraphrasing the newspaper account]: "In a May Day speech to 12,000, the President said the volunteers had been instructed to mass outside his place to hear his orders. Said foreign countries which intervene in Asian affairs are blamed for the continual trouble in the Far East. Said foreign countries, especially the United States, oppose him, and cited as proof the fact that American magazine, Whisper, printed a picture of him with a nude woman to show how bad I [Sukarno] am."*

> *Bundy: (Laughter)*

> *LBJ: Never heard of Whisper.*

> *Bundy: Never heard of Whisper. (Laughter)*

Sukarno's call for volunteers to "crush Malaysia" was part of his belligerent policy towards Malaysia during the period known as Confrontation or Konfrontasi from 1963 to 1966.

Sukarno opposed the creation of Malaysia in 1963, when Malaya, a former British colony, formed a federation with Singapore, Sarawak and Sabah. At that time, Singapore, Sarawak and Sabah were part of the British Empire. Sukarno called the project a neo-colonial plot and alleged the formation of Malaysia was a pretext for Malayan expansionism and continuing British influence in the region. As a result, in 1963, Sukarno began his policy of Konfrontasi, which included a breaking of relations with Malaysia and low-level military conflict between both nations. During this period, small bands of Indonesian troops infiltrated Malaysia. Coming to Malaysia's defence were forces from Australia, New Zealand and Britain.

Declassified US government documents revealed that from 1963 to 1968, there were mounting fears within the Johnson administration over the rise of the Indonesian Communist Party or Partai Kommunis Indonesia (PKI), as well as Sukarno's close ties to China. Crucially, declassified US government documents show evidence of decisions by US intelligence to undertake covert operations in Indonesia to counter the influence of Communism and China, which the US government believed to be inter-related, while trying to maintain utmost secrecy.

Indonesian President Sukarno and Chairman Mao Zedong: Sukarno's friendliness with Chinese Communist leaders made Washington uneasy

Source: VCG

The Johnson administration also linked the ending of Sukarno's Confrontation with Malaysia to defeating Communism in Indonesia. From the mid-1960s onwards, the US government considered the death of Sukarno to be a strong possibility. All this was indicated in a note from Robert W. Komer of the National Security Council Staff to the President's Special Assistant for National Security Affairs McGeorge Bundy, dated 19 November 1964:

We've growing evidence that quite a domestic flap is brewing in Indonesia between PKI and anti-PKI groups, perhaps to a degree the start of jockeying for power in anticipation of Sukarno's demise.

At any rate (US Ambassador to Indonesia, Howard) Jones argues eloquently that this is all the more reason for renewing our efforts to defuse Malaysia crisis, lest this be used by (Indonesian Foreign Minister) Subandrio and PKI (with or without Sukarno) as excuse for re-imposing unity.

This US Intelligence Memorandum of 2 December 1964 also links ending Confrontation to containing Communism within Indonesia:

For the first time in several years there are the faint stirrings of an anti-Communist movement in Indonesia. Provoked by increasing boldness on the part of the Indonesian Communist Party (PKI) and by Sukarno's own increasing reliance on the party, several non-Communist figures have raised a new banner called "Sukarnoism." Its main purpose appears to be that of combating PKI influence in the government and throughout the country.

Sukarnoist spokesmen are urging the US Embassy to take steps to encourage UK-Indonesian or Indonesian-Malaysian talks. They state that unless the Malaysia issue is peacefully settled, the new non-Communist movement will be smothered in the continuing anti-Malaysia clamor, and efforts to remedy Indonesia's deteriorating economy will continue to be frustrated.

The Indonesian Communist Party (PKI) had shifted its allegiance from the Soviet Union to China, as indicated in this memorandum of a conversation on 27 October 1964 that included US State Secretary Dean Rusk and British Foreign Secretary Patrick Gordon Walker:

> *The (British) Foreign Secretary inquired about our assessment of Sukarno's relations with Peking. The (State) Secretary replied that while Sukarno privately speaks of the Chinese Communist threat, the Indonesian Communist Party has swung from Moscow to Peking. The Secretary explained to the Foreign Secretary that our Joint Chiefs of Staff believe it is important to continue our training contacts to the extent possible with the Indonesian Army.*

The US government was increasingly alarmed at the PKI's rising power, as revealed in this US Political Action Paper of 19 November 1964:

> *The fulcrum of political power in Indonesia is sustained by Sukarno through the adroit balancing of power organizations and personal loyalties. The principal identifiable power entities in point are the Indonesian Army and the Partai Kommunis Indonesia (PKI).*
>
> *During the years 1951–1964, the PKI has increased from 12,000 to a claimed membership of three million. This growth has been encouraged and assisted by Sukarno, who has benefited from its highly organized support of his regime and its objectives.*
>
> *The PKI still needs Sukarno to protect it while it consolidates its gains, and it probably hopes he will survive a few more years but no longer. Within that time, if present trends continue, PKI infiltration of national and local government and Communist organizations of the peasantry will have become so effective that at Sukarno's death the party can make a bid for power with good chances of success."*
>
> *The Indonesian Army currently is the only organized entity capable of resisting the trend described above.*
>
> *Sukarno, seeking to maintain his own pre-eminent position, to preserve national unity, and to advance Indonesia internationally at the*

expense of the West, finds it totally inexpedient to challenge the PKI.
His tactics, combined with Communist single-mindedness, seem likely
ultimately to bring Indonesia under Communist control.

The US Political Action Paper of 19 November 1964 urged the US government to intervene in Indonesia to stem the Communist tide:

> *In essence, therefore, unless extraneous factors intrude, a Communist-oriented Indonesia can be expected within the not too distant future. What is clearly required is a program designed to separate legitimate national aspiration, Sukarno chauvinism and PKI ambitions so that forces inimical to the United States can be distinctly identified and countered.*
>
> *That the current trend of events and configuration of forces in Indonesia will result in increasing PKI prestige, influence and size, unless positive as well as negative action measures are taken.*

The US Political Action Paper of 19 November 1964 explicitly called for covert US action in Indonesia, including propaganda to paint China as neo-imperialist:

> *To counter these trends, a covert action program including the following objectives is stipulated:*
>
> *Through indirect means, take action to create an image of the PKI as an increasingly ambitious, dangerous opponent of Sukarno and legitimate nationalism. The role of the PKI and its associated organizations as instruments of neo-imperialism, especially Chinese neo-imperialism, would be consistently emphasized.*
>
> *Encouragement and coordination of covert assistance to individuals and organizations prepared to take obstructive action against the PKI.*
>
> *Development of a broad-gauge ideological common denominator, to which practically all political groupings in Indonesia, except the PKI can adhere, so that the cleavage between the PKI and the residue of Indonesian society can be widened.*
>
> *Identification and cultivation and where possible, coordination of potential leaders within the present and future Government of Indonesia,*

to insure orderly and non-Communist succession upon Sukarno's death or removal from office.

Identification and assessment of anti-regime elements, in order to monitor their activities and strength, and be in a position, in the event of a non-Communist successor regime, to influence them to support such a regime.

This memorandum dated 23 February 1965 provides further evidence of US covert action in Indonesia, with an explicit aim of containing China:

This program has been coordinated in the Department of State with the Assistant Secretary for Far Eastern Affairs and with the U.S. Ambassador to Indonesia.

The aim of this political action program is to reduce the influence on Indonesian foreign and domestic policies of the PKI and the Government of Red China and to encourage and support existing non-Communist elements within Indonesia.

The main thrust of this program is designed to exploit factionalism within the PKI itself, to emphasize traditional Indonesian distrust of Mainland China and to portray the PKI as an instrument of Red Chinese imperialism. Specific types of activity envisaged include covert liaison with and support to existing anti-Communist groups, black letter operations, media operations, including possibly black radio, and political action within existing Indonesian organizations and institutions.

One of the main factors bearing on the problem is the close affinity between the current objectives of Sukarno and Red China and the support provided to Sukarno by the PKI in contrast to the lack of coordination and common ground for action among the various anti-Communist elements within Indonesia.

Operational objectives

Portray the PKI as an increasingly ambitious, dangerous opponent of Sukarno and legitimate nationalism and instrument of Chinese neo-imperialism.

Provide covert assistance to individuals and organizations capable of and prepared to take obstructive action against the PKI.

Encourage the growth of an ideological common denominator, within the framework of Sukarno's enunciated concepts, which will serve to unite non-Communist elements and create cleavage between the PKI and the balance of the Indonesian society.

Develop black and grey propaganda themes and mechanisms for use within Indonesia and via appropriate media assets outside of Indonesia in support of the objectives of this program.

Identify and cultivate potential leaders within Indonesia for the purpose of ensuring an orderly non-Communist succession upon Sukarno's death or removal from office.

Identify, assess and monitor the activities of anti-regime elements for the purpose of influencing them to support a non-Communist successor regime.

This operational program has been approved by Assistant Secretary of State for Far Eastern Affairs and by the US Ambassador to Indonesia.

The following memorandum reveals the US government suspected Sukarno had serious health problems and considered his death in the near future a real possibility. Sukarno was to live for several more years till 21 June 1970. Fears of Sukarno's death temporarily subsided, as indicated in this memorandum of a conversation on 11 December 1964 in New York that included US State Secretary Dean Rusk, Indonesian Deputy Prime Minister Subandrio and Indonesian Ambassador to the US Zairin Zain:

The Secretary Rusk began the meeting by asking about President Sukarno's health. Deputy Prime Minister Subandrio said that an X-ray taken in Vienna some months ago had revealed there was a stone in President Sukarno's right kidney. Inasmuch as his other kidney is already affected, Subandrio said, the X-ray had given rise to real concern. Subsequent examination, however, had shown that the second kidney stone was not serious. As a result, the concern over President Sukarno's health had in general disappeared.

Nonetheless, the CIA feared the death of Sukarno was a strong possibility, which probably would lead to chaos and Communist domination of Indonesia. The CIA believed that even if he did not die so soon, Communist influence in Indonesia would increase. All this is indicated in this special memorandum by the Director of the Office of National Estimates of the Central Intelligence Agency, Sherman Kent, on 26 January 1965:

We are now faced not only with known and growing danger from Sukarno, but with the uncertainties of a possible Indonesia without Sukarno. If this ailing dictator should indeed die in the near future, his bequest to Indonesia would be international outlawry, economic near-chaos, and weakened resistance to Communist domination. Yet if Sukarno lives on for some time to come, the chances of the Communist Party (PKI) to assume power will probably continue to improve. We do not believe that a Communist Indonesia is imminent, or that Sukarno will initiate war. In our view, however, there is sufficient chance of such developments over the next year or two to warrant especial US intelligence and planning attention.

The beginnings of a scramble for succession to Sukarno are already evident. Should Sukarno leave the scene in the near future, we believe that the initial struggle to replace him would be won by Army and non-Communist elements.

Sukarno will probably take various rash actions to lessen his remaining ties with the West and to continue his dalliance with Peiping (Beijing). He apparently believes that long-run trends are working to weaken US/Western influence in Southeast Asia, that this provides Indonesia with the opportunity for considerable profit, and that division of the spoils with Communist China is a problem which can be safely managed at some later date. If persisted in, these views will prove ill-conceived and costly, susceptible of upset by UK/US force, Chinese Communist guile, and domestic deterioration.

This US intelligence memorandum of 1 July 1965 reveals Sukarno knew he could not win militarily in his Confrontation with Malaysia. The memorandum reiterated US fears of rising Communist influence in Indonesia and Sukarno's close ties with China. From the US national intelligence memorandum of 1 July 1965:

> *The principal development in Indonesia over the past year has been the sharply accelerated growth of the Communist Party (PKI) role in government. This trend is likely to continue as long as Sukarno is in control.*
>
> *Sukarno's campaign to destroy Malaysia, now in its third year, will almost certainly continue at varying levels of intensity. There is little prospect of an Indonesian military victory and Sukarno knows it. This realization has led him to denounce and harass the entire Western presence in Southeast Asia, and indeed in the Afro-Asian world.*
>
> *We look for a continuation of Indonesia's hostile attitude toward the US, though chances are less than even that Sukarno will go so far as to break diplomatic relations. Ties with Communist China are likely to become closer, since Sukarno sees no immediate Chinese threat to Indonesian ambitions. The desire of the Indonesian military to continue receiving Soviet arms aid will probably induce Sukarno to maintain relatively friendly relations with the USSR.*
>
> *If Sukarno dies or becomes incapacitated in the next year or so, the immediate successor government would probably be an ostensibly non-Communist coalition.*
>
> *Malaysia is totally dependent on British military support and its foreign policy is closely allied to that of the UK and its Commonwealth partners. The UK, and to a lesser extent Australia and New Zealand, have committed a considerable military force to the defense of Malaysia.*

In a coup that took place on 30 September and 1 October 1965, a handful of Indonesian generals were killed by a group that called itself the 30 September Movement. The movement was led by Lieutenant Colonel Untung, a battalion commander in President Sukarno's bodyguard.

This memorandum to US President Johnson on 1 October 1965 described the beginning of the coup that would lead to Sukarno's downfall and the massacre of hundreds of thousands of suspected Communists in Indonesia, paving the way for the pro-US General Suharto to take over as Indonesian President:

> *A power move which may have far-reaching implications is under way in Jakarta.*
>
> *A group which calls itself the "30 September Movement" claims to have forestalled a "Generals' coup" in Indonesia. A number of unnamed generals and politicians have been arrested, and the homes of Defense Minister General Nasution and Army Commander General Yani are under guard.*
>
> *A decree issued on 1 October by Lieutenant Colonel Untung, Commander of the Presidential Bodyguard, stated that the government would be administered by an Indonesian Revolution Council.*
>
> *No mention has been made of any active role by Sukarno. The government radio initially announced that the 30 September Movement was organized to "save President Sukarno whose health was in danger." It later commented that he was safe and "continues to carry out the leadership of the state."*
>
> *The 30 September group claims that the alleged Generals' plot was American inspired. The US Embassy's external telephone line was cut three hours before the Indonesian Radio announced that the "coup" had been thwarted. Troops are stationed at the Embassy.*
>
> *The immediate purpose of the 30 September Movement appears to be the elimination of any political role by anti-communist Army elements and a change in Army leadership.*

The following US telegram reveals that only a few days into the coup, the US government already knew anti-Communist forces were gaining the upper hand and Sukarno might be on the way out. This US telegram urged covert US support for anti-Communist forces in Indonesia including Suharto and the spreading of anti-Communist propaganda, while making efforts to keep this secret. This telegram also reveals the Soviet Union to be on the side of the US and against China over the issue of Indonesia, which was a reflection of Soviet rivalry with China. This telegram was sent from the US embassy in Indonesia to the US Department of State dated 5 October 1965:

1. *Events of the past few days have put PKI and pro-Communist elements very much on defensive and they may embolden army at long last to act effectively against Communists.*
2. *At same time we seem to be witnessing what may be the passing of power from Sukarno's hands to a figure or figures whose identity is yet unknown, possibly bringing changes in national policy and posture in its wake.*
3. *Right now, our key problem is if we can help shape developments to our advantage, bearing in mind that events will largely follow their own course as determined by basic forces far beyond our capability to control.*
4. *Following guidelines may supply part of the answer to what our posture should be:*

   A. *Avoid overt involvement as power struggle unfolds.*
   B. *Covertly, however, indicate clearly to key people in army such as Nasution and Suharto (my italics) our desire to be of assistance where we can, while at same time conveying to them our assumption that we should avoid appearance of involvement or interference in any way,*
   C. *Maintain and if possible extend our contact with military.*
   D. *Avoid moves that might be interpreted as note of nonconfidence in army (such as precipately moving out our dependents or cutting staff).*
   E. *Spread the story of PKI's guilt, treachery and brutality (this priority effort is perhaps most needed immediate assistance we can give army if we can find way to do it without identifying it as solely or largely US effort).*
   F. *Support through information output and such other means as becomes available to us unity of Indonesian armed forces.*

G. *Bear in mind that Moscow and Peking are in basic conflict regarding Indonesia, and that Soviet Union might find itself even more in line with our thinking than at present.*

H. *Continue to consult closely with friendly embassies extending our line of credit and enhancing our image generally through them as a constructive influence here.*

I. *Continue for time being to maintain low profile and be restrained about any apparent opportunities to rush in with new, overt programs (although need for stepped-up information effort will be great).*

This telegram sent from the US State Department to the US embassy in Indonesia on 6 October 1965 reveals US covert operations in terms of media and propaganda in Indonesia:

We plan and are already carrying out VOA (Voice of America) and information program based on citation Indonesian sources and official statements without at this stage injecting U.S. editorializing. At least in present situation we believe ample such material pointing finger at PKI and playing up brutality of September 30 rebels is available from Radio Djakarta and Indo press.

This US intelligence memorandum of 6 October 1965 sheds more light on the coup and reveals General Suharto as the leader of the anti-Communist forces and a rival of President Sukarno:

The Indonesian army, having countered what appears to have been a leftist coup on 1 October, is for the time being firmly in control of Indonesia. It would like to use the opportunity to take strong steps against the Indonesian Communist Party (PKI) and elements allied with it.

By the early evening of 1 October Army General Suharto, commander of the Army Strategic Reserve (KOSTRAD), informed all military areas that in the absence of Army Commander General Yani, who had been kidnapped, he was assuming command of the army. He was doing so with the understanding and cooperation of the navy in order to destroy the "30 September Movement."

During the night of 1 October, Lieutenant Colonel Untung apparently fled to Central Java where he apparently hoped to establish a position with pro-Communist elements in that province.

Suharto, long regarded as apolitical and possibly an opportunist, emerges in the present situation as a strong military leader and apparently a firm anti-Communist.

The US Embassy in Djakarta has a confirmed report that Sukarno's palace guards and air force troops are protecting Sukarno and (Indonesian Air Marshal Omar) Dani in Bogor. Reportedly, Suharto's troops have their guns trained toward the palace. The US Embassy now believes that Suharto's forces are allowed access to Sukarno for bargaining and tape recording Sukarno's statements but they do not control him.

Sukarno has rejected army suggestions for firm measures against leaders of the "30 September Movement" and the Communist Party. On 4 October he told the army generals that the situation basically involves political issues, that tranquillity and order are needed for a solution, and that the generals should "leave the political settlement to me."

Apparently a few hours prior to this 4 October meeting between Sukarno and the generals, Suharto made an unusual public statement which strongly implied both doubt and criticism of the president and accused the air force and the Communists of complicity in the "30 September Movement".

That US intelligence memorandum dated 6 October 1965 shows Suharto took control of the Indonesian army very rapidly, just a few days after the coup started. This suggests Suharto probably anticipated the coup. If Suharto and other anti-Communist Indonesian officers were taken by surprise, they would not have organised the Indonesian army so quickly with Suharto at the helm. The fact that Lieutenant Colonel Untung fled on the very first night of the coup shows how quickly the coup had faltered, how weak the Communists were and how strong the opposition from the Indonesian army was. This suggests the Indonesian army was well prepared for the coup. Since the US had already initiated covert action in Indonesia before the coup began on 30 September 1965, was the rapid failure of the coup and the swift counter-attack partly due to US covert action?

US embassy officials in Indonesia believed it was highly likely that Sukarno feared the generals who were murdered in the coup were themselves plotting a coup against him, as revealed in this telegram from the US Embassy in Indonesia to the US State Department on 26 October 1965. This telegram also raises the possibility that Sukarno tacitly supported the coup which killed the generals:

Movement forced into early retreat by quick reaction under General Suharto of Strategic Command (Kostrad) and dwindling support for Untung. During evening October 1, Suharto, joined by cavalry battalion from Adjie's Siliwangi division recaptured strategic points and secured city. Rebel troops retreated to Halim; Untung and Air Force Chief Omar Dani flew to his Swahjudi air force base near Madiun early October 2. Sukarno went to Bogor Palace.

Many knowledgeable Indonesians join most foreign diplomats here in believing Sukarno (was) involved in September 30 Movement, although extent (of) his complicity (is) not clear. Sukarno's long-term political record of close association with PKI merged over past year into virtual public identification with PKI. On September 29 in speech to Communist youth, he referred to former "loyal generals" who had become "protectors of counter-revolutionary elements. These we must crush." Important circumstantial evidence lays critical questions at Sukarno's door. His actions during and after coup are suspect, including his lack of any real public remorse over murdered generals. There are reservations, but odds seem overwhelming that, at very least, Sukarno knew what was afoot and had given tacit blessing to seizure of generals, probably having let himself be convinced (not a hard job) that they (were) planning coup against him.

The following telegram from the US Embassy in Indonesia to the US Department of State on 14 October 1965 reveals that the Indonesian army was starting to detain suspected Chinese businessmen and was investigating the Chinese embassy in Jakarta:

Aide said that army is now rounding up suspect Chinese businessmen and seeking to find out through Chinese just what role ChiCom (Chinese Communist) Embassy here played in aborted coup. Aide cautioned

*however that, even if army got the goods on Peking, Djakarta would
have to be very careful about its relations with China. Army could not
go after the ChiComs frontally, he said, but made a gesture with both his
hands as if to suggest a subtle envelopment technique.*

The following telegram from the US Embassy in Indonesia to
the US Department of State on 17 October 1965 claims the
Indonesian army and sections of the Indonesian public suspect the
involvement of China in the coup. Whether China was actually
involved or not, bloody reprisals against Chinese people, whether
of Chinese or Indonesian citizenship, would soon follow.

*There are now two power centers in Indonesia, not one. These are
Sukarno and the army. Each needs the other and at the same time
each is trying to undermine the other. But in true Indonesian fashion
they are trying to reach an agreed settlement which will give the
outward impression that all is well and that national unity has been
preserved.*

*The present political jockeying takes place in an atmosphere of con-
siderable national tension. The attacks on PKI installations which
started in Djakarta have spread to other regions of Indonesia. In some
areas it could strike a spark leading to the outbreak of real conflict.*

*The army and large sections of the Indonesian public suspects
Communist China's hand behind recent events. Sukarno does not, or at
least he will not admit this possibility. However, as one general said,
"We already have enough enemies. We can't take on Communist China
as well." The September 30 affair will almost certainly cause strains
between Djakarta and Peiping (Beijing), but close cooperation will probably continue because both parties find it useful. But there (is) latent
explosiveness against the Chinese in the minds of many, particularly
strong Moslem elements, among the Indonesians.*

*One side of deal may be that army will hush up any indications of
Sukarno's involvement in September 30 affair. We have in fact already
noted that army sources are now playing this down following earlier
open talk that President was involved.*

This following telegram from the US Department of State to the US Embassy in Indonesia on 29 October 1965 points out the suspicion among senior Indonesian army officers that Beijing was behind the coup:

> *Relations with Red China are increasingly strained, and given the suspicion of Army leaders that Chinese Communists were behind the coup, and the course Army must take — i.e., destruction of PKI — a break with China cannot be ruled out. The Soviet Union has begun to exert pressure on Army to call off its campaign against the left, even hinting aid would be cut off. Army cannot capitulate to this pressure without endangering its whole position.*

This memorandum prepared by the CIA on 9 November 1965 indicates tentative steps by the US to aid the Indonesian military in its attempts to wipe out Communist influence in Indonesia, while trying to maintain secrecy over US action:

> *The requests of the Indonesian military leaders for covert assistance in their struggle against the Partai Kommunis Indonesia (PKI), create a definite risk for us of deliberate assistance to a group which cannot be considered a legal government nor yet a regime of proven reliability or longevity.*
>
> *In short, we must be mindful that in the past years we have often wondered when and if the Indonesian Army would ever move to halt the erosion of non-Communist political strength in Indonesia. Now that it has seized upon the fortuitous opportunity afforded by the PKI's error in the 30 September affair and is asking for covert help as well as understanding to accomplish that very task, we should avoid being too cynical about its motives and its self-interest, or too hesitant about the propriety of extending such assistance provided we can do so covertly, in a manner which will not embarrass them or embarrass our government.*

This US intelligence memorandum of 22 November 1965 shows the Indonesian army factions which opposed the coup were against

China, but not the Soviet Union, which highlights the rift between China and the Soviet Union, even though both were Communist states:

For six weeks the Indonesian Army has been engaged in a major campaign against the Communist Party of Indonesia (PKI). Party members and sympathizers are being rounded up and interned by the military; others are being purged from local government positions; and in Central Java PKI adherents are reported to be shot on sight by the army.

A well-placed army source recently told the US Embassy that the army was anti-Chinese and anti-PKI, but not anti-Communist.

Finally, the army believes the PKI's ties to Peking make it in effect the agent of a foreign power. For all these reasons the army finds the PKI a threat to its own power position. But it also finds in these factors useful arguments in the propaganda war it is now waging against the PKI. It is claiming the party is out of phase with Indonesian ideals and a "traitor" to the Indonesian revolution, and is emphasising Chinese Communist involvement in the 1 October uprising. This last argument is particularly effective, given the Indonesians' general antipathy to the numerous Chinese merchants living in their midst.

Whatever its feelings about Peking, the army certainly wants no break with Moscow. It has been careful to exclude the Soviet Union from its recent denunciations of the PKI and of the Chinese Communists. A recent report suggests that Defense Minister Nasution has worked out an understanding with the Soviets whereby Soviet arms would continue to reach Indonesia while the army attempted to eradicate pro-Chinese influence within the PKI.

Moscow has been playing the recent events in Indonesia in a low key in its current propaganda. It has been making the minimum noises necessary when Communist Party members are being harried and shot by government forces. (Soviet) arms deliveries have continued to reach Indonesia without interruption over the past six weeks. There is no indication that they will be cut off.

The army leaders may also feel that continued evidence of Soviet good will, as expressed in uninterrupted arms shipments, may infuriate the Chinese Communists and lead to recriminations that the army could then use to advantage in its attempt to orient Indonesia away from Peking.

Furthermore, it is likely that the Soviets themselves do not particularly wish to become entangled in the thickets of Indonesian politics. They have before them the clear example of Peking's involvement in this manner — an involvement which has led to a diminution of Chinese influence in Indonesia.

This US government memorandum of 14 February 1966 revealed the Soviet Union would allow pro-US forces to take over in Indonesia, because of its rivalry with China:

The Russians are in the embarrassing situation where an Army in which they have a large investment is actively suppressing a Communist Party, but at the same time they are not displeased with the destruction of the power of a thoroughly ChiCom (Chinese Communist) oriented Communist Party. The Soviets probably would not object to a situation developing in Indonesia somewhat analogous to India, with both the U.S. and the USSR providing aid and with Communist China out of the picture.

The Secretary noted that if the US were ever able to play a role in Indonesia again, particularly in regard to providing economic assistance, there were two important prerequisites: some satisfactory resolution of the Malaysian confrontation irritant, and some rational policy toward US oil companies.

This telegram sent from the US Embassy in Indonesia to the US Department of State of 22 December 1965 indicates both Sukarno's position and China's ties with Indonesia were weakening:

Indonesian politics has continued to move in "right" direction. PKI is no longer a significant political force, and Djakarta-Peking axis is in tatters. Meanwhile, army has gained in political experience and has further consolidated its position. Most notable change, however, has been further weakening of Sukarno's prestige and marked failure of his mid-November bid to get full authority back in his own hands. This failure has opened real possibility of far-reaching changes in local power structure during next few months, but many problems and hazards remain.

This telegram from US Ambassador to Indonesia Marshall Green to the US State Department of 27 May 1966 reveals Suharto's attitude, as he was about to take power in Indonesia. This telegram reveals that Suharto wanted to end Sukarno's policy of Confrontation against Malaysia and replace Confrontation with cooperation between Indonesia and its neighbours, Singapore and Malaysia. This telegram also revealed that Suharto viewed China as "the enemy":

My scheduled hour meeting with General Suharto May 26 ran 20 minutes overtime. Suharto, who seemed buoyant and confident, spoke of success in crushing Communists but there is still a job to be done.

Containment of China through SEA (Southeast Asian) Cooperation.

Discussion of this topic revolved almost entirely around Confrontation issue, with Suharto attempting to defend Indonesian policy along conventional GOI (government of Indonesia) lines of argumentation but ended with a firm statement of Indonesia's intention now to bring Confrontation to close. Sole reason Suharto advanced for GOI desiring end of Confrontation was in order (to) pave (the) way for closer association with neighboring countries against menace of Communist China. However, he argued this point with real conviction.

I said we welcomed ending of confrontation for reasons he cited as well as others. As far as Peking concerned, it had ever since late summer 1963 greatly welcomed Indonesian confrontation policy which served to divide and weaken areas over which Peking sought to extend domination. I referred to intelligence reports about how (Chinese foreign minister) Chen Yi, on visit to Indonesia in August 1965, had pressed for continuation of confrontation and non-recognition of Singapore and Malaysia. Peking seemed genuinely concerned at that time that

Indonesia might be tiring of confrontation policy, and in any event Peking wanted to isolate Singapore from Malaysia and Indonesia in order to weaken its economy and promote rise of the Barisan Socialists (a left-leaning Singapore political party).

Significantly, Suharto emphasized Pantjasila (the philosophical foundation of Indonesia created by Sukarno) rather than Sukarno as Indonesia's unifying force and he did not refer to Sukarno once either directly or indirectly.

It was a useful overall exchange, most heartening for Suharto's clear awareness of Peking's threat to Southeast Asia. He referred throughout to China as "the enemy."

This US government memorandum of 17 June 1966 contains a request for the US to provide intelligence communications equipment to Suharto:

On 26 February 1966, representatives of an intelligence organization responsible to General Nasution and attached to the former Armed Forces Staff (SAB), requested that High Frequency (HF) communications equipment be provided for a special link between that intelligence organization, General Nasution and General Suharto. This request for additional equipment has the support of the U.S. Ambassador to Indonesia, and is concurred in by the State Department's Bureau of Far Eastern Affairs.

By July 1966, Sukarno was on his way out, as revealed in this intelligence note from the Director of the Bureau of Intelligence and Research (Thomas Hughes) to Secretary of State Rusk dated 25 July 1966:

The new cabinet whose composition was announced by General Suharto on July 25 represents a major step in the campaign to ease President Sukarno out of effective power and into a figurehead role. Taken together, these developments represent a major blow to Sukarno's position and influence, a blow which he seems to be accepting without a fight.

Hundreds of suspected Communists were killed in the reaction to the Indonesian coup. Those killed included ethnic Chinese and young people who were not serious Communists, but joined the Communist party for social reasons, like meeting the opposite sex, according to various accounts. The slaughter of hundreds of thousands is confirmed in this memorandum from US Secretary of State Rusk to US President Johnson on 1 August 1966:

> *On October 1, 1965, the Indonesian Communist Party joined with elements of the armed forces in an effort to stage a coup by assassination. Six of Indonesia's most prominent generals were killed. Loyal Army elements under General Suharto rallied and crushed the coup attempt within 48 hours. This was the beginning of one of the most dramatic political reversals in recent history. A major nation, which was moving rapidly toward a domestic Communist takeover and was intimately associated with Communist China, within three months destroyed the Communist threat and altered significantly its domestic and foreign orientation.*
>
> *The first element in this political change was the destruction of the Indonesian Communist Party, the fourth largest in the world. The Army hunted down and executed the principal Communist leaders. In the small cities, towns and villages groups of youths, encouraged by the Army and motivated by religion, historic local grievances, and fear of their own fate had the Communists taken power, embarked on a systematic campaign of extermination of Communist Party cadres. **While the exact figure will never be known, an estimated 300,000 were killed.***
>
> *The second aspect of this political revolution was a systematic reduction of the powers of President Sukarno with the object of retaining Sukarno as the historic revolutionary figure and symbol of Indonesian unity, but depriving him of the power to govern. This process proceeded in stages. In March, Sukarno was forced to delegate extraordinary powers to Suharto, and Subandrio, (Indonesian deputy prime minister Chairul) Saleh and others who in the past have done Sukarno's bidding were removed from power and imprisoned. This was followed in July by a meeting of the People's Consultative Council in which General Suharto's mandate was confirmed and Sukarno was stripped of his position as lifetime President. On July 25 a new cabinet, led by General*

Suharto and purged of remaining pro-Sukarno figures, was formed. Sukarno remains on the scene, has a capability to obstruct and delay, but has lost the power to initiate or act.

On the international side there has been a rapid deterioration of Indonesia's relations with Communist China and the Asian Communist states, and a corresponding improvement in Indonesia's relations with the United States and the West.

Anti-Chinese riots have intimidated this important entrepreneurial community and caused an exodus of Chinese businessmen and a flight of Chinese capital.

Our traditional interest in Indonesia has been to keep the country out of the hands of its domestic Communists and out of the orbit of Communist China. This objective has, through the events of October 1 and their aftermath, for the time being been achieved.

Confrontation between Indonesia and Malaysia ended when both nations signed an accord on 11 August 1966 in Jakarta, which re-established bilateral relations. The end of Confrontation enabled the US to improve relations with Indonesia under Suharto, who turned out to be a strong ally of the US.

Sukarno was dismissed as Indonesian President on 12 March 1967, while Suharto was appointed acting president. Subsequently, Sukarno was put under house arrest in Bogor Palace, where his health deteriorated due to the denial of adequate medical care. He died of kidney failure in Jakarta Army Hospital on 21 June 1970 at the age of 69.

Suharto would rule Indonesia from 1967 to 1998, when he resigned under pressure from the Asian financial crisis and riots at home. Indonesia suspended diplomatic relations with China on 30 October 1967. Suharto resumed diplomatic relations with China in August 1990.

It is not known how top US officials including President Johnson felt about the massacre of hundreds of thousands of suspected Communists in the violent backlash against the coup of 1965. However, it is clear that the US leaders were pleased with the outcome of the bloody events of 1965 and 1966, which saw the downfall of Sukarno, an Indonesian leader friendly to China, and the Communists and his replacement by Suharto, an anti-Communist, anti-China, pro-US leader.

Both the US and Sukarno played dangerous balancing games, as revealed in declassified US government documents. The US wanted to support elements of the Indonesian military which could provide a useful counterpoint against Sukarno and the Communists, but tried not to upset the British, who were supporting Malaysia in the Confrontation against Indonesia.

The following US government document shows the delicate balancing game the US played with its ally Britain over Confrontation and the US government's desire to support the Indonesian army to counter Communism. From a US government document dated 28 July 1965:

> *(British) Ambassador Patrick Dean said he had been instructed to convey to the (US State) Secretary the British Government's unhappiness about the US decision to permit the sale of communications equipment for use by the Indonesian Army. The Ambassador said he understood the US problem but the British were faced with the situation of trying to prevent other friendly countries from supplying military equipment to the Indonesians.*

Playing upon Sino-Soviet rivalry, the US government was happy to see the Soviets continuing to supply weapons to the Indonesian military, which was killing and finishing off the Indonesian Communists.

Sukarno tried to counterbalance the Indonesian military against the Communists. However, the antagonism between both factions was too great. The Communists launched a coup in October 1965, killing a handful of generals, and the Indonesian military struck back swiftly with vicious, overpowering strength, wiping out the Communists in a bloody massacre involving hundreds of thousands of lives. Sukarno lost his balance and fell.

The traditional Indonesian shadow theatre, "Wayang Kulit", features the shadows of leather puppets projected against a screen by a light source. In some scenes, these shadow puppets would fight each other. Sometimes the outcome is not one side defeating the other, but a balance of forces. The US intelligence forces and Indonesian Communists operated like shadow puppets in their struggle against each other, while Sukarno tried to be a puppet master, manipulating the Indonesian army and Communists in a precarious balance. Although balance was a desired goal in Indonesian shadow theatre, it was lost in the bloody events of 1965 and 1966, with the anti-Communists crushing the Communists and the US emerging as a key beneficiary.

Tensions between the US and China over Indonesia and Southeast Asia continues in the 21st century. This was demonstrated in US State Secretary Hillary Clinton's visit to Indonesia and China in September 2012. While in Indonesia, Clinton called for a code of conduct for all claimants to disputed islands in the South China Sea, including China.[278] She also pressed ASEAN to insist on China agreeing to a multilateral mechanism to reduce risks of conflict and come to final settlements over sovereignty.[279] Clinton's stance put the US at odds with China, which wanted disputes to be resolved individually with each country, conditions which would give China greater leverage than if it were to deal with a bloc.[280]

Days before Clinton's visit to Indonesia, China's official Xinhua News Agency ran an editorial saying that the trip was "aimed at curbing China's growing influence," "stirring up disputes" and perpetuating the "surreal ambition of ruling the Asia-Pacific and the world." When Clinton arrived in China after visiting Indonesia, Chinese Foreign Ministry spokesman Hong Lei warned the US not to take sides in South China Sea disputes.[281]

---

[278] *The Nation*, "South China Sea disputes: Clinton urges ASEAN to be united", 5 September 2012.
[279] Ibid.
[280] Ibid.
[281] Andrew Quinn and Chris Buckley, *Reuters*, "China warns US not to take sides in sea disputes as Clinton flies in", 4 September 2012.

6.3 Singapore

On Indonesia's Independence Day on 17 August 1964, Indonesian President Sukarno gave his national day speech, which he termed "the year of living dangerously", adapted from the Italian phrase "vivere pericoloso". His choice of words was remarkably prescient. The following year or so was indeed "a year of living dangerously", for the Indonesian leader, Indonesia itself as well as the new-born state of Singapore.

About 14 months later, in October 1965, a coup and counter-coup would occur in Indonesia, which would lead to Sukarno's downfall and the massacre of hundreds of thousands of suspected Communists through 1966 and 1967. In his speech, Sukarno reiterated his call to "crush Malaysia", which at that time included Singapore, as part of his Confrontation with Malaysia. On 10 March 1965, a bomb placed by Indonesian commandos exploded in the HSBC building in Singapore, also known as MacDonald House, killing three people and injuring dozens. This attack was one of an estimated 29 bombs set off by Indonesian commandos in Singapore during the period of Confrontation from 1963 to 1966.

During Confrontation, the local Singapore army comprised a few regiments, with no substantial navy or air force to speak of. If not for the British naval base in Singapore, as well as the presence of the armed forces of Britain, Australia and New Zealand, it was quite conceivable that the Indonesian armed forces could have taken Singapore with ease in a matter of days.

Amidst such perilous conditions, Singapore was born on 9 August 1965, an unwanted orphan ejected from Malaysia. When announcing Singapore's separation from Malaysia on television, Singapore Prime Minister Lee Kuan Yew was shown weeping and wiping away tears with his handkerchief.

Malaysia spat out Singapore less than two years after the merger on 16 September 1963. The Malaysian government, dominated by a Malay Muslim leadership, decided it could not digest Singapore, a city where Chinese formed the majority while Malays, the native ethnic group, were a minority. The Malaysian government's decision to expel Singapore came in the wake of racial riots between Malays and Chinese that rocked Singapore in July and September 1964, which left dozens dead and hundreds injured.

In Singapore's multiracial society, tensions existed not only between Malays and Chinese, but also among the Chinese themselves. Broadly speaking, the Singapore Chinese could be divided into two main groups, the English-educated and the Chinese-educated.

The English-educated Singaporeans of Chinese ethnicity include the late Lee Kuan Yew, the father of independent Singapore, and myself. Many English-educated Singaporean Chinese, having studied in British institutions, looked up to their former British colonial masters. Lee Kuan Yew, who bore the Western name Harry, and had a degree in law with first class honours from Cambridge University, has been called the finest Englishman east of Suez.

Within the group of English-educated Singaporeans is a sub-group of ethnic Chinese, called the Straits Chinese or Peranakan, who have settled in Singapore and Malaysia for generations, absorbed local Malay ways, and often spoke English and Malay better than any Chinese language or dialect.

Although Lee Kuan Yew's ancestors were Hakkas from Guangdong province, his background was Peranakan. He grew up speaking Malay and English, and it was only in his adult years that he mastered Mandarin Chinese with the aid of tutors. I count myself among the Singaporean Chinese who are English-educated, given that my command of English is better than my command of Chinese, which is why I am writing this book in English.

In Singapore, the other group of Chinese consisted of those who studied in Chinese language schools and thus were steeped in Chinese culture. Often they were recent immigrants, nicknamed "Sin Keh" (new guests), who have retained their language and culture from China more than the Peranakans. During the 20th century, many Chinese-educated Singaporeans, influenced by tumultuous events in China, including the anti-Japanese war and the Communist revolution, were sympathetic to Communist

China. The actual extent of involvement of Communist Chinese agents in Singapore is still a matter of debate and speculation, but what is beyond dispute is China's influence on Singapore's Chinese-educated population.

An understanding of the Chinese-educated Singaporeans' sympathy for China can be seen in an encounter I had with a Chinese man in his eighties in Hong Kong in 2012. Although he was born in Indonesia, this man typified the idealistic Chinese-educated of Southeast Asia including Singapore, who were drawn to the land of their ancestors. He told me that as a young man, he had gone to China to volunteer with the Communist army during the Chinese civil war between the Communists and Nationalists. He then lived in Beijing for decades before settling in Hong Kong. He spoke to me in Mandarin Chinese with a thick Beijing accent, despite being a descendant of immigrants from the southern Chinese province of Fujian, the ancestral province of many Singaporeans. He proudly told me of the young Chinese men who grew up in affluent homes in Southeast Asia, but gave up their comfortable existence to join the Communist cause in the Chinese Civil War or the Korean War.

Chinese-educated students supported the Hock Lee bus riots which flared up in Singapore on 12 May 1955. The Hock Lee Amalgamated Bus Company was one of the bus companies operating in Singapore during the 1950s. In February 1955, hundreds of workers of the Hock Lee Amalgamated Bus Company joined the Singapore Bus Workers' Union (SBWU), led by its Secretary Fong Swee Suan, a graduate of a Chinese school.[282] In April 1955, workers of the Hock Lee bus company who were affiliated with SBWU went on strike. In retaliation, the management of the bus company dismissed 229 workers affiliated with SBWU.[283] The sacked workers continued to strike. In a show of support, students from Chinese schools joined the strikers.

---

[282] Singapore Infopedia.
[283] Singapore Infopedia.

On 12 May 1955, the strike escalated into a riot, when four people were killed and 31 injured. The riots subsided the next day.
Later that day, the Singapore government closed three Chinese
schools, namely the Chinese High School, Chung Cheng High
School and its branch school. The students reacted by taking control of the Chung Cheng School and staging a sit-in. On 14 May
1955, an agreement was reached between the Hock Lee Amalgamated Bus Company, the SBWU and the Hock Lee Bus Employees'
Union, which ended the strike.

The British colonial authorities were critical of Singapore's
Chief Minister at the time, David Saul Marshall, a Jew, for not tak-
ing tougher action against the strikers. Hence, the British rejected
his proposal for Singapore's independence in 1956, claiming
Marshall's government was unable to maintain internal security.
As a result, Marshall resigned on 6 June 1956 and was replaced by
Lim Yew Hock as Chief Minister.

To stem the influence of Communism in Singapore, Lim
arrested leftists and banned pro-Communist organisations between
September and November 1956.[284] He de-registered the Singapore
Chinese Middle School Students' Union on 24 September 1956,
which was declared by then Singapore Minister for Education
Chew Swee Kee as "nothing less than a Communist front organisation". About 5,000 Chinese school students responded by seizing
control of their schools on 25 September 1956 and threatening a
sit-in until the union was reinstated. Thousands of students held
protest meetings at other Chinese schools.[285]

On 10 October 1956, Singapore Education Minister Chew
ordered 11 Chinese schools to expel 142 students and terminate the
service of two teachers, while seven other teachers were given
warnings.[286] In response, about 1,000 Chinese High School students
and 3,000 Chung Cheng High School students seized control of
their schools, putting up anti-government posters and holding

---

[284] HistorySG website.
[285] HIstorySG website.
[286] HistorySG website.

meetings that passed resolutions condemning the government's action. Students from other Chinese schools as well as Nanyang University, a local Chinese university, showed up to express support.[287] On 12 October 1956, Chew ordered the schools to close temporarily. However, the schools remained occupied by students, with food and other forms of support supplied by the students' parents, members of the SBWU and other sympathisers.[288] The protest spread to other schools, with outbreaks of violence. As a result, an island-wide curfew was imposed. Between 25 October and 31 October 1956, 2,219 people were arrested.[289] By November 1956, classes resumed in all schools.

Marshall lost the post of chief minister because the British colonial authorities saw him as being soft on Chinese-educated students. Lim, an English-educated Singaporean Chinese, lost the chief minister position partly because the Chinese community thought he was too hard on the Chinese-educated students. In the general elections of 1959, his Labour Front Party lost to the People's Action Party headed by Lee Kuan Yew, who became Prime Minister.

Nonetheless, Singapore leaders, including Lee Kuan Yew, remained wary of Chinese-educated students, suspecting them of being potential sympathisers or supporters of Communist China.

In 1963, the Singapore authorities invoked the threat of Communist subversion to arrest more than 100 people, including many politicians and trade unionists who were Chinese-educated, although those of other races were also among the detained. This series of mass arrests, which began in February 1963, was called Operation Cold Store. Lee Kuan Yew, who was then Singapore Prime Minister, ordered the detention without trial of over 100 left-wing activists, including members of the left-leaning Singapore opposition party Barisan Sosialis, newspaper editors, trade unionists and university students. The operation was authorised by the

---

[287] HistorySG website.
[288] HistorySG website.
[289] HIstorySG website.

Internal Security Council, which comprised representatives from the British, Malaysian and Singapore governments. Those detained in Operation Cold Store included students of Nanyang University, a Chinese university founded in 1956, funded by donations from the local Chinese community. In a speech on 9 December 1963, Singapore Prime Minister Lee Kuan Yew said that in Nanyang University, "a situation is developing which if left unchecked will make it more a University of Yenan than of Nanyang," referring to the Chinese Communist revolutionary base of Yan'an. Lee added, "Indeed the problems of Nanyang can never be resolved until the political abuse the Communists make of it is exposed and stopped."

In 1980, Lee Kuan Yew's government merged Nanyang University with Singapore University, Singapore's main university, which upset sections of Singapore's Chinese community.

Although Prime Minister Lee Kuan Yew's cabinet included Chinese-educated Singaporeans like Jek Yuen Thong and Ong Pang Boon, he generally suspected the Chinese-educated populace had greater potential for breeding sympathisers of Red China compared to the English-educated. Despite Lee Kuan Yew's suspicion of Chinese-educated students, he sent all three of his children to Chinese schools, including his eldest son Lee Hsien Loong, who became Singapore's Prime Minister in August 2004. While Lee Kuan Yew distrusted the leftist tendencies of Singapore Chinese-educated students, he forged a close relationship with the late Taiwan President Chiang Ching-kuo, a son of the late Nationalist Chinese leader Chiang Kai-shek.[290] Such friendship between Lee Kuan Yew and Chiang Ching-kuo is not surprising, given that both leaders shared an opposition to Communist China until Lee's rapprochement with Beijing in the 1970s. As a result of the friendship between Singapore and Taiwan, Singaporean troops have been training in Taiwan since the 1970s.

---

[290] *China Post*, "Taiwan-Singapore ties rely on trust, wisdom to endure", 10 March 2012.

After US President Richard Nixon visited China in 1972, Singapore began friendly but unofficial ties with China, culminat- ing in formal diplomatic relations in 1990.

During the 1970s, before Singapore formally recognised China in 1990, then Singapore Prime Minister Lee Kuan Yew increasingly realised China was a rising power to be reckoned with. During his visit to the UK in 1974, Lee told British officials that China would need 10 more years to build up an effective nuclear second strike capability, after which China would begin to exert its influence glob- ally, according to British government documents. During his trip to the UK on 18 June 1974, Lee told British Member of Parliament David Ennals that Singapore cannot avoid establishing diplomatic relations with China, but he would make the decision on the timing, according to a report of The National Archives (TNA) of the United Kingdom on the Foreign and Commonwealth Office (FCO) at the Public Record Office (PRO).[291]

Lee told Ennals "The advantage for China in establishing rela- tions with Singapore was that she would be able to infiltrate a group of men, some thirty of whom would have diplomatic immunity, into the heart of Southeast Asia."

Lee told Ennals that 15 to 16 percent of Singaporeans would sup- port the Chinese Communist Party, 20 percent would support the Nationalist government in Taiwan and 55 to 60 percent were unde- cided. Lee said Singapore must assure other Southeast Asian nations that Singapore would not become a Trojan Horse for China to extend its influence in the region, hence Singapore will not be hasty in establishing diplomatic relations with China.

In 1978, Chinese leader Deng Xiaoping visited Singapore, as part of his overseas tour to gain ideas for the reforms he would implement in China. According to Lee Kuan Yew's book *The Singapore Story: 1965– 2000*, Deng sought ASEAN's support against Vietnam and the Soviet Union, which were then China's foes. Lee Kuan Yew pointed out to

---

[291] TNA: PRO FCO 15/1909, 18 June 1974, Record of Conversation between Mr Lee Kuan Yew Prime Minister of Singapore and the Minister of State and the Parliamentary Under Secretary of State at the Foreign and Commonwealth Office on 18 June at 10.15 a.m.

Deng there were no "overseas Russians" who launched communist insurgencies in Southeast Asia, but there were "overseas Chinese" supported by the Chinese government that threatened peace and stability in Thailand, Malaysia, Singapore and the Philippines. According to the book, Lee Kuan Yew told Deng, "China has to stop the radio broadcast of CPM (Communist Party of Malaya) and Indonesian communists in southern China." Deng agreed to Lee's request.

Reversing the far-left policies of his predecessor Mao Zedong, Deng's economic reforms launched China's meteoric rise as an economic superpower. Since then, Singapore's leaders no longer saw China as a base for subversive threats but an economic opportunity. Trade between Singapore and China grew 23 times from S$5.2 billion (US$3.8 billion) in 1990 to S$121.5 billion in 2014, according to official Singapore data. In 2013, China overtook Malaysia as Singapore's biggest trading partner.

At a national day rally speech on 18 August 2002, then Singapore Prime Minister Goh Chok Tong said, "So how should we respond to the China challenge? My response is: see China as an opportunity, not a threat. Also, China has stepped up its 'Venturing Out Policy'. The stock of China's outward investments is now more than US$27 billion, up from almost nothing just 25 years ago. We should try to get a fair share of these investments."

On June 2016, the Monetary Authority of Singapore (MAS) announced it would be including its yuan financial investments as part of its official Foreign Reserves from June 2016 onwords.

"This move recognises the steady and calibrated liberalisation of China's financial markets, and the growing acceptance of yuan assets in the global portfolio of institutional investors," said MAS.

As China grew in economic might, Lee Kuan Yew realised China was a force not to be trifled with, and reversed his earlier hostility to Communist China. In 2008, Lee Kuan Yew, no longer Prime Minister but holding the title Minister Mentor, stressed it would not be wise to provoke China the way some had by launching protests against China's Olympic torch relay and talking of boycotting the Beijing Olympic Games that year.[292] The Chinese

---

[292] *Channel NewsAsia*, "Boycott Olympics at a cost: MM", 9 May 2008.

would remember those who tried to frustrate the Chinese government's efforts to make the Olympic Games a success, he warned "Beijing uses its economic and political clout to counter acts it sees as against its interests."[293]

Lee Kuan Yew recalled that his son, then Singapore Deputy Prime Minister Lee Hsien Loong, had annoyed Beijing by visiting Taiwan in 2004.[294]

"Beijing objected and suspended all government-to-government negotiations with us. Our Free Trade Agreement with Beijing has still not been signed after four years," Lee Kuan Yew said in May 2008.[295]

Singapore and China resumed negotiations over their free trade agreement in August 2008 and signed the agreement on 23 October 2008. The Singapore government's attitude towards China has come a long way since its crackdown on local Chinese-educated students who were suspected of being sympathetic to China.

Singapore-China relations further improved in November 2014, when the Singapore Armed Forces and the People's Liberation Army conducted their first joint military exercise in Nanjing, China.[296] Singapore Defence Minister Ng Eng Hen said China and Singapore would increase their military cooperation. Around the time of that joint military exercise, Ng and Chinese Defence Minister Chang Wanquan discussed ways to increase the scope and frequency of joint military drills between both nations.[297] The armed forces of both nations would also work together in counter-terrorism and maritime security drills, and set up closer links between military academies on both sides.[298] Ng told reporters that the move "goes beyond motherhood statements" and reflected the confidence and goodwill that both sides had for each other.

---

[293] Ibid.
[294] Ibid.
[295] Ibid.
[296] *New Paper*, "S'pore China troops in first land war drill", 10 November 2014.
[297] Jermyn Chow, *Straits Times*, "Singapore and China agree to expand military relations", 14 November 2014.
[298] Ibid.

Singapore-China relations have come a long way since the 1970s, when Singapore troops started regular training in Taiwan, which was then an implacable foe of China. Even as Singapore military units have begun joint military exercises with the Chinese People's Liberation Army, Singapore soldiers continue to train in Taiwan, while it is an open secret that the US maintains substantial military, naval and intelligence facilities in Singapore.

Yet tensions continued between Singapore and China. On 7 December 2015, the US and Singapore announced increased military cooperation between both countries in an agreement that included Singapore hosting US military surveillance planes. The very next day, the Chinese Foreign Ministry publicly criticised the enhanced military ties between Singapore and the US, saying a stronger US military presence in Singapore did not "conform to the common and long-term interests among the countries in the region". In his Facebook posting on 11 December 2015, Singapore Defence Minister Ng engaged in a bit of sabre-rattling with his comments on Exercise Forging Sabre, an exercise involving Singapore Air Force jets at Luke Air Force base in Phoenix, Arizona, USA.

"Applause and congratulations at the Command Post at Luke Air Force Base, as missiles fired from our F-15SG and F-16C/D fighter aircraft, and AH-64D Apache helicopters hit all targets. The success of this exercise is a huge confidence booster as it shows that our integrated systems of troops on the ground, Heron-1 UAVs, AH-64D helicopters and fighter aircraft can work in unison to spot and take out mobile targets — even at night!" said Ng in his Facebook posting in praise of the US jet planes, helicopters and missiles supplied to the Singapore Air Force.

China's protests against the enhanced Singapore-US defence cooperation treaty and the Singapore Defence Minister's praise of Singapore-US military cooperation showed Singapore was caught in the middle of military tensions between China and the US.

As can be seen, Singapore's relations with China during the 1960s was marked by the Singapore government's suspicion of China, given the atmosphere of the Cold War and the Singapore government siding with the US and Britain against the Communist bloc. Within Singapore during that period, there were tensions between the Singapore government and the Chinese-educated who were suspected by the government of being sympathetic towards Communist China. During the 1970s, when the US ended its hostility towards China, Singapore followed suit. Since the 1980s, trade between Singapore and China boomed. Even then, mistrust and differences between Singapore and China have not completely disappeared. Like other Southeast Asian countries, Singapore is trying to maintain friendly relations with both the US and China, which is not always easy, given the tensions between these two superpowers.

Large numbers of mainland Chinese have been migrating to Singapore since the 1990s. As their numbers grow, they may form an increasingly significant social group that can potentially have an impact on Singapore society and politics. Despite China being an authoritarian state, many mainland Chinese immigrants do not shy away from opposing the authorities, as evidenced by continual reports of social unrest in that vast country. Some mainland Chinese immigrants may bring with them their habits of fomenting unrest to Singapore. Whether of their own accord or encouraged by unknown interested parties, some mainland Chinese immigrants may possibly stage dissent in their adopted home. If this happens, the Singapore authorities will find it harder to suppress them than the Chinese-educated students and activists in the 1950s and 1960s. An increasingly assertive and economically influential China will stand up for its citizens abroad, in contrast to the 1950s and 1960s when China was contained by the US.

6.4 Vietnam

Like Myanmar and Singapore, Vietnam's relations with China are ambiguous, and Vietnam maintains a balancing act in its relations with China and the US. The history of this Southeast Asian country, at first sight, might suggest Vietnam may be unambiguously hostile towards China, but this turns out not to have been the case.

The Chinese ruled Vietnam for about 1,000 years, from 111 BC to 938 AD. As typical of relations between colonial master and subject, Vietnam adopted many features of Chinese civilisation including Confucianism and Chinese administration, but fought long and hard to kick the Chinese out, just as India adopted the rule of law, democracy, cricket, the English language and Christianity from the British, but were only too glad to see the British leave.

Vietnam underwent nearly 2,000 years of struggle against Chinese rule and Chinese invasion.

Just as Joan of Arc led the French to defeat the English during the Hundred Years' War, Vietnam had its equivalent in two sisters, Tru'ng Trac and Tru'ng Nhi. The Tru'ng sisters were Vietnamese military leaders who ruled Vietnam for three years after rebelling against Chinese rule in 40 AD. Their reign was short-lived, however, as the Chinese gathered an expeditionary army under the Chinese General Ma Yuan to crush the rebellion. The Tru'ng sisters were defeated and committed suicide by drowning themselves in the Hát River in 43 AD. The sisters are highly revered in Vietnam today. Many temples are dedicated to them, and a holiday in February commemorating their death is observed by many Vietnamese. A district in Hanoi called the Hai Bà Tru'ng District is named after them. In addition, streets in major cities and many schools are named after them.

In 938, a Vietnamese rebel leader, Ngô Quyền, defeated a Chinese fleet at the Battle of Bach Dang. He then proclaimed himself King Ngô and began the era of independence for Vietnam, ending over 1,000 years of Chinese rule. Since then, China under the Song, Yuan, Ming and Qing dynasties, spanning a period of nearly 1,000 years, repeatedly tried to invade Vietnam, but failed, except for a 20-year Chinese occupation of Vietnam from 1407 to 1427.

Vietnam has many historical monuments in memory of wars against China, which is a sign of the Vietnamese identity shaped by the concept of China as the enemy. Historical monuments in Hanoi and Ho Chi Minh City celebrate Vietnamese heroes who fought Chinese invaders over the centuries. At a corner of Hoan Kiem Lake in Hanoi is Den Ngoc Son, "Temple of the Jade Mound". This small temple was founded in the 14th century and is dedicated to several gods, including General Tran Hung Dao, who defeated the Mongols in 1288. In Ho Chi Minh City, there is a statue of Tran Hung Dao, a Vietnamese General and prince during the Tran Dynasty. Prince Tran, who lived from 1228 to 1300, repelled three Mongol invasions of Vietnam. Also in Ho Chi Minh City, there is an equestrian statue of General Tran Nguyen Han, who served under Vietnamese Emperor Le Loi during the war against the Chinese in the middle of the 15th century. Vietnam has more monuments built for its heroes who fought the Chinese than those dedicated to heroes who fought the French and Americans.

American Cold Warriors failed to appreciate the deep-rooted Vietnamese suspicion of China which had become ingrained over centuries, otherwise the history of the US war in Vietnam might have been different. Although many US policymakers saw North Vietnam and Communist China as partners during the Vietnam War, war between China and Vietnam flared up just a few years after North Vietnam conquered South Vietnam in 1975.

In 1979, China and Vietnam went to war over their border. Chinese leader Deng Xiaoping had vowed to "teach Vietnam a lesson" for invading Cambodia in December 1978. Cambodia was then under the brutal Khmer Rouge regime, an ally of China. In February 1979, the Chinese People's Liberation Army crossed the border and invaded Vietnam. The Chinese army made some initial advances into northern Vietnam, but soon got bogged down. Both sides were believed to have suffered heavy casualties. In March 1979, the Chinese withdrew, with both sides claiming victory. China failed to prevent Vietnam from driving the Khmer Rouge from most of Cambodia and installing a pro-Vietnamese government in Phnom Penh.

Despite the history of conflict between China and Vietnam, trade between both nations has soared more than a thousand-fold from US$32 million in 1991 to US$36 billion in 2011.[299] By 2013, China had become Vietnam's biggest trading partner, with bilateral

---

[299] Ramses Amer, "Vietnam's relations with China — a multifaceted partnership", *China Policy Institute Blog, Nottingham University*, 17 March 2014.

trade growing at a robust 22 percent from the previous year to US$50.21 billion, according to Vietnam Customs.

Chinese investment in Vietnam has also grown, but lags behind countries like Japan and South Korea. Cumulative Chinese direct investment in Vietnam for the period of 1988 to 2012 shows 893 projects with registered capital approaching US$5 billion.[300] This is much smaller than the US$22.34 billion of total foreign direct investment in Vietnam for the year of 2013 alone, according to the Vietnamese Ministry of Planning and Investment's Foreign Investment Agency. In 2013, Japan topped foreign direct investment in Vietnam with over US$5.87 billion, followed by Singapore at US$4.76 billion and South Korea at US$4.46 billion, according to the agency. When I visited Hanoi in 2011 and Ho Chi Minh City in 2012, I do not recall seeing any Chinese companies in these cities.

One of the reasons why Chinese firms did not win more deals in Vietnam could possibly be the historical Vietnamese suspicion of China. An example is the Vietnamese government's rejection of offers by Chinese state-owned firms to build a high speed railway between Hanoi and Ho Chi Minh City, opting instead for Japanese high speed railway, which was much more expensive and took longer to build. This was a 1,570 km high-speed railway planned by the Vietnamese government to connect the capital Hanoi with Ho Chi Minh City in southern Vietnam, which was scheduled to be fully operational by 2025.

At a railway conference in Hong Kong in July 2010, a Vietnam Railways official, Nguyen Manh Hien, said his country's rail operator had chosen a US$55 billion Japanese model for the high-speed railway. The Japanese high-speed railway would be more costly and take longer to build than the Chinese version. For comparison purposes, it is estimated that the 1,318 km Beijing-Shanghai high-speed railway cost 221 billion yuan (US$35.5 billion) and took three years to build.[301]

---

[300] Ibid.

[301] Toh Han Shih, *South China Morning Post*, "Vietnam shuns China's high-speed express", 19 July 2010.

Nonetheless, Vietnam would stick with the Japanese high-speed railway, Hien insisted, "We studied China's high-speed railway. It is not advantageous."[302] One factor in Japan's favour is its 40-year history of high-speed railway with no accidents, Hien explained.

According to the Chinese-language magazine *Yazhou Zhoukan*, some Vietnamese politicians opposed adopting Chinese high-speed rail technology for fear that China might use high-speed trains to transport the People's Liberation Army to invade Vietnam.

6.5 Maritime tensions

Historical tensions between Vietnam and China have continued in the 21st century, especially over the South China Sea. China faced tensions not only with Vietnam, but also the Philippines, over this body of water. In the South China Sea, the Spratly and Paracel islands face competing claims in part or in full by China, Vietnam, Malaysia, Taiwan, the Philippines and Brunei.

In 2009, China formalised its historic claims to the Spratly Islands, insisting much of that area was part of its exclusive economic zone. Between 2009 and 2011, China's efforts to consolidate its maritime claims heightened tensions in the region.[303] The simmering tensions came to the fore in June 2010 when US State Secretary Hillary Clinton told a regional meeting that the US could act as a mediator in the South China Sea, a move supported by some other Asian governments.[304] According to officials present at the meeting, Yang Jiechi, China's Foreign Minister, responded angrily that the proposal was an "attack on China" and told the nations that supported the US intervention: "China is a big country and other countries are small countries, and that is just a fact."[305]

---

[302] Ibid.
[303] M. Taylor Fravel, "China's Strategy in the South China Sea", *Contemporary Southeast Asia*, Volume 33 Issue 3, 1 December 2011.
[304] Geoff Dyer, *Financial Times*, "Beijing's elevated aspirations", 10 November 2010.
[305] Ibid.

At the Shangri-La Dialogue in Singapore in June 2010, divisions intensified between Chinese and US officials which manifest themselves in open exchanges, while Southeast Asian nations discreetly raised alarms about a fresh push from Beijing to scupper a regional approach to finding solutions for peace and stability.[306] At the dialogue, US Secretary of Defence Robert Gates described the matter as a "growing concern".[307] Gates said, "We oppose the use of force and actions that hinder freedom of navigation".

At Chinese meetings with ASEAN, Beijing told Southeast Asian countries that it would not tolerate attempts to raise the South China Sea issue.[308] The Chinese government preferred to deal with countries individually — a move that apparently put China in the strongest position.[309] In 2010, Vietnam, then Chairman of ASEAN, was desperately trying to force discussion on a legally binding code of conduct.[310] China had discouraged such moves, according to several diplomats.[311]

"On this issue, China is determined to rule ASEAN by dividing it," one regional envoy said.[312]

On 15 June 2010, Greg Torode wrote in *the South China Morning Post*, "Old allies and newer friends in the region are quietly urging the Pentagon not to back away from East Asia, voicing alarm at China's new assertiveness."

Torode quoted a US Obama administration official saying, "We are given some very strong messages behind the scenes. They may never say it publicly, but they certainly say it."

Torode added, "Vietnam's defence minister, for example, spoke of the ongoing 'comradeship and good neighbourliness' with their former enemy, Beijing. Behind the scenes, however, Vietnamese gen-

---

[306] Greg Torode, *South China Morning Post*, "US-China ties in troubled waters", 7 June 2010.
[307] Ibid.
[308] Ibid.
[309] Ibid.
[310] Ibid.
[311] Ibid.
[312] Ibid.

erals are rapidly exploring a range of new cooperation with the US and other regional powers, saying they fear their sovereignty is now at risk from China's assertiveness in the South China Sea." The US navy held a joint drill with its former foe, Vietnam, in the summer of 2010, 35 years after US troops withdrew from Saigon. In August 2011, the US navy returned to Vietnam's Cam Ranh Bay, where US forces had built a vast air and sea base during the Vietnam War.[313] In a little-noticed move, a US military supply ship USNS Richard E. Byrd anchored in Cam Ranh Bay that month for maintenance.[314]

Notwithstanding tensions between China and other nations over the South China Sea, the Chinese government has at times struck a conciliatory note to calm the waters. At a regional meeting in Vietnam in November 2010, Chinese Premier Wen Jiabao talked of creating a "sea of peace and co-operation" in the South China Sea.[315]

The US government has responded to China's conciliatory overtures. In late 2010, the US postponed a naval drill with South Korea and refused to label China as a currency manipulator despite pressure from some US politicians.[316]

"China appears to have recognised the cost of its actions and is taking steps to repair its image, such as restarting military-to-military ties with the US," says Massachusetts Institute of Technology Associate Professor Taylor Fravel. "Even if these steps represent only tactical shifts, they do underscore how China must continue to be sensitive to regional sentiments."[317]

Vietnam has also at times made reconciliatory overtures towards China. For instance, in October 2011, Vietnamese Communist Party General Secretary Nguyen Phu Trong visited China to cool tensions

---

[313] Greg Torode, *South China Morning Post*, "US navy returns to Cam Ranh Bay", 27 August 2011.
[314] Ibid.
[315] Geoff Dyer, *Financial Times*, "Beijing's elevated aspirations", 10 November 2010
[316] Ibid.
[317] Ibid.

that had flared up earlier. In May and June 2011, Chinese vessels had twice cut cables towing the sonar array of boats of the state-owned Vietnam Oil and Gas Group (Petrovietnam) in Vietnam's exclusive economic zone under the 1982 United Nations Convention on the Law of the Sea (UNCLOS).[318] These incidents had sparked public protests in Vietnam,[319] with China and Vietnam accusing each other of violations of territorial waters. The Vietnamese party leader's trip to China was deemed to be an olive branch, when he called for China to set up a hotline to prevent misunderstandings between both countries.[320]

Fravel was quoted in *Diplomat* magazine saying Beijing's diplomatic initiatives should be acknowledged.

"Although (Chinese People's Liberation Army) PLA-affiliated media commentators, such as Major General Luo Yuan, have called for China to adopt a more forceful response, (Chinese) officers such as Ma Xiaotian and Liang Guanglie have not. . . . Of course, China will continue to assert its claims. But the PLA's support for a diplomatic approach and limiting the potential for escalation should be noted," Fravel told the magazine in June 2012.

On 2 September 2012, a Chinese People's Liberation Army delegation, led by the Deputy Chief of General Staff Ma Xiaotian, visited Vietnam, Myanmar, Malaysia and Singapore, with the aim of easing tensions over the South China Sea.[321] The Chinese military and Foreign Ministry have conducted a number of exchanges with Asia Pacific nations in 2012, in the hope of reducing suspicion towards China's intentions.[322]

On 4 September 2012, a Chinese state newspaper, *China Daily*, a state mouthpiece, reported, "A flurry of diplomacy by People's Liberation Army officials is conducive to reducing miscalculations

---

[318] Austin Ramzy, *Time*, "A Step Back From the Brink in the South China Sea", 12 October 2011.
[319] Ibid.
[320] Ibid.
[321] Zhao Shengnan and Wang Chenyan, *China Daily*, "PLA diplomacy to ease tensions", 4 September 2012.
[322] Ibid.

amid recent territorial disputes and neighbours' concerns about China's military strength, analysts said."

Notwithstanding Vietnam's long history of enmity towards China, it has been cultivating ties with both the US and China. For instance, US Defence Secretary Leon Panetta visited Cam Ranh Bay in Vietnam on 3 June 2012, but in an interview published in the *South China Morning Post* the previous day, Vietnamese Deputy Defence Minister Nguyen Chi Vinh told the Hong Kong newspaper that Hanoi and Beijing recognised that increased military links between both sides had contributed to their relationship, and it was "very important" to have good relations with China.

Even as it conducted drills with the US navy, Vietnam has also held military exercises with the Chinese.[323] For instance, the Vietnamese Defence Ministry announced on 25 March 2016 that final preparations were underway for the third Vietnam-China Border Defence Friendship Exchange programme. This joint military exercise was scheduled for 28 to 31 March 2016 in Lang Son Province in Vietnam and Guangxi Province in China, under the joint command of Vietnamese General Phung Quang Thanh and Chinese Defence Minister Chang Wanquan, the Vietnamese Defence Ministry noted.

On 26 and 27 August 2014, the Standing Secretary of the Vietnamese Communist Party Le Hong Anh visited China. Official Vietnamese media declared the trip's main motive was restoring relations between both countries.[324] Anh's trip was regarded as a signal from Vietnam that it did not want a confrontation with China, despite the first visit to Vietnam made by the US Chairman of the Joint Chiefs of Staff, General Martin Dempsey, since 1971.[325] Anh, who ranked fifth in the Vietnamese Politburo, met numerous high-ranking Chinese officials including President Xi Jinping.[326]

---

[323] Geoff Dyer, *Financial Times*, "Beijing's elevated aspirations", 10 November 2010.
[324] An Dien, *Thanh Nien News*, "Vietnam Party official heads to China to defuse tensions", 25 August 2014.
[325] Ibid.
[326] Carl Thayer, *The Diplomat*, "China and Vietnam Eschew Megaphone Diplomacy", 2 January 2015.

During his talk with Xi, Anh said Vietnam would do its utmost to enhance mutual understanding and trust, and consolidate the comprehensive strategic partnership with China.[327]

"Both countries are aware that the increase in defence-to-defence relations can prevent confrontation and conflict," Anh said.

However, relations between China and Vietnam deteriorated again in May 2014, when a Chinese oil rig appeared in waters claimed by both countries. China's move drew criticism from Vietnam, which dispatched ships to confront the rig, leading to a series of ramming incidents between Chinese and Vietnamese vessels. Later that month, in an angry reaction to the Chinese oil drilling, thousands of Vietnamese set fire to foreign factories and rampaged through industrial zones in Vietnam.[328] The violence led to one of the worst breakdowns in Sino-Vietnamese relations since their border war in 1979. Yet ironically, the brunt of the damage was borne by Taiwanese firms which were mistaken for Chinese companies.[329]

Shortly after the oil rig incident in May 2014, the Vietnamese government appeared to be courting the US as a counterweight against China. On 21 July 2014, Hanoi Party Chief Pham Quang Nghi visited the US, where he met the President pro tempore of the US Senate Patrick Leahy.[330] On 14 August 2014, US Army General Martin Dempsey became the first Chairman of the Joint Chiefs of Staff to visit Vietnam in more than four decades.

Despite efforts by Vietnam and China to smooth their relations, mutual distrust continued to linger. In early December 2014, Vietnam sent a statement to The Hague's Permanent Court of Arbitration, making three claims in opposition to China's stand on the Spratly and Paracel islands in the South China Sea.[331]

---

[327] Ibid.

[328] Ho Binh Minh and Manuel Mogato, *Reuters*, "Vietnam mobs set fire to foreign factories in anti-China riots", 14 May 2014.

[329] Truong-minh Vu and Nguyen Thanh Trung, "A US-China Alliance or (still) a US-China-Vietnam Triangle?", *International Policy Digest*, 3 October 2014.

[330] Ibid.

[331] Kristine Kwok and Zuraidah Ibrahim, *South China Morning Post*, "Beijing rejects Hanoi's legal challenge on Spratly, Paracel islands disputes", 13 December 2014.

Subsequently on 12 December 2014, Chinese Foreign Ministry spokesman Hong Lei dismissed the Vietnamese action, describing its claims over the Spratly and Paracel islands as invalid.[332]

On 19 February 2016, Vietnam protested to China as a result of a "serious violation" of its sovereignty due to Beijing's apparent deployment of an advanced missile system on a disputed South China Sea island, Woody Island, while Australia and New Zealand urged Chinese restraint.[333] Tensions between China and its neighbours over maritime territory have risen since Taiwan and US officials said Beijing had placed surface-to-air missiles on Woody Island.[334] Earlier, Australian Prime Minister Malcolm Turnbull had urged claimants to refrain from island-building and militarisation in the South China Sea.[335]

"It is absolutely critical that we ensure that there is a lowering of tensions," said Turnbull, speaking after a meeting in Sydney with New Zealand counterpart John Key.

Given such longstanding tensions between China on one side and Vietnam, the US and other Southeast Asian nations on the other, military conflict cannot be ruled out. If war breaks out over the South China Sea, Vietnam will be the first nation to be embroiled, given its location next to China and the South China Sea, its strong military as well as its history of war with China. The Philippines, another country adjacent to the South China Sea, may be the next country to be drawn into war with China. The US might possibly intervene in any potential conflict that breaks out, which would escalate the situation. As for Southeast Asian countries further away from China, like Singapore, Indonesia and Malaysia, they will be unlikely to actively participate in any such war that might break out. However, the chances of war breaking out are mitigated by other nations which would probably urge restraint on

---

[332] Ibid.
[333] Martin Petty and Colin Packham, *Reuters,* "Vietnam protests China missile deployment, Australia, NZ urge restraint", 19 February 2016.
[334] Ibid.
[335] Ibid.

all sides, such as the example of Australia and New Zealand calling for restraint in February 2016.

Fravel wrote in a paper,[336] "As China continues to accumulate military capabilities, it will feel more confident about managing its claims, less threatened by other states in these disputes, and less likely to use force. At least in China's past territorial disputes, China has been much less willing to use force against its weaker neighbours. What could change China's calculations, however, might be improved security ties between other claimants and the US. If coupled with what China might view as increasing assertiveness by these states in the dispute, China might then view its position as weakening and be more likely to use force. Nevertheless, the other states are so weak when compared to China now and in the future that even closer ties with the United States may not shift China's assessment of the strength of its own claim."

Vietnam's desire to maintain friendly relations with both China and the US is another deterrent to war between China and Vietnam. Like other Southeast Asian countries, Vietnam wants to benefit from economic ties with the US and China, and avoid having to choose between these two superpowers.

6.6 China reaches out to Southeast Asia

The examples of Myanmar, Indonesia, Singapore and Vietnam show that in general, Southeast Asian countries want to maintain a balancing act of having good relations with China and the US. Since 2012, Myanmar has opened up to investment from the US, Europe, Japan and other nations, but China will continue to have substantial economic ties with Myanmar for the foreseeable future. In Indonesia, the Suharto regime initially broke diplomatic ties with China and imposed restrictions on the Indonesian Chinese community, but Indonesia subsequently re-established diplomatic relations with China. The Singapore government

---

[336] M. Taylor Fravel, "China's Strategy in the South China Sea", *Contemporary Southeast Asia*, 1 December 2011.

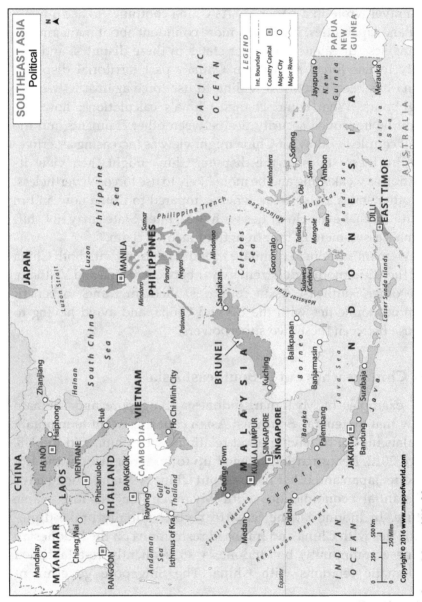

Source: Maps of World

clamped down on Communism and was suspicious of Chinese students from the 1950s to 1970s. Since 2014, the Singapore Armed Forces started training with the Chinese People's Liberation Army even while US forces maintained a presence in the city-state. In contrast to minimal economic exchanges during the Cold War, the Singapore government now welcomes Chinese investment and Singapore is a major investor in China. Despite the long history of war between Vietnam and China as well as tensions between both nations over the South China Sea, Vietnam has military links with both the US and China, while Sino-Vietnamese trade has grown tremendously. Laos and Cambodia have close economic ties to China, while Malaysia maintains friendly ties with both the US and China.

Since 2009, China has overtaken Japan, the EU and the US to become the biggest trading partner of ASEAN. Trade between China and ASEAN has soared nearly ninefold from US$54.8 billion in 2002 to US$446.3 billion in 2013, according to official Chinese data. Some Southeast Asian folk handicrafts, which were supposed to be unique local products, were actually made in Chinese factories because it was cheaper, according to anecdotal accounts.

Beijing has been spending billions of dollars building infrastructure to connect its provinces with Southeast Asia, especially in the southern Chinese Provinces of Yunnan and Guangxi.

On the south coast of Guangxi, Fangchenggang was built as a port in 1968 to ship military supplies to North Vietnam during the Vietnam War, some of which got sent down the Ho Chi Minh Trail to Vietcong guerrillas in South Vietnam.[337] Fangchenggang has since become a port conducting peaceful trade with Vietnam, which has become the biggest trading partner of Guangxi, which shares a common border with Vietnam.[338] On 12 August 2010, the

---

[337] Toh Han Shih, *South China Morning Post*, "Guangxi in major push for regional trade", 21 August 2010.
[338] Ibid.

South China Morning Post reported that the Chinese government supported infrastructure and transport projects totalling 1.5 trillion yuan (US$240 billion) in Guangxi to boost links with Southeast Asia, including port facilities and roads.

On 19 November 2011, the *South China Morning Post* reported that the Chinese government planned to spend 500 billion yuan (US$80.6 billion) on infrastructure in Yunnan to create a gateway to Southeast Asia. The Chinese government has called for the completion of a railway between Dali in Yunnan and Ruili on the China-Myanmar border.[339]

"China sees Southeast Asia as its backyard, as part of its attempt to claim the status of regional power. This could have something to do with its competition with other powers including the US and Japan, to gain a firmer foothold in Burma and Laos," Pavin of the Institute of Southeast Asian Studies said.[340]

"China is trying to accomplish several goals via infrastructure and energy projects in Yunnan," Paul Donowitz, Campaigns Coordinator of Earthrights International, an advocacy group on human rights and environmental issues, said.[341] "One goal is to decrease dependence on the Straits of Malacca, where 80 percent of its oil imports currently pass through."

In October 2013, a 2,520 km oil and gas pipeline, estimated to cost US$2.5 billion, which ran between Yunnan and the west coast of Myanmar, started operations. The pipeline, built and operated by CNPC, the largest Chinese state-owned energy conglomerate, transports gas from the Shwe gas fields, Myanmar's largest gas project, as well as oil carried by tanker from Africa and the Middle East.[342] In October 2009, 115 organisations and political parties from 20 countries submitted an open letter to Chinese President Hu

---

[339] Toh Han Shih, *South China Morning Post*, "Yunnan, the new gateway", 19 November 2011.
[340] Ibid.
[341] Ibid.
[342] Toh Han Shih, *South China Morning Post*, "Joint pipeline with junta sparks rights debate", 9 August 2010.

Jintao calling for the suspension of the pipeline to prevent human rights abuses and regional instability and avoid financial and reputational risks for China.

"We are gravely concerned for the communities living along the pipeline," the letter stated. "Based on experience in Myanmar, partnerships with MOGE (the Myanmar State Oil and Gas Company) on infrastructure projects lead to forced displacement, forced labour and loss of livelihood."

Matthew Smith, Senior Consultant at EarthRights International, said, "Land in some surrounding parts of the pipeline was forcibly confiscated from local villagers. Some villagers were promised compensation, but some villagers received far less than what was promised to them, while others have received nothing."[343]

Smith expressed concerns over a lack of checks and balances as well as low transparency with regards to the massive revenues to be generated by the project. The project was expected to provide the Myanmese junta with at least US$29 billion over 30 years, according to an estimate from Christian Solidarity Worldwide, a human rights organisation with its headquarters in Britain.

Chinese plans for infrastructure to connect to Southeast Asia have experienced delays and political roadblocks. For instance, there had been talk for many years of creating a railway to link southern China to peninsular Southeast Asia, reaching all the way down south to Singapore, but progress has been painfully slow.

"High-speed trains may happen in Malaysia in 10 to 15 years, but not in two to three years. The main problem is high-speed rail is too expensive as new rail lines need to be laid," said Afzar Zakariya, a Senior Manager at Keretapi Tanah Melayu, the Malaysian state railway.[344]

In November 2009, around the time of Chinese President Hu Jintao's visit to Malaysia, the Malaysian government announced it

---

[343] Ibid.
[344] Toh Han Shih, *South China Morning Post*, "Costs and political sensitivities hit hopes of a pan-Asia rail link", 22 March 2010.

would award a US$2.1 billion railway project in southern Malaysia to a Chinese consortium including China Railway Engineering Corporation, a state-owned firm. But the Chinese group encountered delays in the Malaysian project. On 9 March 2010, former Malaysian Finance Minister Daim Zainuddin met Li Changjin, President of China Railway Engineering Corporation, in Beijing. In the meeting, Li expressed to Daim his hope that both sides would implement their joint project as soon as possible.[345] Daim replied that while the Malaysian government had signed a letter of intent on the project, much work remained to be done by both sides.[346]

Some Chinese infrastructure projects in Southeast Asia have also met with local opposition. In 2011, China Southern Power Grid, a Chinese state-owned power company, pulled out of controversial dam projects in Cambodia after local villagers protested that the dams would ruin their fisheries.[347]

Notwithstanding delays and opposition, China's infrastructure links to Southeast Asia will have a profound impact on the region. One example is the oil and gas pipeline between Myanmar and China. With this pipeline connecting Myanmar and China, oil and gas no longer needs to be transported only through the Straits of Malacca, Singapore and the South China Sea to China, but straight from Myanmar to China. The question is, will the Chinese government sponsor or build a canal through the slim Isthmus of Kra in Thailand, to further circumvent the shipment of goods and commodities through the Straits of Malacca? After all, if a Chinese company can build a canal through Nicaragua, Chinese firms can conceivably build a canal through the Isthmus of Kra. If such a canal is ever built through the Isthmus of Kra, it will have important implications for Southeast Asia including Singapore, which is located at the strategic tip of the Straits of Malacca.

---

[345] Ibid.
[346] Ibid.
[347] Toh Han Shih, *South China Morning Post*, "Controversial Chinese projects in Cambodia bow to pressure", 3 September 2011.

Chapter 7

Lenin Revisited

The Chinese Communist Party was founded upon the theories of Karl Marx and Vladimir Lenin. Long after the Chinese leader Deng Xiaoping launched China's capitalist reforms in the 1980s, the Chinese government continued to pay lip service to Marxist–Leninism, despite China having adopted many features of capitalism. Lenin, the leader of the Bolshevik Revolution and the first leader of the Soviet Union, had written a book, *"Imperialism: The Highest Stage of Capitalism"*, which was published in 1916. Soviet and Chinese propaganda labelled the Americans as imperialists during the Cold War. In Indochina, local Communists invoked the bogey of imperialism when they fought US forces during the Vietnam War.

According to Lenin's book, imperialism has five essential features:

1. The concentration of production and capital developed to such a high stage that it created monopolies which play a decisive role in economic life.
2. The merging of bank capital with industrial capital, and the creation, on the basis of this financial capital, of a financial oligarchy.

3. The export of capital, which has become extremely important, as distinguished from the export of commodities.
4. The formation of international capitalist monopolies which share the world among themselves.
5. The territorial division of the whole world among the greatest capitalist powers is completed.

The British Empire was obviously one of the empires Lenin had in mind when he wrote his book in the early 20th century, given that Britain was the most powerful empire at that time. China in the 21st century shares some, but not all, the features of British imperialism in the late 19th and early 20th century.

Lenin's book quoted John Hobson, a British critic of imperialism: "Great Britain grants loans to Egypt, Japan, China and South America. Her navy plays here the part of bailiff in case of necessity. Great Britain's political power protects her from the indignation of her debtors."

China lacks a key element of British imperialism, which is a dominant global navy. China's navy in the 21st century is not powerful enough to play the bailiff or protect China "from the indignation of her debtors", as Lenin had described the British Royal Navy in the 19th century and early 20th century.

Nonetheless, in terms of providing financing throughout the world, China in the 21st century has swopped places with the British Empire in the 19th and early 20th century. In the 21st century, Chinese institutions grant loans to Egypt and South America, and invest in Britain and Japan. Chinese investments in Europe doubled to a record US$18 billion in 2014 from 2013.[348] In the first three quarters of 2014, Chinese investments in Europe soared 218 percent, leapt 150 percent in Japan and jumped 70 percent in Russia.[349] Britain was the European nation that received the most Chinese

---

[348] *Baker & McKenzie report*, "Chinese investment into Europe hits record high in 2014", 11 February 2015.
[349] *KPMG quarterly China* report, third quarter 2014.

investment in 2014 at US$5.1 billion.[350] This is not surprising, given that Britain has been assiduously courting Chinese money.

After incurring Beijing's wrath for meeting the Dalai Lama in 2012, UK Prime Minister David Cameron visited China in 2013 to repair ties and seek investment from China. In 2014, Chinese Prime Minister Li Keqiang visited the UK, which saw deals worth at least 14 billion pounds signed. Li was granted an audience with Queen Elizabeth during his visit. A British official said this was a rare honour for a visitor who was not a head of state. As part of Britain's attempts to further gain economic benefits from China, Prince William, second in line to the British throne, visited China in March 2015. During his visit, Prince William avoided saying anything that might offend his Chinese hosts, and he did not visit Hong Kong, where elements of the local population were seething with resentment against Beijing for not giving Hong Kong greater democracy. In October 2015, Chinese President Xi Jinping made a state visit to the UK, where he was given a lavish red-carpet welcome, including a 103-gun salute and a state banquet in Buckingham Palace. During Xi's visit, deals worth nearly 40 billion pounds were signed between both countries, the British government declared.[351] So grand was the welcome ceremony given by the British for the Chinese leader that it caused discomfort and drew criticism from some quarters of the British establishment and Britain's Western allies.

An article by George Parker and Jamil Anderlini in the *Financial Times on* 18 October 2015 stated, "Britain's traditional allies regard this behaviour as bizarre at best and craven and dangerous at worst, while old China hands at the Foreign Office are in despair."

The *Financial Times* article quoted an unnamed grandee saying, "We will just have to hold our noses."

---

[350] *Baker & McKenzie report*, "Chinese investment into Europe hits record high in 2014", 11 February 2015.

[351] https://www.gov.uk/government/news/chinese-state-visit-up-to-40-billion-deals-agreed.

An unnamed senior advisor to US policymakers described the UK as "the only place where China is truly influential right now because they are so desperate for Chinese investment."[352]

An unnamed senior western intelligence officer said, "The most charitable spin we can put on the current China policy of the British government is to say it is a pure mercantilist, unprincipled, self-serving decision aimed at attracting short-term investment. The big question is whether it actually works."[353]

The Chinese have also switched roles with the British as wealthy tourists in Europe enjoying the fruits of their investments. In the 19th and early 20th century, it was the British and other European investors who took holidays in Europe by living off the income from their investments in China.

Lenin quoted Hobson: "In the South of England, in the Riviera, and in Italy and Switzerland, wealthy aristocrats drawing dividends and pensions from the Far East. Reflect upon the vast extension of such a system which might be rendered feasible by the subjection of China to the economic control of financiers, investors, and political and business officials, draining the greatest potential reservoir of profit the world has ever known, in order to consume it in Europe."

The situation reversed in the 21st century, where wealthy Chinese are buying property in England and the Riviera. Chinese individuals and companies have emerged as major buyers of real estate in the UK, where they have fuelled a housing shortage and were accused of driving up property prices, the *Daily Mail* reported in April 2014.[354]

"September 15, 2010 was an historical day for China on the French Riviera. On this day, a Shanghainese entrepreneur signed the agreement which made him the owner of a luxury villa, with amazing sea views in the City of Nice. This transaction was

---

[352] George Parker and Jamil Anderlini, *Financial Times*, "Britain's red-carpet welcome for Xi baffles traditional allies", 18 October 2015.
[353] Ibid.
[354] Louise Eccles, *Daily Mail*. "Chinese buyers fuelling UK housing shortage: Far East speculators price Britons out of market across the country", 4 April 2014.

apparently the very first ever recorded purchase by a private Chinese citizen on the French Riviera," wrote French luxury property specialist Phillippe Benoit Du Rey in the luxury property website PropGOLuxury.com.

By 2012, Chinese ranked second behind Americans as buyers of luxury residential property in France.[355]

Some Chinese-owned luxury villas in the south of France acquired notorious associations. During the trial of Bo Xilai in August 2013, a Chinese businessman, Xu Ming, admitted he owned a six-bedroom luxury villa in Cannes on the French Riviera. In September 2013, Bo, a former Chinese Commerce Minister and Party Chief of Chongqing, was jailed for life for bribery, embezzlement and abuse of power. Xu testified in court that Bo's wife Gu Kailai told him in 2000 that she wanted to buy a villa in France, for which Xu provided US$3.23 million. In his trial, Bo said he was "completely unaware" of the villa. French court documents revealed that the villa was once managed by Neil Heywood, a British businessman who was murdered by Gu. In August 2012, Gu was given a suspended death sentence by a Chinese court for murdering Heywood.

Just as China in the 21st century shares some (but not all the) elements of imperialism with the British Empire, China and the US exhibit some, but not all, of Lenin's five attributes of imperialism. Let us examine these five features, starting from the fifth.

On **the fifth point**, the territorial division of the world between China and the US, such a division of the world has not occurred in the 21st century.

Lenin wrote, "The characteristic of imperialism is not industrial capital, but finance capital. It is not an accident that in France it was precisely the extraordinarily rapid development of finance capital, and the weakening of industrial capital, that, from 1880 onwards, gave rise to the extreme extension of annexationist (colonial) policy."

---

[355] Peta Tomlinson, *South China Morning Post*, "More Asians buying into dream of owning property in France", 26 September 2012.

This is not true of the US or China in the 21ˢᵗ century. The international order and public opinion in the 21ˢᵗ century makes it unthinkable for any superpower to annex another country without strong justification, given the memories of two world wars and fears of a nuclear third world war.

Lenin wrote, "The principal spheres of investment of British capital are the British colonies. In this case, enormous exports of capital are bound up with the possession of enormous colonies."

This is not the case in the 21ˢᵗ century. Although military incursions occur, world opinion in the 21ˢᵗ century would not stand for any country invading vast territories to create "enormous colonies". US companies invest in many countries but these are not American colonies. Similarly, Chinese companies are making increasingly large investments around the world, but China is not colonising other countries.

Regarding **the fourth point** on international monopolies "which share the world among themselves", this is only partly true of the US and China in the 21ˢᵗ century. Both countries have huge companies with extensive international presence. For US companies, think of technology giants like IBM with facilities and operations in many countries. During the late 20ᵗʰ century and early 21ˢᵗ century, US Internet giants like Facebook and Google reach most of the world through the Internet. Some, but not all, large US companies are monopolies. Microsoft, Google and Facebook dominate their niches, with no company powerful enough to effectively challenge them. Likewise, China's huge SOEs have operations in many countries. For instance, CNPC, the largest Chinese state-owned energy company, provides oilfield and engineering services in 67 countries, according to its website.

The largest Chinese dam builder, Sinohydro, has construction projects in more than 80 countries, according to its website. As of 2015, the state-owned firm commands 50 percent share of the international hydropower market, according to International Rivers. Sinohydro's overseas revenue has leapt more than tenfold from less than US$500 million in 2005 to over US$6 billion in 2014, while its international orders soared sixfold from US$2 billion in 2005 to over US$12 billion in 2014, according to the company's website.

Notwithstanding the fact that China is the biggest dam builder in the world, Sinohydro is not a monopoly but faces competition from another Chinese state-owned dam builder, Gezhouba. At the start of the 21st century, few or no Chinese companies can be completely characterised as monopolies. US and Chinese companies are not so dominant as to "share the world among themselves". There are many large companies with extensive international operations of different nationalities, including the British, Dutch, German, French, Italian, Japanese and South Korean.

On **the third point**, where a hallmark of imperialism is the export of capital, this is true of the US and is increasingly true of China in the 21st century. The US is the largest overseas investor globally. China rose from the world's sixth largest foreign investor in 2011 to the world's third largest foreign investor in 2012, behind the US at number one and Japan at number two, according to official Chinese data. In 2014, China became a net capital exporter for the first time, with its overseas direct investment (ODI) at US$140 billion exceeding foreign direct investment (FDI) of US$120 billion, according to the Chinese Ministry of Commerce.

As Lenin wrote, "Imperialism is capitalism in that stage of development in which the dominance of monopolies and finance capital has established itself, in which the export of capital has acquired pronounced importance. The capital exporting countries have divided the world among themselves in the figurative sense of the term. But finance capital has also led to the actual division of the world."

In the 21st century, the financial muscle of China and the US has not led to a division of the world in the actual sense. But with the global clout of Wall Street, as well as China's rapidly growing loans and investments in Africa, Latin America, Asia, Europe and the US, the two main capital exporting countries in the 21st century, namely the US and China, can be said to have divided the world among themselves in the figurative sense of the term.

The second point on the partnership of banks with industry, as well as the dominance of a financial oligarchy, is largely true of the US and China in the 21st century. Chinese state-owned policy lenders like China Development Bank and China Exim Bank lend billions to finance many overseas projects of Chinese SOEs. Both within and outside China, large Chinese SOEs regularly receive loans from Chinese state-owned banks on favourable terms with little difficulty. The Big Four Chinese state-owned banks (Bank of China, Industrial and Commercial Bank of China, China Construction Bank and Agricultural Bank of China) plus the two Chinese state-owned policy lenders, China Development Bank and China Exim Bank, form a Chinese financial oligarchy which plays an increasingly important role in global finance.

The US has the world's largest stock exchanges as well as the world's biggest and most influential financial hub in New York City. Wall Street is first among equals in an international financial oligarchy that also includes the financial institutions of the UK, Japan, Switzerland and increasingly China. Such is the global importance of US capital, that when the subprime mortgage crisis broke out in the US and Lehman Brothers collapsed in 2008, most of the world suffered from a global financial crisis that lasted a few years. The description of Wall Street as a financial oligarchy with huge global impact is difficult to dispute.

During the run up to the US Presidential elections of 2016, the Democratic candidates Hillary Clinton and Bernie Sanders both publicly attested to the dominance of Wall Street.

In a speech on 5 January 2016, Sanders said, "(The American people) also know that a handful of people on Wall Street have extraordinary power over the economic and political life of our country. We will no longer tolerate an economy and a political system that has been rigged by Wall Street to benefit the wealthiest Americans in this country at the expense of everyone else."

In a tweet on 25 March 2016, Clinton said, "The top 25 hedge fund managers make more than all of the kindergarten teachers in America combined. That's not acceptable."

The first point, with regards to the concentration of production and capital in monopolies, is largely, but not wholly, true of the US and China in the 21st century. China has massive SOEs where the number of employees, scale of business and financial assets are huge, ironically originating from the state control of companies under Communist doctrine. For example, China Railway Group, a Chinese state-owned rail builder, had 289,547 employees as of the end of 2013, while its assets totalled 628 billion yuan or approximately US$100 billion, according to its 2013 annual report. In 2013, the Hong Kong and Shanghai-listed firm built 4,843 km of railroad and 1,008 km of roads, while earning 540.39 billion yuan of revenue, according to its 2013 annual report. China Railway Group has built more than 230 overseas projects including railway, roads, bridges and airports in more than 55 countries, according to its website. A Chinese e-commerce company, Alibaba Group, had market capitalisation on the New York Stock Exchange of more than US$200 billion in early 2015.

As for the US, huge multinationals like GE, ExxonMobil, Boeing, Microsoft, IBM and Apple have become leading global brands. GE had 307,000 employees around the world at the end of 2013, according to its website.

However, in early 21st century, many large Chinese SOEs were not monopolies, especially in view of the Chinese government's policy of encouraging competition. For example, there are two competing state-owned rail construction firms, namely China Railway Group and China Railway Construction Corporation.

Similarly, many US multinationals are not monopolies. The US has antitrust laws to prevent monopolies. Microsoft, which virtually monopolises its personal computer software niche, had run-ins with US antitrust laws. In a US court case that lasted from 1998 to 2001, Microsoft was ruled by a US judge as being a monopoly, but was not forced to break up and only had to pay a fine.

Although most US multinationals are not monopolies, when the largest US firms in each sector are grouped together, for example, the US oil majors, US technology giants including Google,

IBM, Microsoft and Cisco Systems, or the major US banks including Morgan Stanley and Citi, their combined economic clout is so huge that it can be said fairly that they do play a "decisive role" in the economic life of the world, as mentioned in Lenin's first point of imperialism. Likewise, the three major Chinese state-owned energy firms (CNPC, Sinopec, CNOOC) combined together, are wielding increasing influence on the world stage.

Although China had a substantial private sector by the early 21st century, the large Chinese state-owned firms pretty much set the direction of the Chinese economy, and play an increasingly important role in the global economy. The international clout of the Chinese state-owned firms is magnified by the much larger role of the Chinese government in these companies compared to the US government. The visits of Chinese leaders to other countries are routinely accompanied by the signing of billions of dollars of deals in energy or infrastructure for Chinese state-owned companies. As the scale of the overseas business of Chinese state-owned firms grow, the point will be reached where Chinese state-owned firms can be described as playing a "decisive role" in the world economy. Ilon Alon, a Director of the China Centre at Rollins College in Florida, forecasts Chinese ODI will soar to US$1 trillion by 2025,[356] a tenfold increase from China's ODI of US$102.9 billion in 2014.

To recapitulate, for China and the US in the 21st century, it is obvious that the fifth point on territorial division of the world is not true, as China and the US have not carved up territories around the world between them. The third point on capital export is true, given that China and the US export investments and loans to various countries. The second point on financial oligarchy is largely true for the US and China, given the important role of Wall Street and the increasing international influence of Chinese state-owned banks.

The fourth and first points on international monopolies are only partly true, because virtually no Chinese or US company can

---

[356] Toh Han Shih, *South China Morning Post*, "Overseas investments raise key China questions", 17 December 2014.

be described as a monopoly though some firms are so huge that they are internationally influential. Nonetheless, some large Chinese and US companies in the 21st century share some, albeit not all, the attributes of monopoly as described by Lenin. It is instructive to see how Lenin characterised monopolies:

"Firstly, monopoly arose out of a concentration of production."

"Secondly, monopolies have accelerated the capture of the most important sources of raw materials, especially for the coal and iron industries. The monopoly of the most important sources of raw materials has enormously increased the power of big capital."

"Thirdly, monopoly has sprung from the banks. Some three or five of the biggest banks in each of the foremost capitalist countries have achieved the personal union of industrial and bank capital, and have concentrated in their hands the disposal of thousands upon thousands of millions which form the greater part of the income of entire countries. A financial oligarchy, such is the most striking manifestation of this monopoly."

"Fourthly, monopoly has grown out of colonial policy. Finance capital has added the struggle for sources of raw materials, for the export of capital, for spheres of influence, i.e. for spheres for profitable deals, concessions, monopolist profits and so on."

The development of the Chinese economy and Chinese SOEs largely fit Lenin's pattern, except for the fourth point on colonialism. The scale of production in a large Chinese SOE is so massive as to justifiably be described as "a concentration of production". For example, the assets of Petrochina, a listed Chinese state-owned energy company, grew 178 percent from 99.48 billion Euros in 2007 to 321.57 billion Euros in 2014, according to Statista, a statistics portal. While most Chinese SOEs are not monopolies, the vast scale of their operations gives them a far greater economic influence than the numerous small and medium Chinese manufacturers. In 2013, Chinese overseas direct investment grew 18 percent year-on-year to US$96 billion, of which 79 percent came from SOEs, according to A Capital, a European-Asian private equity fund.

Lenin's second point of monopolies acquiring vast supplies of raw materials around the world aptly describes CNOOC, a Chinese state-owned energy firm. In 2013, CNOOC completed its US$15.1 billion acquisition of Canadian oil company Nexen, giving the Chinese firm access to offshore production in the North Sea, Canada, the Middle East, the Gulf of Mexico and West Africa.[357]

China's economy has an insatiable appetite for raw materials, including coal and iron. In early 21st century, China has become the world's largest coal producer and yet is one of the world's largest coal importers, because it is the world's largest coal consumer. China is the world's largest net importer of petroleum and also the world's largest importer of iron ore; China is the world's largest consumer and producer of copper and also the world's biggest metals producer. Chinese SOEs have invested billions of dollars around the world to lock in China's access to raw materials. China's overseas investments in resources soared more than six-fold from US$8.2 billion in 2005 to US$53.3 billion in 2013, according to the American Enterprise Institute and the Heritage Foundation. Chinese firms have invested a total of US$20 billion in copper mines in Chile as at the end of 2014, Chinese state television CCTV reported.

The American need for raw material is not as great as China's because much of US manufacturing has been outsourced to China.

We have just discussed Lenin's second point on monopolies seeking raw materials. Let us now turn to Lenin's third point on monopoly springing from banks. His book states, "Again, the final word in the development of banks is monopoly. The close ties that exist between the banks and industry are the very things that bring out most strikingly the new role of the banks. At the end of 1909, the nine big Berlin banks controlled about 83 percent of the German bank capital."

---

[357]Euan Rocha, *Reuters*, "CNOOC closes $15.1 billion acquisition of Canada's Nexen", 25 February 2013.

Although Chinese and US banks are not monopolies, they command a significant share of finance in their respective countries in the 21st century, they can almost be described as financial oligarchies.

China's Big Four state-owned banks, namely Bank of China (BOC), Industrial and Commercial Bank of China (ICBC), China Construction Bank (CCB) and Agricultural Bank of China (ABC), accounted for 58 percent of total retail deposits in China in 2011, while their share of China's banking market plus that of Bank of Communication (BoCom) was 49.2 percent, according to PIM, a US consulting firm.

"The sheer size of these institutions is breathtaking. ICBC and ABC have over 400,000 employees each, nearly as many as Volkswagen, the world's biggest carmaker," *the Economist* stated in an article on 31 August 2013.

In 2012, the world's biggest bank was ICBC with US$2.8 trillion in assets, followed by two US banks — JP Morgan with US$2.4 trillion in assets and Bank of America with US$2.2 trillion in assets, according to *The Banker*, a trade publication. CCB ranked fifth in 2012, while another US bank, Citigroup, was sixth, BOC ranked ninth and ABC was 10th. However, from 1998 to the third quarter of 2013, the assets of the top five banks in China as a share of the total fell from 63 percent to 44 percent.[358]

A measure of how much a country's five biggest banks dominate its banking industry is the asset concentration ratio 5 (CR5), which represents the assets of a country's biggest five banks as a percentage of the national total. In contrast to China, the US CR5 has risen from less than 15 percent in the late 1980s to 63.2 percent in 2013.[359] The CR5 of Austria and Holland was above 90 percent in 2013, while it was more than 80 percent for Germany and Canada, and over 70 percent for Spain, France, UK and Italy.[360] So it can be fairly said that the five biggest banks play dominant roles in the US and European nations.

---

[358] Yang Kaisheng, *Caixin*, "Do China's big banks enjoy a monopoly", 6 March 2014.
[359] Ibid.
[360] Ibid.

Outside China, Chinese banks have been playing an increasingly significant role on the international stage.

Two Chinese state-owned banks, China Development Bank (CDB) and China Exim Bank, have been financing the overseas projects of Chinese companies. These two policy lenders granted loans of at least US$110 billion to other developing countries' governments and companies in 2009 and 2010, compared with the World Bank's loan commitments of US$100.3 billion from mid-2008 to mid-2010.[361] China Exim Bank has funded most of China's overseas dams, including dams in Africa, Latin America, Myanmar and Cambodia, according to International Rivers. By 2013, CDB became the world's largest financial institution for overseas loans, overtaking both the World Bank and Asian Development Bank.[362]

Chinese banks completed 38 foreign mergers and acquisitions (M&A) totalling US$20.24 billion between 2002 and 2011, according to Deloitte. In 2013, ICBC was the most aggressive Chinese bank in terms of expanding overseas, setting up 239 subsidiaries and branch offices in 31 countries and jurisdictions.[363] In July 2012, ICBC became the first Chinese bank to acquire a controlling stake in a US bank, by buying 80 percent of the US subsidiary of Bank of East Asia, a Hong Kong bank.[364] By the end of 2010, BOC had US$351.6 billion in overseas assets.[365]

Both China in the 21st century and the European empires of Lenin's day follow a similar chronological pattern of evolution from the export of manufactured wares to the export of capital, as well as the shift from many smaller firms competing with each other towards the dominance of large conglomerates.

---

[361]Geoff Dyer, Jamil Anderlini and Henny Sender, *Financial Times*, "China's lending hits new heights", 17 January 2011.
[362]George Chen, *South China Morning Post*, "China Development Bank grabs chance for aggressive global loan expansion", 13 March 2013.
[363]Jonathan Calkins, "Banking abroad: the globalization of Chinese banks", *CKGSB Knowledge*, 28 March 2013.
[364]Ibid.
[365]Ibid.

Lenin outlined the history of European capitalism and imperialism: "The principal stages in the history of monopolies are the following: (1) 1860–1870, the apex of development of free competition, (2) after 1873, the development of cartels, but they are still the exception, (3) the end of the 19th century and the crisis of 1900–1903, cartels became one of the foundations of economic life. Capitalism has been transformed into imperialism."

"Under the old capitalism, when free competition prevailed, the export of goods was the most typical feature. Under modern capitalism, when monopolies prevail, the export of capital has become the typical feature."

As an example of competition typified by the export of goods, Lenin cited an the example of England in the middle of the 19th century, which "claimed to be the workshop of the world, the great purveyor of manufactured goods to all countries, which in exchange were to keep her supplied with raw materials." .

What Lenin said about European imperialism, particularly British imperialism, in the late 19th century finds echoes in China in the late 20th and early 21st century. From the late 20th century to 2010, China was the world's factory, supplying much of the world's manufactured goods. The manufacturing of light industrial goods in China was dominated by many small and medium enterprises, so there was competition among them. After 2010, China's status as the world's factory diminished as an increasing number of factories shifted to lower cost countries, although China remained a major manufacturing powerhouse. It was approximately around 2010 that large Chinese state-owned firms started making increasingly large acquisitions around the world, accompanied by large Chinese state-owned banks extending billions of dollars of loans overseas. Such cross-border acquisitions and financing is the export of capital which Lenin mentioned.

Lenin wrote that the union between banks and industry culminated in the union between both banks and industry with the state.

He quoted the German economist Otto Jeidels, "Seats on the supervisory board are freely offered to persons of title, also to ex-civil servants, who are able to do a great deal to facilitate relations with the authorities. Usually on the supervisory board of a big bank there is a member of parliament or a Berlin city councillor."

Senior directors of Chinese state-owned banks and companies are regarded as Chinese government officials, ironically a legacy of China's Communist system. Top Chinese officials shuttle between Chinese state-owned firms and the government. For instance, Guo Shuqing was appointed the head of a Chinese government agency, the State Administration of Foreign Exchange (SAFE) in 2001, and subsequently appointed Chairman of CCB in 2005, which was followed by his appointment as Chairman of another Chinese government body, the China Securities Regulatory Commission, in 2011.

A similar situation exists in the US, an avowedly capitalist economy. Robert Rubin joined Goldman Sachs in 1966, then served as Assistant to the President for Economic Policy from January 1993 to January 1995, and was US Treasury Secretary from January 1995 to July 1999. After leaving office in 1999, Rubin joined Citigroup as a board member. Another example is Timothy Geithner, the US Treasury Secretary from January 2009 to January 2013. In 2014, Geithner joined US private equity firm Warburg Pincus as President and Managing Director.

In the later stages of capitalism, finance becomes increasingly dominated by fewer and fewer financial institutions which become increasingly monopolistic, according to Lenin. The increasing concentration of huge amounts of finance capital in fewer financial institutions is linked to the capital markets, as Lenin wrote, "Finance capital, concentrated in a few hands and exercising a virtual monopoly, exacts an enormous and ever-increasing profits from the floating of companies, issue of stock, state loans etc., tightens the grip of financial oligarchies and levies tribute upon the whole of society for the benefit of monopolists."

Ferguson would agree with Lenin on the importance of capital markets to the success of an empire. In Ferguson's book, *The Ascent of Money*, he argues that the Dutch Empire in the 17th century and the British Empire in the 18th century had a competitive advantage by virtue of their capital markets which were relatively more sophisticated compared to other European nations. This enabled the British and Dutch to raise money more easily to finance their wars and imperial expansion, while the Spanish and French empires struggled with financial defaults, according to his book.

Just as the 17th century Dutch Empire and 18th century British Empire possessed the most sophisticated capital markets of their time, in the 21st century, the US and China are the two biggest capital markets in the world. As of 31 January 2015, if you combined the stock exchanges within each country, the US would be the biggest stock market in the world by market capitalization followed by China, according to the World Federation of Exchanges. Adding the New York Stock Exchange and Nasdaq, which are the two leading US stock markets, gave a total market capitalization of US$27 trillion as of 31 January 2015, 55 percent more than the 2014 US GDP figure of US$17.42 trillion, while the total market capitalization of the Shenzhen, Shanghai and Hong Kong stock exchanges was US$9.6 trillion, close to China's GDP figure of US$10.35 trillion in 2014.

On the basis of individual exchanges, the Hong Kong Stock Exchange ranked sixth globally in market capitalization as of 31 January 2015, while the New York Stock Exchange was number one in the world. However, Hong Kong overtook the New York Stock Exchange as the world's biggest market for initial public offerings (IPOs) in 2015, according to data from Thomson Reuters. Companies, mostly Chinese, raised US$25 billion in IPOs in Hong Kong in 2015, surpassing the US$19.4 billion raised in the New York Stock Exchange, according to Thomson Reuters. This shows Hong Kong, with its international, open and relatively sophisticated capital market, has become an important financing conduit for Chinese companies, just as the London stock exchange and the Amsterdam stock exchange previously financed the British and Dutch empires respectively.

The US capital markets finance the operations of US-listed companies within the US and abroad, while China's capital markets, especially Hong Kong's international capital market, provide the funds to drive the overseas expansion of Chinese companies.

Unfortunately, capital markets have proven to suffer from their share of abuses.

As Lenin wrote, "But the holding system not only serves to increase enormously the power of the monopolists; it also enables them to resort with impunity to all sorts of shady tricks to cheat the public. The "democratisation" of the ownership of shares, the "democratisation of capital" is, in fact, one of the ways of increasing the power of financial oligarchy."

Lenin cited an example, "The Spring Steel Company of Kassel was regarded some years ago as being one of the most profitable enterprises of Germany. Through bad management, its dividends fell within the space of a few years from 15 percent to nil. It appears that the board, without consulting the shareholders, had loaned 6 million marks to one of the subsidiary companies."

"This typical example of balance sheet jugglery, quite common in joint stock companies, explains why their boards of directors are more willing to undertake risky transactions than individual dealers. Modern methods of drawing up balance sheets not only make it possible to conceal doubtful undertakings from the average shareholder, but also allow the people most concerned to escape the consequences of unsuccessful speculation by selling their shares in time."

Sounds familiar? Think of the Enron and WorldCom scandals in the US. When Enron, a US energy company, went bankrupt with an estimated US$23 billion in debt and caused the loss of 20,000 jobs on 2 December 2001, it was the largest US bankruptcy at that time, until it was surpassed by the bankruptcy on 21 July 2002 of WorldCom, which was once the second largest US long distance telephone company.

In 2002, WorldCom's internal auditors as well as the US Securities and Exchange Commission (SEC) began investigating allegations of fraud in the company. By the end of 2003, it was estimated that WorldCom's total assets had been inflated by US$11 billion, making it the largest accounting fraud in US history at that time, according to an SEC report.

Once the seventh largest US company, WorldCom's share price on the New York Stock Exchange collapsed, going from US$90 on 23 August 2000 to 12 US cents on 11 January 2002, causing shareholders to lose nearly US$11 billion. On 15 March 2005, Bernard Ebbers, who resigned as WorldCom Chief Executive Officer in April 2002, was found guilty of all charges and convicted of fraud, conspiracy and filing false documents with regulators. Ebbers was sentenced to 25 years in jail.

On 25 May 2006, a US jury found Enron founder Kenneth Lay guilty of all six counts of conspiracy and fraud, while in a separate US trial, Lay was found guilty of four counts of fraud and making false statements. Lay died on 5 July 2006 before sentencing could be passed.

An example of the "balance sheet jugglery" that Lenin talked about comes in the form of Jeffrey Skilling, who was Enron Chief Executive Officer during the scandal. Skilling hid the company's losses using a technique called mark-to-market accounting, which values assets based on current market prices. By using mark-to-market accounting, Enron could write off any loss without hurting its bottom line.[366] Skilling resigned as Enron Chief Executive Officer on 14 August 2001, after being appointed to that post only six months earlier. On 25 May 2006, a US jury found Skilling guilty of one count of conspiracy, one count of insider trading, five counts of making false statements to auditors and 12 counts of securities fraud. On 23 October 2006, he was sentenced to 24 years and four months in prison, and fined US$45 million. In reaction to the Enron scandal, US Congress passed the Sarbanes-Oxley Act on 30 July 2002, which imposed tougher rules on corporate governance.

Since China took to the capitalist road in the 1980s, corruption has been rife in the country. The number of Chinese corruption and fraud cases is too large to describe in detail. One notable example of stock market fraud involved Zhou Zhengyi, a Shanghai tycoon, and Chen Liangyu, the former Party Chief of

---

[366] Investopedia.

Shanghai. Zhou, who also went by the Cantonese name of Chau Ching-ngai, had business operations in Shanghai and Hong Kong. He controlled two Shanghai-linked companies that were listed in Hong Kong, Shanghai Land Holdings and Shanghai Merchants Holdings.

In 2003, Zhou was arrested on suspicion of improperly obtaining bank loans. In 2004, Zhou, who was then China's 11th richest businessman, was given a three-year jail sentence for stock market fraud in a mainland Chinese court. The punishment was considered light, causing speculation that some powerful Chinese officials, possibly in Shanghai, helped him. He spent his sentence in a Shanghai prison.

Zhou was released from prison in May 2006, but five months later, he was detained again while Chinese prosecutors investigated a Shanghai social security fund scandal. The fund scandal brought down a number of high-ranking officials including the then Shanghai Party Chief Chen Liangyu. It was also in 2006 that Chen was dismissed from his post. On 11 April 2008, Chen was sentenced to 18 years in prison for accepting bribes and abuse of power as well as stock manipulation, financial fraud and his role in the Shanghai pension fund scandal.

In November 2007, Zhou was sentenced by a mainland Chinese court to a much longer prison term of 16 years. In his second sentence, Zhou was found guilty of five charges including misappropriation of funds, bribery and forging value-added tax (VAT) receipts. This time, Zhou was accused of bribing officials of the Shanghai Futures Exchange as well as managers of Chinese state banks in attempts to obtain loans for his businesses, according to Chinese media reports. Zhou was also accused of bribing a senior prison official so that he enjoyed special treatment during his first jail term in Shanghai, Chinese media reported. Several prison officials were sentenced for granting Zhou perks in prison, such as TV, an air conditioner, refrigerator and frequent visits by friends, according to reports in the Chinese media.

Another casualty of the scandal was Liu Jinbao, the former Chief Executive of the Hong Kong branch of the Bank of China. Liu was dismissed from the Chinese state-owned bank in May 2003 for approving a HK$1.77 billion loan to New Nongkai, a company owned by Zhou. This is an example of the close ties between banks and big business as described by Lenin. Investigations of Liu over the Zhou scandal led to his being given a suspended death sentence in a mainland Chinese court in August 2005 on charges of accepting bribes and embezzlement, which were unrelated to Zhou's case.

The Zhou scandal had a social dimension involving land and property. Zhou made a fortune from tearing down old tenements in Shanghai and replacing them with modern towers.[367] In China, land is owned by the state and developers are only allowed to buy 75-year leases on plots of land from local authorities. Through close ties with senior Chinese officials, soft loans from Chinese state banks and opaque property deals, Zhou became one of the richest men in his home city.[368]

In 2002, when Zhou redeveloped several areas along Shanghai's Suzhou Creek, 10,000 residents in those areas were told to vacate their homes, but they rebelled.[369] Several hundred tenants filed a lawsuit claiming Zhou had failed to compensate them properly and complained they were offered inadequate alternative accommodation.[370] Hundreds of tenants who Zhou tried to evict hired a Chinese lawyer, Zheng Enchong, to press their case. Zheng went to court in May 2002, accusing Shanghai officials of colluding with Zhou. Zheng complained of favouritism and corruption, alleging the city's officials had skimmed off a big share of the compensation payments offered to his clients.[371]

In 2003, the same year that Zhou was given a light three-year jail sentence in Shanghai, Zheng was arrested and found guilty

---

[367]Peter Goodspeed, *National Post*, "Tenant protests expose Chinese corruption: millionaire developer probed over loans", 1 November 2003.
[368]Ibid.
[369]Ibid.
[370]Ibid.
[371]Ibid.

of "illegally obtaining state secrets" in a closed-door trial in a mainland Chinese court. Zheng was jailed for three years and released in 2006, the same year that Zhou got out of his first jail sentence and Shanghai Party Chief Chen Liangyu was dismissed for corruption.

The land controversy surrounding Zhou echoes what Lenin wrote in his book on imperialism, "Speculation in land in the suburbs of rapidly growing towns is a particularly profitable operation for finance capital. Frantic speculation in suburban building lots, collapse of building enterprises, underhand agreements with the police and the Berlin administration for the purpose of getting control of building sites, tenders, building licenses etc. American ethics, which the European professors and well-meaning bourgeois so hypocritically deplore, have, in the age of finance capital, become the ethics of literally every large city, no matter what country it is in."

"No matter what country," wrote Lenin. As this book argues, that includes the US and China in the 21st century.

Again, American ethics, or the lack of it, was partly responsible for the creation and subsequent collapse of the US housing bubble in 2007, which led to the global financial crisis of 2007 and 2008. The bubble was caused by people borrowing money on very cheap terms to buy homes while financial institutions packaged these housing loans and sold them off, claiming they were sound financial products when in reality these debts rested on shaky foundations. In the years after the global financial crisis of 2008, the US authorities punished various leading financial institutions, including Citigroup and Goldman Sachs, for selling these dubious financial products based on housing loans.

Despite their flaws, scandals and abuses, capital markets are an important source of finance, including the export of capital, one of Lenin's five elements of empire. In turn, an empire's export of capital is linked to its building of railways overseas, as argued in Lenin's book. In this respect, Lenin was in agreement with Hobsbawm. As discussed in Chapter 2, Hobsbawm wrote that British imperialism was characterised by the construction of railway around the world, a trait shared by China in the 21st century. This applies not only to the construction of railway, but all sorts of infrastructure including ports, roads, airports, dams, buildings and power stations around the world.

Lenin wrote, "The possibility of exporting capital is created by the fact that numerous backward countries have been drawn into international capitalist intercourse; railways have been built or are being built there."

"Railway statistics provide remarkably exact data on the different rates of the development of capitalism and finance capital in world economy. The development of railways has been more rapid in the colonies and in the independent and semi-independent states of Asia and America. Here, the finance capital of the four or five biggest capitalist states reigns undisputed. Thus, about 80 percent of the railways are concentrated in the hands of the five Great Powers (US, the British Empire, Russia, Germany and France). But the concentration of the ownership of these railways, of finance capital, is much greater still: French and English millionaires own an enormous amount of stocks and bonds in American, Russian and other railways. Thanks to her colonies, Great Britain has increased the length of her railways by 100,000 km, four times as much as Germany."

While the five Great Powers that accounted for 80 percent of the world's railways were Western in Lenin's time, China has joined the ranks of the world's major builders, suppliers and financiers of railway in the 21st century. By 2014, China had the world's third longest rail network at 112,000 km, behind Russia and the leader, the US, according to official Chinese data. That year, China boasted the world's longest high speed rail network at 16,000 km. Unlike Lenin's time, virtually all the railway in China were built by Chinese state-owned firms and financed by Chinese capital, while abroad, Chinese state-owned firms like China Railway Rolling Stock Corporation hold their own against Western rolling stock manufacturers like Alstom of France, Siemens of Germany and Bombardier of Canada.

In 2014, Chinese state media nicknamed Prime Minister Li Keqiang "China's high-speed rail salesman", as he went abroad trying to convince countries like Thailand and Britain to adopt Chinese high-speed railway. This was part of the Chinese government's long-term ambition of creating an intercontinental high-speed rail network connecting China, Russia and Europe, and a high-speed railway that would traverse southern China and peninsular Southeast Asia all the way south to Singapore. In his state-of-the-nation report in 2015, Chinese Premier Li included rail equipment makers as one of seven sectors which the Chinese government prioritised for export.

"We will encourage Chinese companies to participate in overseas infrastructure development projects and engage in cooperation with their foreign counterparts in building up production capacity," Li said.

China's rail equipment exports accounted for 10 percent of global market share in 2014.[372] China's exports of railway equipment rose 22.6 percent to US$4 billion in 2014, with major markets that include Asia, South Africa and Latin America, according to official Chinese data. Chinese companies signed contracts for overseas rail projects worth US$24.7 billion in 2014, Commerce Ministry official Zhi Luxun told reporters on 5 February 2015 in Beijing.

Lenin wrote, "Finance capital has created the epoch of monopolies, and monopolies introduce everywhere monopolist methods. The most usual thing is to stipulate that part of the loan that is granted shall be spent on purchases in the country of issue."

Between 1890 and 1910, France often resorted to this method, Lenin pointed out. "The export of capital abroad thus became a means of encouraging the export of commodities. In these circumstances, transactions between particularly big firms assume a form that bordered on corruption. Krupp in Germany, Schneider in France, Armstrong in England are examples of firms which have close connections with powerful banks and governments and cannot be ignored when arranging a loan. The construction of Brazilian railways is being carried out chiefly by French, Belgian, British and German capital. In the financial operations connected

---

[372] Lan Lan, *China Daily USA*, "China takes 10% of global rail market", 6 February 2015.

with the construction of these railways, the countries involved also stipulate for orders for the railway materials."

In Chinese infrastructure projects around the world, Chinese SOEs building infrastructure, including railway, would stipulate that the equipment came from China. For example, China Railway Construction Corporation won a US$12 billion contract in November 2014 to build a railway in Nigeria. Chinese state media quoted CRCC Chairman Meng Fengchao saying this project would adopt Chinese technological standards which subsequently led to the purchase of another US$4 billion of Chinese construction machinery, trains and other equipment. Chinese state-owned banks like China Exim Bank and China Development Bank finance the overseas infrastructure projects of Chinese SOEs with huge loans on easy terms, making it difficult for the foreign client to reject Chinese participation in the project.

Infrastructure projects like the construction of railway and ports requires huge amounts of capital, which the governments of developing countries normally could not afford by themselves. However, China has vast supplies of capital to finance such infrastructure projects in the form of loans on easy terms which are affordable for the governments of these countries. Lenin characterised imperialism as "an enormous superabundance of capital (that) has accumulated in the advanced countries."

Indeed, China has an "enormous superabundance of capital" in the 21st century. China overtook Japan as the world's second largest economy behind the US in 2010. According to China's State Administration of Foreign Exchange, between the first quarter of 2011 and the second quarter of 2014, China's cumulative assets from outbound direct investment nearly doubled from US$323.4 billion to US$640.2 billion. As of June 2014, China has accrued additional foreign assets through outbound trade credit, lending, and currency and deposits totalling US$1.25 trillion.

Lenin wrote, "The supremacy of finance capital over all other forms of capital means the predominance of the rentier and of the financial oligarchy; it means the crystallisation of a small number of financially powerful states from among all the rest. We see standing out in sharp relief four of the richest capitalist countries. Two of these countries, England and France, possess the most colonies; the other two, the US and Germany, are in the front rank as regards rapidity of development and the degree of capitalist monopoly in industry. Together, these four countries own nearly 80 percent of the world's finance capital. Thus, nearly the whole world is more or less debtor to and tributary of these four international banker countries, the four pillars of world finance capital."

The Asian Infrastructure Investment Bank (AIIB) is an example of China's emergence as a major lender to the world and one of the "pillars of world finance capital".

AIIB is an international financial institution proposed and led by China but includes other nations as members. The purpose of this multilateral development bank is to finance railway and other infrastructure projects in Asia. During a visit to Jakarta on 2 October 2013, Chinese President Xi proposed to Indonesian President Susilo Bambang Yudhoyono to establish AIIB to promote interconnectivity and economic integration in the region. Beijing would put up US$50 billion of its own money for AIIB. Xi expressed the hope that this bank would supply some of the funds needed to upgrade infrastructure in the region.

AIIB will help meet Asia's enormous infrastructure needs, which are well beyond the capacity of institutional arrangements to finance, wrote US Economics Noble Laureate Joseph E. Stiglitz.[373] Multilateral institutions like the World Bank and the Asian Development Bank (ADB) have neither the political will nor the funds to meet the challenge.[374] The ADB lent just US$13 billion in 2014. Yet a 2010 ADB report estimated Asia would need to spend US$8 trillion on infrastructure in the next decade. This is where China's financial muscle and political will comes in.[375] China has

---

[373] Joseph Stiglitz, *MarketWatch*, "America's childish opposition to Asian infrastructure bank", 13 April 2015.
[374] Cary Huang, *South China Morning Post*, "China-led Asian bank challenges US dominance of global economy", 11 April 2015.
[375] Ibid.

US$3.9 trillion in foreign reserves, more than any other country, and decades of infrastructure construction experience.[376]

Not all Southeast Asian countries were enamoured with AIIB. Speaking at the Asian Financial Forum in Hong Kong in January 2015, former Thai Foreign Minister, Kasit Piromya, expressed grave reservations about the bank.

"The origin of AIIB is part of the strategy of China to dominate Asia. It's not out of good intentions. It deals with the geopolitics of how China will cope with the US and Japan, as well as South Korea, Taiwan and Australia," he said.

"Strings attached to Chinese money will come back to haunt developing countries, like Japanese money a few decades ago. That must not be the case with AIIB. With AIIB, China will dictate terms that will weaken ASEAN as a whole. The Chinese bilateral assistance to some ASEAN countries has weakened and split ASEAN," warned Kasit Piromya.

"AIIB, ADB and World Bank are political-economic institutions. A lot of politics come into play. I tell the US and Japan to accommodate the Chinese. China is a world power now, and it must cooperate with the international community. I'm very worried about China's go-it-alone style," he added.

Nonetheless, by 2 April 2015, almost all Asian countries and most major countries outside Asia had joined the AIIB. By 15 April 2015, AIIB officially approved 57 nations as prospective founding members, including Sweden, Israel, South Africa, Portugal and Poland. The US and Japan, which had tense relations with China, were not among those 57 member nations of AIIB. China's invitation to other countries to join AIIB was met with scepticism by the US.[377] The Obama administration voiced misgivings about the bank's transparency, governance and potential conflicts with existing institutions, particular the ADB.[378]

Britain was the first major European nation to join AIIB.

---

[376] Ibid.
[377] Ibid.
[378] Ibid.

"The Cameron government embraced the AIIB in exchange for the right to become the European clearing house for the Chinese yuan. Within days, France, Germany and Italy had become founding members. The carrot in their case was the promise they could help write the new bank's lending rules," wrote Matthew Fisher in an opinion column in the National Post on 31 March 2015.

"Joining South Korea in the stampede, Australia Prime Minister Tony Abbott submitted Canberra's application Sunday, just beating the March 31 deadline for charter members to sign up. His reasons are clear. Australia's trade with China reached US$127 billion in 2013, while free-spending Chinese tourists are rapidly becoming the mainstay of its important tourism industry," wrote Fisher.

In an article published by the Brookings Institution on 17 March 2015, Philippe Le Corre, a visiting fellow at the US think tank, wrote, "Already the largest recipient of Chinese investment in Europe since 2014 (£10 billion), Britain now appears in a stronger position than some of its European neighbours to befriend China. Prime Minister David Cameron has spent much time cosying up to China. China has said it intends to further invest in British infrastructure, including railways, energy and water. It has already purchased nearly 10 percent of Thames Water, the country's largest water company, as well as 10 percent of the firm that owns Heathrow International Airport. In addition, the City of London wants to become the world's largest international exchange platform for the yuan, China's currency. Several large Chinese banks, such as China Merchant Bank and China Minsheng Bank, have recently opened subsidiaries in London."

"Having tried to lobby its allies against joining AIIB, the Obama administration now appears to be the main loser. On the other hand, China seems to have won the show. This once again demonstrates that China's ability to divide Western nations among themselves is stronger than sometimes assumed," wrote Le Corre.

"Europeans, for their part, are mainly concerned with trade and investment issues. Their governments are now competing among themselves to attract Chinese investors," Le Corre noted.

From 2010 to 2013, British exports to China surged 80 percent, pointed out Harsh Pant, a Professor at King's College London, in *Daily News & Analysis* on 3 April 2015.

"At a time when the rise of China is shaking up the global economic and security architecture, Britain seems to have decided that it is best to hedge its bets as a potential rivalry between the US and China looms large on the horizon. By deciding to join the AIIB, London has heralded the beginning of a new era in global politics. No wonder, Washington is annoyed," wrote Pant.

In March 2015, just after Britain joined AIIB, the White House issued a statement expressing disapproval of this move by a country with which the US had enjoyed a "special relationship" since World War II. "The special relationship" was a term coined by British Prime Minister Winston Churchill during World War II, when Britain and the US fought shoulder to shoulder against Germany, Japan and Italy. With AIIB, Britain apparently preferred Chinese money over the special relationship. The White House statement read, "This is the UK's sovereign decision. We hope and expect that the UK will use its voice to push for adoption of high standards."

One unnamed American source accused Britain of "constant accommodation" of China, Stiglitz wrote.

"Covertly, the United States put pressure on countries around the world to stay away (from AIIB). In fact, America's opposition to the AIIB is inconsistent with its stated economic priorities in Asia. Sadly, it seems to be another case of America's insecurity about its global influence trumping its idealistic rhetoric — this time possibly undermining an important opportunity to strengthen Asia's developing economies. China itself is a testament to the extent to which infrastructure investment can contribute to development. The AIIB would bring similar benefits to other parts of Asia, which deepens the irony of US opposition. President Barack Obama's administration is championing the virtues of trade; but, in developing countries, lack of infrastructure is a far more serious barrier to trade than tariffs," Stiglitz added.

"But in a world with such huge infrastructure needs, the problem is a financial system that has excelled at enabling market manipulation, speculation, and insider trading, but has failed at its core task: intermediating savings and investment on a global scale. That is why the AIIB could bring a small but badly needed boost to global aggregate demand. So we should welcome China's initiative to multilateralize the flow of funds. Indeed, it replicates American policy in the period following World War II, when the World Bank was founded to multilaterize development funds that were overwhelmingly coming from the US," argued Stiglitz.

"America's opposition to the AIIB is not unprecedented; in fact, it is akin to the successful US opposition to Japan's generous New Miyazawa Initiative of the late 1990s, which offered $80 billion to help countries in the East Asian crisis. Then, as now, it was not as if the US were offering an alternative source of funding. It simply wanted hegemony," Stiglitz pointed out.

Commenting on AIIB, Lawrence Summers, a former US Treasury Secretary, wrote on his website on 5 April 2015, "This past month may be remembered as the moment the United States lost its role as the underwriter of the global economic system. But I can think of no event since Bretton Woods comparable to the combination of China's effort to establish a major new institution and the failure of the US to persuade dozens of its traditional allies, starting with Britain, to stay out of it."

Since the end of World War II in 1945, American-dominated institutions have been the cornerstone of the global economic order. Rising from the rubble of World War II, the Bretton Woods pact to establish a global monetary order paved the way for institutions such as the World Bank, IMF and ADB. The IMF traditionally mixes US and European influence; the ADB is an American fiefdom shared with Japan.[379] China and other major emerging economies have long been dissatisfied with the slow pace of the Bretton-Woods system in giving them a greater say in the global financial

---

[379] Ibid.

system.[380] AIIB is the first Asian-based international bank to be independent of the Western-dominated Bretton Woods institutions, namely IMF and the World Bank.

"With China's economic size rivaling America's and emerging markets accounting for at least half of world output, the global economic architecture needs substantial adjustment. Political pressures from all sides in the US have rendered it increasingly dysfunctional," wrote Summers, a Harvard Economics Professor.

"Largely because of resistance from the right, the US stands alone in the world in failing to approve the International Monetary Fund governance reforms that Washington itself pushed for in 2009. It would come closer to giving countries such as China and India a share of IMF votes commensurate with their new economic heft. Meanwhile, pressures from the left have led to pervasive restrictions on infrastructure projects financed through existing development banks, which consequently have receded as funders, even as many developing countries now see infrastructure finance as their principle external funding need," Summers argued.

"With US commitments unhonoured and US-backed policies blocking the kinds of finance other countries want to provide or receive through the existing institutions, the way was clear for China to establish the Asian Infrastructure Investment Bank," Summers wrote.

The AIIB is a sign of China's challenge to the US in the global financial order, which is only one facet of the complicated relationship between the US as the top superpower and China as a rising superpower. The following chapter looks at this complex relation between the incumbent superpower and the rising superpower.

---

[380]Ibid.

Chapter 8

The Dragon and the Eagle

8.1 Economic embrace

The US has a special relationship with Britain, a term coined by British Prime Minister Winston Churchill during World War II, born of their alliance in fighting the Axis powers. In the 21st century, the US is in a different sort of relationship with China, locked in a marriage of convenience entwined by mutual economic interests that affect the world.

British historian Niall Ferguson and German economist Moritz Schularick invented the term "Chimerica" in 2006 to describe this intimate economic interdependence between China and America. The word Chimerica evokes Chimera, a mythical beast in Greek mythology that is a combination of lion, goat and dragon. Explaining their choice of the word Chimerica, Ferguson and Schularick said savings by the Chinese and overspending by Americans had led to an incredible period of wealth creation not just in the US and China, but throughout the world. The duo said that Chimerica enabled the world to enjoy "a spectacular boom in asset prices" from 2002 to 2007.[381] Unfortunately, this unhealthy

---

[381] Niall Ferguson and Moritz Schularick, "Chimerica" and the global asset market boom", *International Finance*, Volume 10, Issue 3, 2007.

marriage between China and the US led to the global financial crisis of 2007 and 2008.

Ferguson and Schularick wrote in a Harvard Business School paper, titled "The end of Chimerica", in 2009, "For the better part of the past decade (2000 to 2009) the world economy has been dominated by a unique geo-economic constellation that we have called 'Chimerica': a world economic order that combined Chinese export-led development with US over-consumption on the basis of a financial marriage between the world's sole superpower and its most likely future rival."[382]

China overtook Japan as the world's second biggest economy in 2010. Hence Chimerica has become a combination of the world's two biggest economies. Many economists believe it is a matter of time when China will overtake the US as the world's biggest economy. Chimerica accounted for 13 percent of the world's land surface, a quarter of its population, more than a third of world GDP, and two fifths of global economic growth from 2000 to 2009, Ferguson and Schularick pointed out.

"For China, the key attraction of this marriage was its potential to propel the economy forward by export-led growth. Thanks to the Chimerican symbiosis, China was able to quadruple its GDP since 2000, raise exports by a factor of five, import Western technology and create tens of millions of manufacturing jobs for the rural poor. For America, Chimerica meant being able to consume more, save less and still maintain low interest rates and a stable rate of investment. Over-consumption meant that between 2000 and 2008, the US out-spent its national income by a cumulative 45 percent, i.e. total U.S. spending over the period was 45 percent higher than total income. Purchases of goods from China in excess of income accounted for about a third of over-consumption," wrote Ferguson and Schularick.

China, the biggest manufacturing nation, manufactured massive amounts of cheap goods and exported them to the US, the biggest consuming nation. US imports from China skyrocketed a

---

[382]Niall Ferguson and Moritz Schularick, *Harvard Business School Working Paper*, "The End of Chimerica", October 2009.

hundredfold from US1.1 billion in 1980 to US$100.1 billion in 2000, according to official US data. US imports from China more than tripled from US$100.1 billion in 2000 to US$321.5 billion in 2007 when the global financial crisis began to strike, according to official US data. China overtook Mexico to be the second biggest exporter to the US in 2003 and became the biggest exporter to the US by 2013.

By dint of the huge volume of low-cost Chinese goods flooding the US market, China exported more to the US than the US exported to China. In tandem with the huge growth of Chinese exports to the US, the US trade deficit with China jumped from US$10.4 billion in 1990 to US$266.3 billion in 2008, according to official US data.

US importers paid Chinese exporters for Chinese-made goods in US dollars. The Chinese exporters exchanged their US dollars with the People's Bank of China for yuan. To maintain the yuan exchange rate with the US dollar within certain limits, the People's Bank of China bought US dollars in exchange for yuan. Since China was a net exporter to the US, the Chinese central bank was a net buyer of US dollars and accumulated vast reserves of US dollars. By the end of 2014, China accumulated US$3.9 trillion of US dollar reserves, accounting for 61 percent of the nation's external financial assets, according to the State Administration of Foreign Exchange, which manages China's foreign reserves.

The People's Bank of China channeled most of China's US dollar reserves into buying US Treasury bonds. Through its holdings of US Treasury bonds, China in effect lent money to the US. That is why US comedians joked about China being both the bank and the factory of the US. As of February 2015, US debt to China was $1.22 trillion, roughly 20 percent of the US public debt owned by foreign countries, according to official US data.

China's holdings of US Treasury bonds more than tripled from less than US$200 billion in 2003 to over US$700 billion in 2008, when China overtook Japan as the biggest holder of US Treasury bonds, according to official US data. By buying US Treasuries, China helped keep US interest rates low. If China stopped buying US Treasuries, US interest rates would rise, which could possibly hurt the US and global economy. Since US consumers buy less when the US economy weakens, it was not in China's interest to sell off large amounts of US Treasuries as that would raise US interest rates. Low US interest rates helped fuel the US housing boom during the first decade of the 21st century, as banks offered cheap loans to Americans to buy property they normally could not afford. As banks gave out more housing loans, Americans bought more real estate and hence property prices rose.

Thus, the US and China were interlocked in a symbiotic relationship, where China gained huge US dollar reserves from selling lots of cheap goods to the US, while US consumers were able to buy cheap Chinese goods and could afford to buy homes thanks to low-interest loans. This led to an export boom in China and a housing bubble in the US. On the surface, both nations appeared to enjoy a win–win relationship.

"For a time, it seemed like a marriage made in heaven. It also seemed like a marriage with positive externalities for the rest of the world. Global trade boomed and nearly all asset prices surged," wrote Ferguson and Schularick.

Before the crisis broke in 2007, in a *South China Morning Post* report of 21 March 2006, Diana Choyleva, then Director of Lombard Street Research, a London think tank, already predicted, "The US and China have been joined at the hip by marriage, which unfortunately is going to end up in tears."

"Mid-2006 to 2007 will be difficult. The US may not be in a recession but will still be in tough times, possibly with many quarters of slow growth. I see a stock market correction starting in the US, with the contagion spreading across the world," Choyleva said in 2006.[383]

That was what happened. From a peak of 14,164.43 points on 9 October 2007, the Dow Jones Industrial Average fell by more than half to 6,594.44 points on 5 March 2009. From 30 October 2007 to 9 March 2008, Hong Kong's Hang Seng Index dropped about 30 percent. The Shanghai Composite index plunged by more than half from 4,380 points in January 2008 to 1,820 points at the end of

---

[383]Toh Han Shih, *South China Morning Post*, "Sino-US Trade Marriage 'bound to end in tears'", 21 March 2006.

2008. Through the year 2008, London's FTSE Index fell 31 percent in its biggest ever drop at that time.

Choyleva predicted in March 2006, "A correction is likely to happen when Americans are less willing to borrow. The consumer slowdown in the US is likely to remove the last support from China's economic expansion."

The housing bubble burst as growing numbers of Americans defaulted on their housing loans, which drove down property prices. This spiraled into a vicious cycle of falling property prices and accelerating numbers of defaults on home loans. The snowballing defaults hurt the US banks that had supplied the loans. The full force of the global financial tsunami was felt when Lehman Brothers went bankrupt in September 2008. With assets of over US$600 billion, Lehman's collapse was the biggest bankruptcy of a US bank at that time.

US real GDP began contracting in the third quarter of 2008 and did not return to growth until the first quarter of 2010. The IMF considered the global financial crisis of 2008 as the worst global recession since World War II, while some economists believed it was the worst economic crisis since the Great Depression of the 1930s. The IMF estimated that large US and European banks lost more than US$1 trillion due to toxic assets and bad loans between January 2007 and September 2009. In 2009, the world's GDP contracted by 0.8 percent while global trade declined by 12 percent, the IMF estimated.

The bursting of the US property bubble drained Americans of their buying power, which reduced their purchases of Chinese goods, hurting Chinese exporters. China faced a temporary plunge in international trade and the prospect of a potential crisis. The port of Hong Kong, which serves as a key conduit for China's exports, suffered year-on-year declines in container throughput of 23.6 percent, 20.6 percent and 18.9 percent in January, February and March 2009, respectively, according to official Hong Kong statistics. The reasons for such a steep drop in Hong Kong port's throughput included decreased buying in the US and a temporary freezing of trade credit arising from loss of confidence. China avoided a recession by launching a 4 trillion yuan stimulus in late 2008.

Other countries fell into recession. Brazil underwent recession from the fourth quarter of 2008 to the first quarter of 2009, the 28-member EU suffered a recession from the second quarter of 2008 to the second quarter of 2009, Japan underwent a recession from the second quarter of 2008 to the first quarter of 2009, and the UK was in a recession from the second quarter of 2008 to the third quarter of 2009.

"Yet, like many a marriage between a saver and a spendthrift, Chimerica was not destined to last. We believe the financial and economic crisis of 2007–2009 has put the marriage on the rocks. The reduction of the imbalance between the United States and China — in short, the dissolution of Chimerica — is now indispensable if equilibrium is to be restored to the world economy. The end of Chimerica is desirable, though the divorce needs to be amicable," Ferguson and Schularick recommended in their paper of 2009.

"In some ways China's economic model in the decade 1998–2007 was similar to the one adopted by West Germany and Japan after World War II. Trade surpluses with the US played a major role in propelling growth. But there were two key differences. First, the scale of Chinese currency intervention was without precedent, as were the resulting distortions of the world economy. Second, the Chinese have so far resisted the kind of currency appreciation to which West Germany and Japan consented," said Ferguson and Schularick.

From 1960 to 1978, the Deutsche Mark appreciated by almost 60 percent against the US dollar, while the Japanese yen appreciated by nearly 50 percent.

"We conclude that Chimerica cannot persist for much longer in its present form. Sizeable changes in exchange rates are needed to rebalance the world economy. The world economy's key structural imbalance is that the second biggest economy in the world (China) has pegged its currency to that of the largest economy (the US) at a strongly undervalued exchange rate," Ferguson and Schularick wrote in 2009.

Six years after Ferguson and Schularick's call for the appreciation of the yuan, the IMF said the Chinese currency was not undervalued. In May 2015, David Lipton, the IMF's first Deputy Managing Director, said, "While undervaluation of the renminbi was a major factor causing large imbalances in the past, our assessment is that the substantial real effective appreciation over the past year has brought the exchange rate to a level that is no longer undervalued."

The statement by this senior IMF official put the IMF at odds with its biggest shareholder, the US, which insisted that China continued to maintain an unfair trade advantage from a currency that Washington considered "significantly undervalued".[384]

Although the yuan has generally appreciated against the US dollar over the years, the Chinese government has longed resisted US pressure to substantially raise the value of the yuan. The Chinese leaders perceived Japan's acquiescence to US pressure to raise the value of the yen as the cause of Japan's "lost decades" of economic stagnation. An article in *People's Daily*, a Chinese state newspaper, in 2010 argued that Japan's "lost decades" was a cautionary tale to China not to go down the same path.

China's relations with the US in the 21st century bears some similarities to Japan's economic relations with the US in the 1980s. During the 1980s, some quarters in the US feared Japan as an upcoming economic rival, just as some Americans now perceive China as a rising threat in the 21st century. Japan was one of the world's fastest growing economies from the 1950s till the mid-1980s. During the 1980s, Japan's exports to the US boomed while Japanese companies invested heavily in the US. In that decade, Japan was the second biggest investor in the US after the UK, while the US ran a huge trade deficit with Japan. Washington sought to reduce the US trade deficit with Japan by getting the yen's exchange rate with the US dollar to rise.

In September 1985, at a G5 meeting in the Plaza Hotel in New York, the G5 nations, comprising US, UK, France, Germany and Japan, declared the US dollar overvalued and called for the appreciation of the Japanese and German currencies. Following the Plaza Accord, the yen appreciated by 30 percent against Japan's trading partners' currencies over 15 months, after adjusting for inflation.

---

[384]Tom Mitchell and Shawn Donnan, *Financial Times*, "China currency is 'no longer undervalued', says IMF", 26 May 2015.

Subsequently, the Japanese property market bubble burst and the Japanese stock market collapsed in 1990. Japan's average annual GDP growth dropped to 1.1 percent between 1990 and 2011.

An IMF paper in April 2011 argued that currency appreciation alone was not the cause of Japan's lost decades.[385] However, the IMF paper admitted that unlike Japan, which had a floating exchange rate, China maintained a managed exchange rate supported by vast US dollar reserves and capital controls which prevented the free flow of funds out of the country. China's more restrictive currency regime should help the country avoid sharp appreciation as in the case of the Japanese yen, the IMF said. In effect, the IMF agreed with the Chinese government's policy of not succumbing to US pressure to let the yuan appreciate too much.

After the marriage between the US and China exploded in an ugly mess in the global financial crisis of 2007 and 2008, how have the two nations been mending their relationship? What is beyond dispute is both countries have been restructuring their economies to prevent a repeat of the unhealthy imbalances that caused the crisis. The question is how successful their efforts have been and what future developments there are. As will be shown later, trade and investment between China and the US continued to grow on a massive scale after the crisis, which meant interdependency between both nations has increased. Despite calls by Ferguson and Schularick for China and the US to divorce, both nations remain wedded to each other. How has this marriage fared since the financial tsunami?

In the run-up to the crisis, China had one of the world's biggest current account surpluses while the US had one of the world's biggest current account deficits. This was one of the main causes of the global financial crisis. A nation's current account is the sum of its trade balance, its net income from abroad and net cash transfers. A country with a current account surplus like China typically sells more than it buys from the rest of the world, and thus owns more foreign assets than foreign liabilities, making it a net lender to the

---

[385] IMF, *World Economic Outlook*, "Tensions from the two-speed recovery: unemployment, commodities, and capital flows", April 2011.

world. Conversely, a country with a current account deficit like the US is a net borrower from the world.

Most of China's foreign lending took the form of buying US Treasury bonds. China's massive holdings of US Treasuries kept US interest rates low, which spurred the US housing bubble that in turn led to the crisis. China's current account surplus as a percentage of GDP jumped from 2 percent in 2002 to 10.8 percent in 2007 when the global financial crisis began, but fell back to 2 percent in 2014.[386] China's current account surplus fell from US$353.2 billion in 2007 to US$213.7 billion in 2014, according to official Chinese data. From a peak of more than 10 percent of GDP in 2008, China's current account surplus plunged dramatically to 1.9 percent in 2012.

Meanwhile, the US current account deficit had halved in 2013 from its peak in 2006. The US current account deficit further narrowed to US$81.1 billion in the fourth quarter of 2013 from US$96.4 billion in the third quarter of 2013, according to official US data. That was the smallest deficit since the third quarter of 1999.

Since the crisis, the US has significantly reduced its debt. US individual debt as a percentage of disposable income fell from a peak of 129.7 percent at the end of 2007 to 102.4 percent at the end of 2014, the lowest level since 2002, according to Marketwatch, a financial information provider which tracks markets. As a percentage of net worth, US personal debt has fallen from a peak of 25 percent to 16.3 percent, the lowest since 2000, according to Marketwatch.

"After rising in nearly every quarter of the preceding half-century, household debt fell between the second half of 2008 and early 2013 by a cumulative amount of nearly US$1 trillion — a phenomenon often referred to as household deleveraging," said the US Federal Reserve.

China has also been learning its lessons from the crisis.

China's holdings of US Treasury bonds soared from under US$200 billion in 2003 to over US$700 billion in 2008, according to official US data. After that, China's holding of US Treasuries continued to rise to

---

[386]Sean Miner, "China's current account in 2014", *Peterson Institute for International Economics*, 8 February 2015.

nearly US$1.2 trillion in 2010. However, from 2010 to 2015, China's holdings of US Treasuries no longer rose rapidly but remained roughly flat around US$1.2 trillion. In contrast, with US imports from China growing faster than US exports to China, the US trade deficit with China widened from US$226.8 billion in 2009 to US$342.3 billion in 2014. Given that the US trade deficit with China increased from 2009 to 2014 while China's holding of US Treasury bonds remained largely unchanged, this indicates China has been diversifying away from holding US Treasury bonds.

The Chinese government has been making an explicit effort to reduce its vast holdings of US Treasury bonds. A column in a Chinese state newspaper, *People's Daily*, on 20 August 2009 noted China sold US$25.1 billion of US treasury bills in June 2009.

"This has gratified people in China. China is in an urgent need to alter its structure imbalance with its Forex reserves, so that the value of reserve assets could be preserved and increased. The reduction of US treasury bonds also shows that China is seeking to diversity its Forex reserves. Such diversification nevertheless poses a complex topic," declared the Chinese state mouthpiece.

Throughout 2014, China cut its US treasuries holdings by US$49.2 billion, reported *Xinhua*. In late 2014, Chinese Premier Li Keqiang said China would promote the diversification of its foreign exchange reserves beyond US Treasury notes.

Hong Hao, Managing Director of Research at Bank of Communications International, said the sale of yuan-denominated bonds by institutions like the AIIB to fund infrastructure projects in developing nations would see China gradually move away from buying of US treasury bonds.[387] A Bank of America Merrill Lynch report on 16 March 2015 said "One Belt One Road", the Chinese government's vision of creating land and sea transport infrastructure connecting China to Asia, Europe and Middle East, would switch a portion of China's foreign exchange reserves from US Treasuries into emerging markets.

---

[387] Carrie Hong, "China's offshore RMB endgame, Part II: China unbound", *Global Capital*, 24 April 2015.

Despite the Chinese government's intention to diversify away from US Treasury bonds, doing so is not easy. China faces the prospect of a capital loss on its huge holdings of US debt, if US Treasury bond prices fall as a result of a huge sell-off of US Treasuries.

"The real constraint to any Chinese desire to shift significantly out of investing in US Treasuries may actually have more to do with the sheer size of the US Treasury bond market relative to other investments. The reality is that, so long as China continues to accumulate reserves at a pace of around US$400 billion a year, there are few relatively safe investments other than US government bond markets that are deep and liquid enough to absorb a significant portion of such massive inflows," Eswar Prasad, a Cornell University Professor, in his testimony to the US-China Economic and Security Review Commisison (USCC) on 25 February 2010.

The US Treasury market will remain for the foreseeable future the most liquid government security market. The amount of marketable US Treasury securities is huge, with US$8.85 trillion in outstanding bills, notes, and bonds as of the end of 2010.[388] Trading in US Treasury securities averaged US$949.8 billion per day in 2010.[389]

Resolving the economic imbalances between China and the US, which precipitated the global financial crisis, is easier said than done. To do so, China would need to open its capital account, liberalize interest rates, and make the yuan fully convertible, wrote Michael Casey in the *Wall Street Journal* on 8 February 2015.

"Those are changes Beijing wants to implement, but they pose an enormous challenge because introducing them unilaterally would unleash sweeping capital flows and financial volatility, which could provoke a Chinese banking crisis and strip manufacturers of their competitive advantage," wrote Casey. [390]

"China has since allowed the yuan's value to appreciate and the current-account imbalances have narrowed. But the world's second

---

[388] Investinginbonds.com.
[389] Investinginbonds.com.
[390] Michael Casey, *Wall Street Journal*, "China is Key If Dollar Keeps Advancing", 8 February 2015.

largest economy remains unhealthily dependent on manufacturing exports and on an investment cycle that is perpetually being doubled down in search of ever-thinner returns," Casey added.

Nevertheless, China has been making progress towards liberalising its currency. At a press conference in March 2015, an official with the State Administration of Foreign Exchange said market forces had played a bigger role in determining the yuan exchange rate.

In June 2015, Pan Gongsheng, the Vice Governor of the People's Bank of China, said China was close to its goal of allowing the yuan to be exchanged for foreign currency without any limits on the amount — a move that will grant greater flexibility to Chinese investment overseas.[391]

"We are not too far away from the yuan capital account full convertibility," said Pan.

Even US government officials agreed that China had been taking steps towards liberalizing its currency. China has committed to limiting its currency interventions to moves countering damaging swings in exchange rates, US Treasury Secretary Jacob Lew said on 24 June 2015 after high-level talks with top officials visiting from Beijing.

Hence, it can be seen that although China and the US have not completely solved all the imbalances in their economic relations, both nations have made significant progress. However, China's antidote for the crisis, namely the splurging of trillions of yuan to stimulate its economy, has generated a dangerous side effect in a huge increase in debt.

In late 2008, to counter the global financial crisis, the Chinese government launched a 4 trillion yuan stimulus which was invested largely in infrastructure projects like the country's hugely expensive high speed railway. This generated trillions in additional spending, saddling the nation with a huge increase in debts. China's debt surged from 130 percent of GDP in 2008 to 200 percent in 2013.[392]

---

[391] Phoenix Kwong, *South China Morning Post*, "China close to its goal of full yuan convertibility on its capital account", 21 June 2015.

[392] Simon Rabinovitch, *Financial Times*, "The debt dragon: Credit habit proves hard for China to kick", 26 August 2013.

Although the world economy had since recovered from the global financial crisis a few years after it began in 2007, 2013 marked the advent of a new cycle, where global imbalances between the US and China moved to imbalances within China, Charles Dumas, Chairman of Lombard Street Research, a British economic research house, noted. "China was exporting its savings and wasting them in the US. Now, it has been wasting its savings domestically."[393]

If China is able to engineer a jump in household income growth and embark on massive reforms and capital account liberalization, the global economy will be rebalanced, Dumas explained. Failure would trigger global deflation amid an inevitable Chinese credit crisis in the coming years, warned Dumas in 2013.

In a Reuters column on 3 September 2013, Andy Mukherjee addressed the question, "Is China condemned to suffer a Japanese 'lost decade'?"

China's economy in 2013 bore three similarities with Japan in the late 1980s, namely high and rising debt, diminishing export competitiveness and an ageing society, Mukherjee noted. "China can avoid slipping into Japan's deflationary hole, but only if it learns from Tokyo's failure to cleanse its banking system."[394]

In 1989, the total private credit in Japan was about 200 percent of GDP, roughly similar for China in 2013, Mukherjee pointed out.

"What overwhelmed the Japanese economy was property mania. Residential land prices in Tokyo tripled between 1985 and 1988 before collapsing. As much of the speculation had been financed by credit, the financial system froze. However, Japan allowed its banks to hide their problems until 2004, when Prime Minister Junichiro Koizumi finally cleaned them up," Mukherjee wrote.

"China's authorities are in a similar bind: the country's local governments have borrowed between US$2.4 trillion and US$2.9 trillion, largely by pledging increasingly valuable land as collateral.

---

[393] Sid Verma, *Euromoney*, "China sows seeds for next global downturn", 16 October 2013.
[394] Andy Mukherjee, *Reuters*, "The lessons for China from Japan's lost decade", 3 September 2013.

But failing to write down dud loans could clog up the system and impede new investment and growth," Mukherjee warned.

"China has some advantages. For one, it is still developing, while Japan's urbanization was largely complete by the 1980s. City dwellers in modern jobs may be able to support more household debt than rural workers. Similarly, increasing labour productivity will boost growth and gradually make China's debt less burdensome. China's controls on domestic deposit rates and on international capital flows also reduce the chances of a short-term debt crisis. That gives the leadership some breathing room to sort out its problems," Mukherjee wrote on a cheery note.

Therefore, it can be seen that the US and China have made significant effort to put their marriage on a healthier footing, but serious challenges remain. Just as heavy household debt threatens a marriage between husband and wife, the massive Chinese debt poses a risk to the marriage between China and America, as well as the world economy.

In 2009, Ferguson and Schularick had called for China and America to divorce. Yet both China's exports to the US and the US trade deficit with China continued to grow massively after 2009.

After falling between 2008 and 2009 during the financial crisis, US merchandise trade with China grew nearly 50 percent from around US$300 billion in 2009 to nearly US$450 billion in 2014, according to official US data. US merchandise imports from China soared from US$296.4 billion in 2009 to US$466.7 billion in 2014, while US merchandise exports to China surged from US$69.6 billion in 2009 to US$124 billion in 2014, according to official US data. The US trade deficit with China widened from US$226.8 billion in 2009 to US$342.3 billion in 2014.

China was the largest source of US merchandise imports in 2014, at US$467 billion.[395] China's share of total US merchandise imports rose from 8.2 percent in 2000 to 20.7 percent in 2014.[396] This

---

[395] Wayne Morrison, "China-US trade issues", *Congressional Research Service*, 17 March 2015.
[396] Ibid.

meant that despite rising wages in China, the country continued to grab market share from other exporting nations with lower wages.

Take US computer equipment imports for example, which constitute the largest category of US imports from China. In 2000, Japan was the largest foreign supplier of US computer equipment, while China ranked fourth.[397] In 2014, China and Japan switched places; Japan's ranking had fallen to fourth, while China was the largest foreign supplier of computer equipment with market share of 64 percent of US computer equipment imports, a big jump from 12 percent in 2000.[398] While US imports of computer equipment from China skyrocketed by 725.1 percent from 2000 to 2014, the total value of US computer imports worldwide rose only 52.4 percent.[399] Again, China took market share from other exporting nations.

Garments are another example where China continues to gain market share in the US. Even in 2014, China did not lose its crown as the biggest supplier of clothing to the US, a position it had maintained for many years. This was despite Chinese labour costs having become higher than that of other developing countries like Vietnam and Bangladesh.

US imports of cotton trousers from China rose from US$3.05 billion in 2009 to US$3.94 billion in 2013, while US imports of cotton knit shirts from China rose from US$2.5 billion in 2009 to US$3.14 billion in 2013, and US imports of bras from China rose from US$791.51 million in 2009 to US$1.24 billion in 2013, according to official US data.

Despite China's rising labour costs, China continued to gain market share in the US clothing market from lower-cost nations. Textile industrialists said China's well-developed supply chain, efficient logistics and economies of scale from the sheer size of its manufacturing more than compensated for its higher wages compared to other countries. China's share of US imports of cotton trousers rose from 27.6 percent in 2009 to 29.9 percent in 2013,

---

[397] Ibid.
[398] Ibid.
[399] Ibid.

while China's share of US imports of cotton knit shirts rose from 20.5 percent in 2009 to 24.5 percent in 2013, and China's share of US imports of bras rose from 45.3 percent in 2009 to 51.5 percent in 2013, according to official US data.

Thus, it can be seen that even after Ferguson and Schularick called for China and America to divorce in 2009, both nations have become more closely entwined through their growing trade. The interdependency between the two countries has further deepened with the rapid rise of China's investments in the US.

For at least two decades since China's economic liberalisation in the 1980s, investment between the two countries was largely a one-way street, dominated by US investment in China for the latter's cheap costs and fast growing market. That trend has changed into a two-way flow of investment between both nations. Since 2010, Chinese investment in the US has grown by leaps and bounds.

Different organisations give different estimates of Chinese investment in the US, but all paint a picture of its blistering growth. Chinese investment in the US soared from an annual average of less than US$1 billion before 2008 to over US$14 billion in 2013, according to the Rhodium Group, a US consultancy. Official Chinese data say Chinese FDI in the US jumped from US$1.9 billion in 2007 to US$17.1 billion in 2012, while official US data estimated that Chinese FDI in the US jumped nearly tenfold from US$585 million in 2007 to US$5.2 billion in 2012. By 2014, annual Chinese investments in the US exceeded US investments in China on an annual basis, according to Rhodium.

"Chinese FDI into the US will be one of the great economic stories of the next decade," said Mike Margolis, a partner at US law firm Blank Rome.[400]

"There is only one economic game-changer on the horizon for Los Angeles: Chinese investment. Political and business leaders in Los Angeles recognise this and are bending over backwards to make Los Angeles more attractive to Chinese investors," said Margolis, who lived in Los Angeles.

---

[400]Toh Han Shih, *South China Morning Post*, "China's surging investments in US heralds new multinational era", 4 August 2014.

In 2014, the municipal government of Los Angeles approved a US$39 million tax credit for Greenland Group, a Chinese property developer, to support its investment in a real estate project in downtown Los Angeles. Greenland Group acquired the site in Los Angeles in July 2013 with a planned total investment of US$1 billion.[401]

"This is being replicated all over the US, as other areas compete for Chinese capital," Margolis said.

US local governments have been sending delegations to China courting investment. California Governor Jerry Brown, during a visit to China in April 2013, announced US$1.5 billion in Chinese investment in Oakland, and sought investment for a high-speed railway in California.[402] In the same month, several US state governors attended a US-China governors' forum in China.[403] In May 2013, four US mayors from North Carolina and Alabama visited China, and President Xi met Los Angeles Mayor Antonio Villaraigosa during the latter's visit to China."[404]

"On the US side, China has begun to be perceived as not only a top exporter but an important investor with cash and job creation potential," said Mao Tong, a partner at US law firm Squire Sanders.[405]

From 2000 to 2014, Chinese firms spent nearly US$46 billion on new establishments and acquisitions in the US, according to a Rhodium report of May 2015. By the end of 2014, there were 1,583 establishments by Chinese firms in the US, Rhodium estimated. The expansion of Chinese companies in the US has resulted in more than 80,000 Americans on Chinese company payrolls by 2015, up from fewer than 15,000 five years ago, the Rhodium report noted.

"Chinese FDI is only at the initial stage Japanese firms reached in the 1980s, and there is tremendous growth potential for Chinese investment, job creation, and other benefits," the Rhodium report added.

---

[401] Ibid.

[402] Toh Han Shih, *South China Morning Post*, "Distressed US cities look to Chinese cash", 1 August 2013.

[403] Ibid.

[404] Ibid.

[405] Ibid.

If the US continues to be a major recipient of China's booming outward investment, it could receive between US$100 billion and US$200 billion of Chinese investment by 2020, the Rhodium report predicted. This could increase the number of full-time US jobs provided by Chinese employers to somewhere between 200,000 and 400,000 by 2020, the Rhodium report forecasted.

"Greater Chinese FDI marks a new chapter in US-China economic relations: Higher levels of investment mark the beginning of an era of US-China economic engagement that brings a wider array of mutual benefits," the Rhodium report noted.

If Rhodium's prediction of 400,000 US jobs provided by Chinese investments by 2020 turns out to be true, China would catch up with Japan in supporting US jobs. Prior to the 1980s, Japanese companies provided practically no jobs in the US, but by 2015, they employed almost 700,000 Americans, making them important contributors to the economies of many regions in the US, the Rhodium report pointed out.

As Chinese companies and investments account for an increasing number of jobs in US, Chinese influence on elections and politics in the US will grow. As Chinese investors account for more US jobs, US politicians will be increasingly reluctant to bash China in their political speeches or adopt a hawkish stance against China.

"FDI can be a catalyst for greater exports of 'Made in the US' goods and services to China: Growing investment creates important linkages which can help local (US) economies reach the Chinese market with their goods and services. FDI from China can also help to facilitate the export of US services — including entertainment, hospitality, and financial and business services — to Chinese consumers," the Rhodium report explained.

If Chinese investments in the US boost US exports to China, this would reduce the US trade deficit with China, which was one of the causes of the global financial crisis of 2007 and 2008.

For years, China has been supplying much of the shoes, toys, clothes and other manufactured goods to US consumers. By 2015, China's export of manufactured goods to the US was starting to be counterbalanced by the rapidly growing US exports of services to China, especially travel services, according to a USCC report of

2 April 2015. US export of services to China grew 10 percent to around US$41 billion in 2014, faster than the 2.6 percent growth in Chinese export of services to the US, according to official US data. The US trade surplus in services with China rose 14.5 percent year-on-year to US$26.8 billion in 2014, partly offsetting the US trade deficit in goods with China of US$342.6 billion.

"By a wide margin, the top US service export and largest service surplus to China in 2014 was travel, which represented 51 percent of US service exports to China in 2014," the USCC report of 2 April 2015 pointed out.

US exports of travel services to China more than doubled from around US$9 billion in 2010 to US$21 billion in 2014, much faster growth than other services, the USCC report noted. The number of Chinese tourists visiting the US surged 21 percent to 2.19 million in 2014, which was faster than the 7 percent growth rate for all tourists to the US which totaled 75 million, according to official US data.

"That reflects increasing tourism by Chinese to the US," said Edmund Sim, a partner at Appleton Luff, an international law firm.[406] US service export dollars are boosted by Chinese tourists purchasing property in the US, Sim pointed out. "The US property market has been a pretty good investment for them."

Property agents in San Francisco and Los Angeles would fly in groups of Chinese investors, sometimes as many as 50 people in one group, to buy property, Robert Pearce, a Director of Blackfish, a company that markets United States real estate in 2013 explained.[407] The Chinese end up buying property as well as luxury brands like Chanel when visiting the US, he said, adding: "What do mainland Chinese have? Cash."

Chinese buyers accounted for 18 percent of the US$68.2 billion that foreigners spent on homes in the US during the 12 months to the end of March, according to the US National Association of Realtors. That is up from 11 percent in 2011 and 5 percent in 2009.

---

[406] Ibid.
[407] Toh Han Shih, *South China Morning Post*, "Chinese flock to California to acquire real estate", 7 October 2013.

The US faces a massive US$8 trillion infrastructure investment bill, and is courting Chinese investors since many of its own local governments are in financial difficulties, according to a US Chamber of Commerce report of October 2013. Some local US governments are desperate for funds, as exemplified by the City of Detroit, which filed for bankruptcy in July 2013, with an estimated US$20 billion in debt in what was then the largest bankruptcy in the US of an American city.[408]

Despite the thirst for cash by local governments and businesses in the US, Chinese investments could give rise to legal and political challenges, the chamber warned. Given the history of many major Chinese companies being partly owned by the state, the issue of state control might result in US regulatory or political scrutiny of Chinese participation in US projects, the chamber noted. If Chinese SOEs account for a significant share of Chinese investments in the US, it can create anxiety among some quarters in the US that the Chinese government is using SOEs to infiltrate and promote Beijing's agenda in the US. Some Americans have argued that the Chinese government provided benefits and support to Chinese state-owned firms, such as subsidies, that give them an unfair advantage in competing in the US market.

One of the biggest challenges for Chinese businesses is US concern over Chinese commercial and state espionage, the chamber pointed out. "The US intelligence community has characterised Chinese intelligence services as among the most capable and persistent intelligence threats against the US, and the US Department of Justice considers Chinese espionage one of its top priorities."

Margolis put such US fears into historical perspective, saying, "We can hear today the same fears that were voiced 25 years ago about Japanese investment; fears that China is taking over the US economically. These tie into the increasing tension between China and the US in foreign affairs."[409]

---

[408] Monica Davey and Mary Williams Walsh, *New York Times*, "Billions in debt, Detroit tumbles into insolvency", 19 July 2013.

[409] Toh Han Shih, *South China Morning Post*, "China's surging investments in US heralds new multinational era", 4 August 2014.

One wild card that may allay US fears of a rising China is a revolution in energy production that benefits the US. At least for a while, it seemed that the shale oil revolution in the US would give the US an edge over China, but some analysts believed the shale oil revolution would be short-lived.

The shale oil revolution pushed US crude oil production to its highest level in the past four decades at 3.4 billion barrels in 2015 from 2 billion barrels in 2010, according to the US Energy Information Administration (EIA). Thanks to the shale oil revolution, US crude oil exports jumped more than eightfold from 42,000 barrels per day in 2010 to 502,000 barrels per day in November 2014, according to EIA. As a result of the rise in US oil production, US imports of crude oil fell from 3.2 billion barrels in May 2005 to 2.2 billion barrels in December 2014, according to the same agency.

The shale oil revolution in the US arose from advances in hydraulic fracturing, called fracking. This is the process of drilling down into the earth, after which a high-pressure fluid, which is a mixture of water, sand and chemicals, is directed at the rock to release the gas inside. Water, sand and chemicals are injected into the rock at high pressure, allowing the gas to flow out to the head of the oil well. Previously, fracking was considered too expensive as a method to extract oil and gas. Over time, the rise in energy prices, combined with improved technology, has made fracking economically viable.

Thanks partly to fracking, the US current account deficit tumbled to a 14-year low in the fourth quarter of 2013.[410] The shale oil revolution resulted in a decline in US oil imports, which in turn shrank the US current account deficit.[411] As discussed earlier in this chapter, the US account deficit was one of the causes of the global financial crisis in 2008. Thanks to the shale oil revolution, the US started exporting crude oil to China in 2013 for the first time since

---

[410]Lucia Mutikani, *Reuters*, "US current account deficit hits 14–year low", 19 March 2014.
[411]Ibid.

2005, giving Washington increased leverage in Sino-US relations with major implications for the global oil market.[412]

"If US oil exports to China increase, the impact on Sino-US relations will be felt. The biggest impact will be on the global energy market," said Li Xin, an analyst at Masterlink Securities in Shanghai.[413]

As US dependence on oil imports decreased, the importance of the Middle East as an oil producer would diminish, Li predicted.

In December 2012, China overtook the US as the world's biggest net importer of oil, as US oil imports fell, the EIA noted. China's crude oil imports rose from less than 3 million barrels per day in 2006 to slightly over 5 million barrels per day in 2011, according to official Chinese data. China's crude oil imports further rose to 6.2 million barrels per day in 2014.

"China will increase its oil imports in the coming years," said Adrian Loh, an analyst at Daiwa Capital Markets in Singapore.[414]

"China's oil import demand is growing at half a million barrels per day each year. China will increasingly be deeply dependent on the stability of the global oil market," said Mikkal Herberg, a research director at the US-based National Bureau of Asian Research, during his testimony before USCC.

"For China, the room for ramping up oil production is limited. China's reliance on oil will increase unless it can find different energy sources," said Lawrence Lau, an Analyst at Bank of China.[415]

China imported 55 percent of its oil in 2014, nearly half of which came from countries in the Persian Gulf.[416] The single largest source of Chinese crude oil imports was Saudi Arabia. In 2010, China imported 893 thousand barrels of oil per day from the Middle Eastern nation, which accounted for 75 percent of

---

[412]Toh Han Shih, *South China Morning Post*, "US gets upper hand on crude oil", 18 April 2013.

[413]Ibid.

[414]Ibid.

[415]Ibid.

[416]Elly Rostoum, *Foreign Policy Association*, "China reaches the equivalent of peak US energy imports dependence", 14 July 2014.

Saudi Arabia's production.[417] China's reliance on oil in the Persian Gulf has increased with its growing demand for oil. The tricky point is Saudi Arabia has been a long-time ally of the US, which has maintained a strong military and naval presence in that region. This gives the US crucial leverage over China and renders China vulnerable to the US.

However, by late 2015, there were signs that the US shale oil boom might have petered out. By that year, the plunge in oil prices had forced half the country's drilling rigs offline and wiped out thousands of jobs in the US.[418] Deutsche Bank and Goldman Sachs predicted that the strong growth of US oil production would end in 2015, at least temporarily. US oil production decreased by 120,000 barrels per day in September 2015 from the previous month, in the lowest oil output in the past 12 months, according to EIA.

If the shale oil boom turns out to be short-lived, then the US advantage over China will be temporary. Nonetheless, regardless of whether the shale oil boom is short-lived or long lasting, the principle remains that a revolution in energy production can give the US a geostrategic advantage over China, provided it lasts long enough. The converse is true. If China enjoys a long-term shale oil boom or invents some game-changing energy technology, China can reduce its reliance on energy imports and its vulnerability to US military superiority, including US naval dominance of most of the world's waters.

8.2 Military standoff

China's heavy dependence on imports of oil, natural gas, minerals, food and other commodities often requires transportation through seas and oceans dominated by the US navy. The question is, will China's intense reliance on imports increase tensions with the US and even lead to war? After all, Japan's heavy dependence

---

[417]Ibid.

[418]Lynn Doan and Dan Murtaugh, *Bloomberg*, "Shale oil boom could end in May after price collapse", 13 April 2015.

on imports was one of the causes of Japanese aggression in World War II.

China's growing dependence on oil and liquefied natural gas transported through the Indian Ocean, Malacca Straits and South China Sea is a key driver of the Chinese navy's modernisation drive towards "blue water" capabilities, "which is setting off alarm bells across the region and contributing to a regional naval arms race", said Herberg in his testimony to USCC.

The US would probably maintain its overwhelming military superiority over China, especially in terms of its Navy, for a very long time. This alone would deter China from starting a war against the US. China will have to accept the fact that the resources and goods it so badly needs would be shipped through waters policed by the US navy.

In fact, China and the US may be convinced that it is in their mutual interest for the US navy to protect shipments of resources and goods to China. The rationale is China and the US are both part of a common international supply chain, where raw material shipped to China gets processed into manufactured goods, which China in turn exports to the US. For instance, Nike sports shoes and Apple iPhones are manufactured in China for Nike and Apple, which are US companies, and shipped to the US where they are sold to consumers.

The prospect of war between China and the US is also softened by the absence of any competing ideologies that pit the US and China in mutual hostility. This stands in contrast to the tensions during the Cold War between the Soviet Union, with its mission to spread Communism to the world, and the US, who was out to save the Free World.

In December 1953, US President Dwight Eisenhower, in his "Atoms for Peace" speech to the UN in New York, referred to the nuclear tensions between the US and the Soviet Union, "To pause there would be to confirm the hopeless finality of a belief that two atomic colossi are doomed malevolently to eye each other indefinitely across a trembling world."

Eisenhower expressed the hope that the US and Soviet Union need not be locked into perpetual hostility, "So my country's purpose is to help us move out of the dark chamber of horrors into the light."

Fortunately, China and the US during the 21st century are nowhere near the tense face-off between the Soviet Union and the US during the Cold War. Trade and investment between the Soviet Union and the US during the Cold War was minimal compared to the large and growing trade and investment between China and the US during the 21st century.

One might joke that war is unlikely to break out between China and the US, because if it did, American soldiers would have no clothes or boots to wear, since China supplies much of the clothes and shoes worn by Americans. More seriously, will the ever-increasing economic links between the US and China be strong enough to prevent war between them?

Prior to World War I, the major European powers, France, Germany and Britain, were highly economically interdependent among each other, yet the strong economic linkages did not prevent World War I from breaking out, a draft paper issued on 5 February 2011 by two academics at the University of California at San Diego, Erik Gartzke and Yonatan Lupu, pointed out.

Even though war broke out, there is evidence to suggest that economic linkages served an important role in averting conflict prior to World War I, Gartzke and Lupu argued. The beginning of the 20th century saw a series of crises among the interdependent states of Western Europe that nevertheless did not result in war, they point out. World War I actually began among the economically backward, non-interdependent states of Eastern Europe in the Balkans, Gartzke and Lupu wrote. Tight alliances between Western European powers and Eastern European nations then effectively handed the foreign policies of Western powers over to the Eastern European countries which were poorly integrated into the world economy, Gartzke and Lupu added. Economic interdependence between West European powers succeeded in averting war where nations were integrated, but was incapable of forestalling conflict in the Balkans where economic integration had yet to occur, they argued. Once conflict was sparked in the Balkans, economic interdependence could not prevent war from spreading through competing networks of military alliances across Europe, Gartzke and Lupu wrote.

For example, despite the bitter rivalry between Germany and France, the two powers remained at peace for 43 years between the Treaty of Frankfurt in 1871 which ended the Franco-Prussian war in Germany's favour, and the outbreak of the First World War in 1914. During this period, manufacturing and finance became highly integrated between these two countries, trade between the two grew significantly, and unprecedented amounts of capital flowed across their borders.[419] One example is the German financing of iron mining in the French region of Longwy-Briey.[420]

Competition for colonies led to tensions among the European powers during the run-up to the First World War, but nonetheless did not break out in war, Gartzke and Lupu pointed out. For instance, in 1905, the German Kaiser Wilhelm II visited Tangier and gave a speech promoting Moroccan independence, provoking the French authorities.[421] France moved troops to the German border while Germany called up its reservists, but the crisis was resolved.[422]

Ironically, the system of alliances, created to deter aggression and reduce the likelihood of war, was an incentive for the economically interdependent powers to shift foreign policy discretion away from themselves towards the non-interdependent powers, namely Austria-Hungary and Serbia.[423] As war broke out in the Balkans, the Western powers felt the cost of backing down from their alliance commitments outweighed the costs of sacrificing their economic linkages, and so were sucked into the First World War, argued Gartzke and Lupu.

---

[419]Erik Gartzke and Yonatan Lupu, "Economic Interdependence and the First World War", draft paper, 5 February 2011.
[420]Ibid.
[421]Ibid.
[422]Ibid.
[423]Ibid.

During the Cold War, the US and the Soviet Union were both entwined in their separate webs of alliances in Europe, the Middle East and Asia. Any war that flared up in a country allied to either superpower threatened to engulf the world in nuclear war. In the Middle East during the Cold War for example, the Soviet Union backed some Arab states against Israel, which was supported by the US. The situation is more relaxed between the US and China in the 21st century. China in the 21st century is an economic partner of both the Arab nations and Israel. This defuses any potential tension between the US and China over the Middle East.

The US is no longer using the Monroe Doctrine to shut out the growing Chinese economic and even military reach in Latin America. For a long time to come, China would be in no position to militarily threaten Europe, and has no reason to do so, given that Europe is one of China's biggest economic partners. If war ever breaks out between the US and China, which is not very likely, it will be in Asia, at flashpoints such as the South China Sea.

One possible scenario is war flaring up between China and Vietnam or Japan, while the US, tied by alliances to Vietnam and Japan, gets drawn into war with China. Perhaps Beijing might wish to see the US end its military alliance with Japan. However, if the US were to withdraw from the Asia Pacific, the US would no longer be able to deter Japanese military expansionism. Japan has the potential to quickly build up a navy and air force that will be far more powerful than the Chinese navy and air force. Given that Japan's planes and aircraft carriers were a match for the US in World War II, Japan can easily build aircraft carriers and combat aircraft that outclass their Chinese counterparts. It is the US presence in Asia Pacific that prevents the resurgence of Japanese military might after Japan's defeat by the US in World War II. China needs the US in Asia to maintain a balance of power.

Even if war were to break out between the US and China, the probability of the war escalating to a global nuclear war is extremely small. China does not seek to conquer the world, but only wishes to do business with the world. The US and China no longer have any serious ideological differences, and China does not seek to impose Communism on any country. The global economy heavily depends on the harmony in Sino-US relations, so if there are threats of war between China and the US, many countries would exert their utmost in pulling China and the US back from the brink of war. As such, there is very little incentive for the US or China to launch a nuclear war against each other.

In the unlikely event of war between the US and China, the bet is on the US winning, given American technological superiority supported by ongoing innovation, which is the fruit of the American values of freedom and openness. Any war between the US and China is unlikely to be prolonged, and likely to be short and sharp. The US must have learnt its lesson from the Vietnam War, not to get bogged down in another long war in Asia. Americans would not stand for another prolonged war that costs a growing number of American lives as happened in the Vietnam War, and would vote out any US government that executes such a war.

A likely outcome of war between the US and China is the US will not occupy large hinterlands in China, because that would be too costly, but seize strategic coastal cities. This is what Britain did in the Opium War by taking Hong Kong. But if this happens, the Chinese government, Chinese people, and many overseas Chinese including some American Chinese, would feel the sting of defeat with great bitterness, haunted by China's "century of humiliation" from the Opium War till World War II.

The bitterness felt by the Chinese in any defeat by the US would poison Sino-US relations. It is conceivable China and the US would continue to do business even after the US defeats the Chinese, just as China traded with Britain after the Opium War. But the resentment of humiliation would cast a pall over Sino-US relations, which would create uncertainty for the rest of the world, since the global economy already depends so much on China and the US.

Most Asian nations are likely to do their utmost to prevent war breaking out between China and the US in their backyard. A Korean proverb goes, "When whales fight, the shrimps get crushed", while there is a Laotian proverb that says, "When elephants fight, the ants die". Asian nations have a stake in keeping the peace between the US and China, which are both important economic partners.

The rest of the world, including Europe, would not want war between the US and China either, even if the fighting happens far away from Europe in Asia, given that the world depends on the economic symbiosis between its two biggest economies. Much of the world, including Europe, will exert great political influence to prevent any such war from happening. The European powers went to war in both world wars through obligations that resulted from their alliances. The Soviet Union and the US threatened to destroy each other and the rest of the world in a nuclear holocaust, again partly over their alliances with other nations. In contrast, Europe and other countries would use their alliances with the US and China to restrain the two superpowers. Thus, despite tensions and potential flashpoints between the US and China like the South China Sea, the chances of war between the two superpowers are remote.

The relationship between China and US is not one that is purely bilateral, but the concern of the global community. The world has a stake in the health of the Sino-US marriage.

Chapter 9

Anti-Imperialist Pseudo-Empires

In the 21st century, the world is witness to two superpowers that possess some, but not all, of the attributes of empire. The US has been the supreme superpower, economically and militarily, since the end of World War II. China emerged as the new superpower in the early 21st century. Both China and the US deny they are empires and profess to oppose imperialism for different reasons arising from their different histories.

In the 21st century, China partially shares the attributes of the British Empire in the 19th century. China is the biggest manufacturing and trading nation in the 21st century, as the British Empire was in the 19th century. Chinese state-owned companies are building railway, roads, dams, power stations and other infrastructure in Latin America, Africa, Asia and Europe. Similarly, building railways around the world was a feature of British imperialism, albeit the British rail-building was led by the private sector. Chinese private businesses and state-owned firms are actively operating and investing in Africa, Latin America, North America and Asia, just as the European empires did in bygone days. What China and the European empires have in common is the quest for economic benefits in going out beyond their borders.

China has some, but not all, the features of Lenin's definition of an imperialistic power. China has become a net exporter of capital and most likely will continue to export an increasing amount of capital to the rest of the world, through loans, investments and other forms of financing. The scale of Chinese companies, especially SOEs, is so massive that their trade, operations and investments overseas can fairly be said to play a decisive role in the world economy. Chinese banks are expanding their operations around the world, and rising in global influence. Chinese state-owned banks work hand-in-hand with Chinese SOEs to make offers that are hard for developing countries to refuse, which often involve the building of infrastructure projects cheaper and faster than competitors, financed by huge loans on easy terms. In this way, the combination of Chinese banks and Chinese companies play an important role in China's global expansion.

African newspapers have criticised Chinese individuals and companies for bad behaviour, African governments for being too friendly to China and the Chinese government for human rights failings. But on the whole, African newspapers mostly do not see China as an evil empire exploiting and colonising their continent, as shown in Chapter 4. English-language newspapers in only five nations were examined, namely South Africa, Zimbabwe, Namibia, Zambia and Angola, but they are a fairly representative sample due to the diversity of political systems and their importance on the continent. The general verdict of African newspapers is: China is not an empire.

China in the 21st century lacks some essential elements of an empire. Although millions of Chinese have settled in Africa, Latin America, Southeast Asia and North America, they cannot create colonies the way the European empires did. Despite the sizeable presence of ethnic Chinese in Southeast Asia, most Chinese in Southeast Asian countries, especially Singapore which has a Chinese majority population, do not identify themselves as Chinese citizens. Chinese soldiers and settlers did not claim sovereignty in these regions, while European armies and colonists did.

Having a navy capable of projecting power globally is a pre-requisite of a dominant world empire. The British possessed such a navy in the 19th century. The US has had such a navy since the

20th century. For a long time to come, China's navy will be unable to match the US navy. Without sufficient military power, China is unable to impose its institutions, government and will upon other countries, the way the European empires were able to.

In contrast to China, the US projects military power throughout the world, with military bases in places such as Diego Garcia, Okinawa, Kuwait, Guantanamo Bay, Western Europe and Australia. While it is true that the US does not occupy entire nations as the European empires did, and the current international ethos generally would no longer allow it, but European nations started building their empires by establishing bases in coastal cities. These outposts were enough for the European empires to exert their influence over large regions without needing to occupy them. It was only at a later stage, mainly in the late 19th century, that European empires conquered large hinterlands. This was the case with the British empire in India, Malaya and Africa, the French empire in Indochina and the Dutch empire in Indonesia. Nevertheless, the US normally does not invade and occupy large land masses for long periods of time or claim perpetual sovereignty over them, unlike earlier empires. In that respect, the US does not possess all the attributes of an empire.

The US professes that its military bases protect the Free World from aggression. The US justified its invasion of countries like Afghanistan and Iraq by invoking the anti-imperialist themes of fighting aggression and terrorism, defending freedom and protecting other nations. By supporting one nation against other, such as South Vietnam against North Vietnam during the Vietnam War, the US claimed it was supporting the right side in the struggle for freedom. But it is not too dissimilar from earlier European empires which supported one local ruler against a local rival, in a divide and conquer strategy.

However, the global projection of US military power has not always been the case throughout American history. Empires cannot be isolationist, yet the US had episodes of isolationist tendencies in its history, especially during the 1930s.

The Office of the Historian of the US State Department said, "During the 1930s, the combination of the Great Depression and the memory of tragic losses in World War I contributed to pushing American public opinion and policy toward isolationism. Isolationists advocated non-involvement in European and Asian conflicts and non-entanglement in international politics. The leaders of the isolationist movement drew upon history to bolster their position. In his Farewell Address, (the first US) President George Washington had advocated non-involvement in European wars and politics."

It took an enemy to prod the US out of its isolationist shell to fight a war. In World War I, it was the German empire. In World War II, it was the Axis powers of Germany, Japan and Italy. During the Cold War, the Communist bloc led by the Soviet Union provided the justification for the US military umbrella around the world. After the terrorist attacks on US homeland on 11 September 2001, the US invaded Afghanistan and Iraq in the name of fighting terrorism or destroying weapons of mass destruction. An enemy, real or perceived, gives the US rationale for saving the world, thus providing the justification for an American semi-empire that is anti-imperialist. Saving the world is part of the US psyche; just look at the many American superheroes who save the world from some villain in American comics and movies. I recall myself as a little boy growing up in Singapore during the 1970s, reading American comics where the heroes were warned that some forces were out to install a government in a foreign country that is unfriendly to the US. The American heroes would foil this plot and "save" that country.

But China in the 21st century is no villain menacing the world in the mold of Nazi Germany or the Soviet Union. China has become a nominal Communist country and has long shed its mission to spread Communism to other countries. The end of the Cold War meant the end of competing ideologies. China is not an enemy of the US in the conventional sense of the term, but that does not mean there is no military rivalry between the two superpowers. China is free to increase its military strength as much as it wants to and is capable of doing so, because it is not under US restrictions on its armed forces the way Japan is. From the end of World War II in 1945 till 1990, Japan's rapid economic growth enabled it to become both an important economic partner and rival of the US, similar to China's economic relations with the US in the 21st century. But the US has imposed limits on Japan's military since it defeated Japan in World War II, while China, free of such constraints, is building up its military capabilities. In that sense, China possesses more of an important ingredient of empire, military power, compared to Japan. For a long time at least, Chinese military power will increasingly challenge but not overtake US military supremacy.

While there are areas of tension between the US and China such as the South China Sea, the likelihood of war between these two superpowers is low. There are not many resources which the US and China compete over. Rather, China complements the US by importing resources from around the world, process them into manufactured goods which it then exports to the US. In this way, the US has outsourced much of its resource extraction to China. While the US no doubt will feel an increasing challenge posed by a Chinese navy that is modernising, the US navy has a vested interest in ensuring the safe passage of ships carrying resources to China as well as goods made from these resources and exported from China, because the US is the destination of many of these Chinese goods. If the US navy blockaded the shipment of oil and other commodities to China, manufactured products like iPhones will end up costlier in the US. This is an example of the coexistence of competition and cooperation, or as it is sometimes called, "co-opetition".

China both competes and cooperates with the US. China and the US compete for international influence, which is demonstrated by the trips of US and Chinese leaders to Africa and Southeast Asia to win support, as mentioned earlier in this book. China competes with the US in influence over the South China Sea, and more generally, in military build-up. China is building up its blue-water naval capabilities and increasing its overall military capabilities. The US, as the world's greatest military power, must not feel comfortable with China trying to catch up with the US militarily. While there are tensions and competition between these two superpowers militarily and geopolitically, there is also cooperation. The visit of Chinese Foreign Minister Wang Yi to Washington DC in February 2016, where he held talks with US Secretary of State John Kerry, serves as an example that encapsulates competition and cooperation in Sino-US relations.

As a CNN article by Nicole Gaouette and Elise Labott on 24 February 2016 states, "The back-and-forth between Kerry and Chinese Foreign Minister Wang Yi reflected the awkward dance of competition and cooperation between the United States and China. The world's two largest economies work together on issues like Iran's nuclear program, the civil war in Syria and climate change, even as they clash over cybertheft, North Korea's nuclear ambitions, missile defense in South Korea and how to handle contested stretches of ocean in Asia."[424]

"We can cooperate in areas where our interests and values are aligned despite the fact that we have differences," Kerry said, while Wang said the US and China "should make the cake or the pie of our common interests bigger."

Wang said the US and China had a "complicated and diversified relationship".[425]

Economically, there is also much cooperation between both countries. As discussed in the previous chapter, economic ties between the world's two biggest economies are only growing stronger. The US and China are among the biggest trading partners of each other. Since China opened up its economy in the 1980s, the US has been one of the major investors in China, with many leading US multinationals like GE, Microsoft and IBM having a substantial presence in China. Chinese investments in the US have been growing rapidly. As mentioned in the last chapter, Chinese investment in the US soared from an annual average of less than US$1 billion before 2008 to over US$14 billion in 2013, according to the Rhodium Group. In just the first two months of 2016, Chinese companies spent at least US$23 billion acquiring US companies, 15 percent more than the US$20.5 billion spent in the whole of 2015, according to Dealogic.

---

[424]Nicole Gaouette and Elise Labott, *CNN*, "South China Sea, North Korea tensions at issue in Kerry-Wang meeting", 24 February 2016. http://edition.cnn.com/2016/02/23/politics/u-s-china-kerry-wang/.
[425]Ibid.

If there was perfect harmony in Sino-US relations, the US and China will form a combined economic powerhouse that will dominate the world. In such a scenario, there will be a new global order of peace and stability under the hegemony of Chimerica, which can be called "Pax Chimerica", just as Pax Romana was a period of peace within the Roman Empire from 27 BC to 180 AD, Pax Britannica was the period from 1815 to 1914, when the British Empire dominated the world's oceans and global trade, and Pax Americana since the end of World War II saw no more world wars, only localised wars. However, the prospect of Pax Chimerica is unlikely to be realised, given the military rivalry between the two superpowers and areas of tensions like the South China Sea.

With so much cooperation between the two superpowers and a significant amount of competition, any conflict between the US and China, if it arises, will not be similar to a confrontation between two cowboys in a Western, facing each other with hands ready to grab their nuclear pistols. A confrontation between two "nuclear cowboys" is an apt description of tensions between the US and the Soviet Union during the Cold War, when nuclear war threatened to engulf the world if Soviet forces just crossed the border from Eastern Europe to Western Europe. Nor will Sino-US relations be like knights in heavy armour clashing the hard steel of their weapons against each other. Sino-US relations is not a contest in hard power. Rather, it is more like "Push Hands", the ancient Chinese martial art based on Taoist philosophy, embodying both conflict and cooperation in soft tension between two players.

In "Push Hands", two players face each other with each player's arms in light contact with the other's arms. Each player moves his or her arms, waist and legs in a circular pattern, while trying to remain in balance.

There is both competition and cooperation in "Push Hands". The competitive aim is to push or pull your opponent out of balance. A player who is pushed or pulled off balance will stumble out of position. But this does not involve using brute force to throw off the other player or grabbing the other player, let alone punching or kicking your opponent.

"Push Hands" involves maintaining light contact with an opponent, while sensing the magnitude and direction of an opponent's force and yielding or responding to an opponent's force partially by giving way, and partially by controlling or guiding the opponent's direction.[426] The goal is to reduce the amount of force needed to neutralise attacks, so that one may defeat speed and strength with skill.[427]

The aim of "Push Hands" is to feel your opponent's energy, intention and movements. You redirect and borrow your opponent's strength to your advantage. To do this you must harmonise with your opponent until both of you fuse into one.[428] Herein lies the element of cooperation, as both players move harmoniously together in a circle. China and America are locked by economic interdependency into Chimerica, a form that is two yet one, moving harmoniously together in a circle.

"Push Hands" embodies the Taoist philosophy of the power of softness and fluidity, like water. The Chinese sage Lao Zi, the founder of Taoism, said, "Water is fluid, soft, and yielding. But water will wear away rock, which is rigid and cannot yield. As a rule, whatever is fluid, soft, and yielding will overcome whatever is rigid and hard. This is another paradox: what is soft is strong."

The late Hong Kong gung fu (martial arts) star Bruce Lee agreed, "I got mad at myself and punched the water! Hadn't this water illustrated to me the principle of gung fu? I struck it but it did not suffer hurt. Again I struck it with all my might — yet it was not wounded! I then tried to grasp a handful of it but this proved impossible. This water, the softest substance in the world, only seemed weak. In reality, it could penetrate the hardest substance in the world."[429]

Like water, China's trade and investments are penetrating the US in ways that Soviet missiles and tanks never could during the Cold War. Beijing can adopt an apparently passive posture in military and political terms, and just let Chinese trade and investment do their work according to market forces, weaving economic webs

---

[426] https://ckchutaichi.com/advanced_training/push_hands/.
[427] https://ckchutaichi.com/advanced_training/push_hands/.
[428] http://www.taichido.com/chi/styles/push.htm.
[429] Bruce Lee, *Artist of Life*, Tuttle Publishing, 1999.

with other countries. This is Wu Wei, another form of soft power in Taoist philosophy. In the Taoist text *Dao De Jing*, Lao Zi described Wu Wei as "do nothing and there is nothing left undone."

The concept of Wu Wei should not be taken literally to mean being totally passive and doing absolutely nothing. Nothing could be further from the truth. The Sage waits in inaction; only when the time is right, does he act.[430] To the uninitiated, it looks like the Sage is doing nothing, then suddenly things are done.[431] This is because he does not do anything unnatural, but follows the natural law; he follows Tao.[432] The Tao of action is to act when action is needed.[433]

China's foreign policy of non-interference in other nations' affairs is a manifestation of Wu Wei. This is in contrast to the US, which has charged around the world in the name of fighting aggression, Communism or terrorism, having fought in Vietnam, Iraq and Afghanistan.

China's policy of non-interference enabled it to be friends and economic partners of both Israel and Arab states, who have had a history of hostile relations with each other. Chinese investments in Israel exceeded US$2 billion in 2015,[434] while Chinese state companies have built a light rail system in Mecca, Saudi Arabia, to transport Muslim pilgrims. In late January 2016, Xi visited Egypt, Saudi Arabia and Iran, where he witnessed deals signed between the companies of these three states and China, while a few days later on 2 February 2016, the first ever Chinese-Israeli private equity fund was announced. The US$200 million Catalyst CEL Fund was a partnership between Catalyst Private Equity, an Israeli investment firm, and China Everbright, a Hong Kong-based subsidiary of a Chinese state-owned firm, China Everbright Group.[435]

---

[430] Ibid.
[431] Ibid.
[432] Ibid.
[433] Ibid.
[434] Hayley Slier, *Channelnewsasia*, "Chinese firms making major investments in Israel", 14 July 2015.
[435] Tova Cohen, *Reuters*, "Israel-China private equity fund raises over $200 million", 2 February 2016.

China's policy of non-interference allows it to be a mediator between two factions which distrust each other. For example, during the G20 summit in Brisbane, Australia in November 2014, US President Obama and UK Prime Minister Cameron snubbed Russian President Vladimir Putin due to differences over Ukraine. However, Chinese President Xi got along comfortably with both sides.

China's apparent lack of ideology means its overtures in the world will not polarise nations into those that support its ideology and those that oppose it. Nations of any political stripe can accept and deal with China. In contrast, during the 1950s, US State Secretary John Foster Dulles, a fierce, scowling anti-Communist, adopted the position that nations were either for the US or the Soviet bloc. Southeast Asian nations are not amenable to Dulles' approach, they generally prefer to have harmonious relations with both China and the US. Given China's ability to build ties with all kinds of countries, it can be argued that China's policy of non-interference is a form of soft power.

Soft power is not unique to Taoist philosophy. Both modern China and the US subscribe to the notion of soft power. Building China's soft power was repeatedly emphasised by Hu Jintao when he was Chinese president from November 2002 to November 2012.[436] In the US, Joseph Nye of Harvard University developed the concept of soft power as the ability to attract others to do your will, without resorting to hard power to coerce them or economic power to benefit or bribe them.

Soft power is essential in ensuring the longevity of an empire. The Mongols used hard power to conquer China and establish the Yuan Dynasty, but this dynasty lasted only 97 years. In contrast, the Tang Dynasty lasted 289 years. Tang Taizong, the second emperor of the Tang Dynasty, was supposed to have said, "I won the empire on horseback, but I cannot rule the empire on horseback." Tang Taizong realized he had to rely not only on the army,

---

[436]Toh Han Shih, *South China Morning Post*, "Experts differ on China's soft power in Africa", 22 July 2013.

but also on an administration of scholar-gentlemen to govern his empire. The empires of two great conquerors, Genghis Khan and Alexander the Great, broke up shortly after their deaths. In contrast, the Roman Empire lasted five centuries, because it possessed the rule of law and a durable political system. If the Chinese pseudo-empire wishes to endure, it must nurture its soft power.

China stumbled when it tried to project soft power in a clumsy manner by pushing an overt ideology like its Confucian Institutes around the world. In 2014, the Toronto District School Board in Canada ended a planned partnership with China's government-funded Confucius Institute. The move follows similar cancellations in the US. In 2014, the University of Chicago said that it had suspended negotiations for the renewal of the agreement for a second term of the Confucius Institute at the University of Chicago.

Confucian Institutes have also been set up in Africa. Bjorn Harald Nordtveit, Associate Professor at the University of Massachusetts in Amherst, said, "One Hollywood blockbuster is probably more influential than a lot of Confucius Institutes. More Africans talk about Hollywood movies than Confucius Institutes."[437]

Hollywood is only one of the many advantages the US enjoys in soft power. US pop music and US brands like Apple and Coke are popular throughout the world. English is the lingua franca of the world, spoken far more than any Chinese language or dialect. US soft power is manifest in its ability to constantly attract talent from all over the world, including China, to study, research and create world-class companies like Google. The US culture of openness, freedom and innovation enables it to possess the world's most advanced military technology and thus maintain its position as the dominant military power.

"French soft power is bigger than China in francophone countries in Africa. France's relation with French-speaking African countries like Senegal is intimate. China is trying to make inroads in French-speaking countries in Africa, but it's hard for China,"

---

[437] Ibid.

said Jean-Pierre Cabestan, Head of Government and International Studies at Hong Kong Baptist University.[438]

In film, literature and music, Africans remain more attracted to Western countries, Cabestan said.

Martyn Davies said, "China has minimal soft power in Africa, mostly due to the fact that its companies in Africa do not possess such soft power in their businesses or brands."[439]

China does not possess soft power in Africa, argued Chamorro, "Soft power is about cultural attraction. China has economic power."[440]

Like China in the 21st century and the British Empire in the 19th century, the US wields enormous economic power. Adding to the US economic clout is the status of the US dollar as the world's reserve currency. The status of the US dollar as the global reserve currency is underpinned by the trust the world places in the US currency. This is an example of soft power, the ability to maintain international trust, which boosts US economic power.

China has a long way to go before its currency can rival, let alone displace, the US dollar as the dominant global reserve currency, wrote Eswar Prasad, a Professor at Cornell University.[441]

"China is missing one crucial ingredient: the world's trust. To achieve currency dominance, China needs more than economic and military might; it requires a broader and more credible set of public and political institutions. And it is here that the US shines — at least relatively speaking," wrote Prasad, who was also a senior fellow at the Brookings Institution.

This was apparent in the aftermath of the global financial crisis in 2008, Prasad pointed out. "Even though America's financial markets nearly collapsed, its public debt levels rose sharply, and the dollar strengthened relative to most other currencies. That is because global investors seeking a safe haven automatically turn to US Treasury securities in times of global financial turmoil."

---

[438] Ibid.
[439] Ibid.
[440] Ibid.
[441] Eswar Prasad, "The dollar is still king", *Project Syndicate*, 14 May 2014.

"Trust in US public institutions is rooted in the open and transparent democratic process that underpins them. Freedom of expression and unfettered media bolster this confidence. The US legal system — independent from the executive and legislative branches of government — further supports the dollar's global role," he wrote.

This contrast with China's single-party system, where the level of government accountability is much lower, Prasad argued.

How can China acquire the advantages in soft power that the US enjoys? Hong Kong, a former colony of the British Empire which returned to China, can help. The British Empire bequeathed to Hong Kong the rule of law and freedom of expression. Hong Kong can pass on these two forms of soft power, rule of law and freedom of expression, to its mother country. Just as Hong Kong entrepreneurs helped develop China's economy after China opened up to the outside world in the 1980s, Hong Kong can help China gain international trust by developing the rule of law.

Hong Kong can help China grow another form of soft power, democracy. When he was China's leader, Deng Xiaoping created Special Economic Zones like Shenzhen to experiment with economic liberalisation, and then Hong Kong investors flocked to Shenzhen to build factories and businesses. This paved the way for economic liberalisation throughout the whole of China. Likewise, Beijing can use Hong Kong as a Special Democratic Zone to introduce democracy and experiment with it. The Chinese government can see what works and what does not work with democracy in Hong Kong, adapt the best practices and implement it throughout China.

Hong Kong's role in the economic reform of China and possible future role in the political reform of China has parallels with the roles played by Amsterdam in the Dutch Empire and London in the British Empire.

During the 17th century, Amsterdam was a hub of financial innovation developing new instruments of financing, which enabled Holland to fund its wars and build up the Dutch Empire, said Ferguson in his book, *The Ascent of Money*. Financial innovation spread from Amsterdam to London, so that by the mid-18th century,

London had a thriving bond market that was more sophisticated than other financial centres of the day, wrote Ferguson. London's financial innovation enabled financing of the British Empire, while the Spanish Empire suffered financial difficulties.[442] Just as financial innovation in Amsterdam and London bankrolled the Dutch and British empires, respectively, Hong Kong's open and international financial market is funding China's overseas economic expansion. In future, innovation in democracy, freedom and the rule of law in Hong Kong can strengthen China's soft power in the world.

So we see that Sino-US relations involve not only rivalry in hard power, but also competition in soft power. China and the US have different forms of soft power. The US arsenal of soft power includes its openness, creativity and the international trust in its currency. China's soft power includes its neutral policy of non-interference in other countries.

In this game of hard power and soft power, how should the US and the rest of the world handle a rising China? To anticipate China's moves, the US and the rest of the world should understand what makes the Chinese government tick. An overriding obsession of the Chinese leadership is maintaining social stability among its population of over one billion. The Chinese psyche is haunted by the Middle Kingdom's long history of rebellion that toppled dynasties. The Chinese leaders' priority is to minimise as much as possible any restive tendencies in the world's most populous nation. This is a prime driver of Beijing's decisions on whether to be nice or nasty to the US or Japan, whether to act aggressively over the South China Sea or be reconciliatory, whether to open its economy to foreign investors or make it more restrictive, whether to increase China's imports or engage in trade wars.

In Chinese history, poverty drove peasants to rise up in rebellion and overthrow the emperor, so an important factor in ensuring social stability is to reduce poverty. World Bank figures show that more than 600 million Chinese have been taken out of poverty

---

[442] Ferguson, Niall, *The Ascent of Money: A Financial History of the World*, Penguin Books, 2009.

since China's economic reform in the 1980s. This is part of the Chinese government's agenda to ensure social stability among its huge population.

Just as China is the world's biggest exporter of goods, it can export poverty reduction to the rest of the world.

"China invested in agriculture to reduce poverty and successful agricultural projects were built up from the grass roots. These were not top-down solutions. The Chinese government and World Food Programme selected the successful agricultural projects and implemented them throughout the nation. Think of the soft power China would gain if it focused this ability and exported it," said Brett Rierson, China representative for the World Food Programme.[443]

"It helps China have a positive image across all strata of society, not just the top leadership [in these countries]. To protect China's interests and those of Chinese citizens abroad, it's in China's interest to invest in soft infrastructure in developing countries," Rierson said.

In May 2005, Beijing, the United Nations Development Programme and other international organisations jointly established the International Poverty Reduction Centre in Beijing. The centre provides information and international collaboration on poverty reduction.

In November 2012, the World Bank and China launched an online knowledge hub to spread knowledge of China's successes in reducing poverty both at home and in other countries, according to the World Bank website.

Commenting on the launch of this knowledge hub, World Bank Group President Jim Yong-kim said, "China has lifted 600 million people out of poverty in the last 30 years. Demand is growing among other developing countries to learn from this remarkable progress. The knowledge hub will play an important role in making China's lessons available to the world and further our common mission to end extreme poverty."

---

[443]Toh Han Shih, *South China Morning Post*, "China's formula to reduce poverty could help developing nations," 29 March 2013.

"The world has seen a dramatic decrease in global poverty from 2005 to 2011 and this is to continue till 2015," wrote Laurence Chandy and Geoffrey Gertz in a paper for the Brookings Institution, a US think tank.

The number of poor people globally fell from over 1.3 billion in 2005 to under 900 million in 2010, wrote Chandy and Gertz. "Poverty reduction of this magnitude is unparalleled in history. Never before have so many people been lifted out of poverty over such a brief period of time."[444]

China cannot impose its poverty reduction programmes on other countries, but must respect their independence and sovereignty. China's successful track record of poverty reduction cannot be a one-size-fits all solution uniformly applied to all countries, given the different histories and circumstances of various nations. Nevertheless, China's achievement in poverty reduction can be a form of soft power to attract other countries to learn from China and adapt it to their own circumstances.

China and the US can work together to reduce poverty around the world. One optimist on the prospect of global poverty reduction is Bill Gates, the billionaire founder of US software giant Microsoft.

"I am optimistic enough about this that I am willing to make a prediction. By 2035, there will be almost no poor countries left in the world. Almost all countries will be what we now call lower-middle income or richer. Billions of people will have been lifted out of extreme poverty," said Gates, one of the world's richest men, in 2015.[445]

The Bill and Melinda Gates Foundation, founded by Gates and his wife Melinda, is expected to give away most of Gates' fortune of around US$67 billion. The foundation's Global Development

---

[444]Laurence Chandy and Geoffrey Gertz, Brookings Institution, "Poverty in Numbers: The Changing State of Global Poverty from 2005 to 2015", January 2011.
[445]Adam Withnall, *The Independent*, "No poor countries by 2035: Bill Gates annual letter says extreme poverty and child mortality could be virtually wiped out in next two decades", 21 January 2014.

Division aims to identify and fund solutions that can help people lift themselves out of poverty.

The foundation's annual letter in 2015 stated, "We can make fighting poverty a priority. We think the next 15 years will see major breakthroughs for most people in poor countries. They will be living longer and in better health. They will have unprecedented opportunities to get an education, eat nutritious food, and benefit from mobile banking. These breakthroughs will be driven by innovation in technology — ranging from new vaccines and hardier crops to much cheaper smartphones and tablets — and by innovations that help deliver those things to more people."

US President John Kennedy, in his inaugural address on 20 January 1961, said, "For man holds in his mortal hands the power to abolish all forms of human poverty and all forms of human life."

"To those nations who would make themselves our adversary, we offer not a pledge but a request: that both sides begin anew the quest for peace, before the dark powers of destruction unleashed by science engulf all humanity in planned or accidental self-destruction."

"Let both sides explore what problems unite us instead of belabouring those problems which divide us. Now the trumpet summons us again, not as a call to bear arms, not as a call to battle, but a call to bear the burden of a long twilight struggle, a struggle against the common enemies of man: tyranny, poverty, disease and war itself. Can we forge against these enemies a grand and global alliance, North and South, East and West, that can assure a more fruitful life for all mankind?"

Hopefully, China and the US will take up Kennedy's challenge. Eradicating global poverty can be an enduring legacy of China and the US, which are empires, yet not empires.

Bibliography

Absher, Kenneth Michael, *Mind-Sets and Missiles: A First Hand Account of the Cuban Missile Crisis* (Strategic Studies Institute, US Army War College, 2009).

All Africa Global Media, "South Africa: Hu Jintao pays Zuma courtesy call", 26 March 2012.

Amazon Watch, "Amazon in Focus", Fall 2014.

Amer, Ramses, "Vietnam's relations with China — a multifaceted partnership", *China Policy Institute Blog, Nottingham University*, 17 March 2014.

An Dien, *Thanh Nien News*, "Vietnam party official heads to China to defuse tensions", 25 August 2014.

Asia Pacific Foundation of Canada report, "China goes global 2013", November 2013.

Associated Press, "China overtakes US to become world's biggest oil importer", 10 October 2013.

Baker & McKenzie report, "Chinese investment into Europe hits record high in 2014", 11 February 2015.

Bassett, D.K., "The 'Amboyna Massacre' of 1623", *Journal of Southeast Asian History*, Volume 1, Number 2, September 1960.

Bearak, Barry, *New York Times*, "Zambia drops case of shooting by Chinese mine bosses", 4 April 2011.

Bloomberg, "China eclipses US as biggest trading nation", 13 February 2013.

Buncombe, Andrew, *The Independent*, "Aung San Suu Kyi urges support for controversial Chinese-backed copper mine", 13 March 2013.

Calkins, Jonathan, "Banking abroad: the globalization of Chinese banks", *CKGSB Knowl*edge, 28 March 2013.

Cargill, Tom, Chatham House Report "Our common strategic interests: Africa's role in the post-G8 world", June 2010.

Casey, Michael, *Wall Street Journal*, "China Is Key If Dollar Keeps Advance", 8 February 2015.

Centre for Chinese Studies, University of Stellenbosch, prepared for the Rockefeller Foundation, "China's Engagement of Africa: Preliminary Scoping of African Case Studies", November 2007.

Chandy, Laurence and Geoffrey Gertz, Brookings Institution, "Poverty in Numbers: The Changing State of Global Poverty from 2005 to 2015", January 2011.

Chang, Rachel, *The Straits Times*, "ST Global Outlook Forum: 'China is already a superpower'", 2 December 2013.

Channel NewsAsia, "Boycott Olympics at a cost: MM", 9 May 2008.

Chen, George, *South China Morning Post*, "US and China both have roles to play: Suu Kyi", 28 January 2013.

Chen, George, *South China Morning Post*, "China Development Bank grabs chance for aggressive global loan expansion", 13 March 2013.

China Daily, "Is this young Kenyan Chinese descendant?", 11 July 2005.

China Post, "Taiwan-Singapore ties rely on trust, wisdom to endure", 10 March 2012.

Chow, Jermyn, *The Straits Times*, "Singapore and China agree to expand military relations", 14 November 2014.

Cohen, Tova, *Reuters*, "Israel-China private equity fund raises over $200 million", 2 February 2016.

Craughwell, Thomas, *The Rise and Fall of the Second Largest Empire in History: How Genghis Khan's Mongols Almost Conquered the World*, Fair Winds Press, 2010.

Darwin, John, *Unfinished Empire*, Allen Lane, 2012.

Davey, Monica and Mary Williams Walsh, *New York Times*, "Billions in debt, Detroit tumbles into insolvency", 19 July 2013.

Davies, Penny, *Diakonia and the European Network on Debt and Development*, "China and the end of poverty in Africa — Towards mutual benefit?", August 2007.

Doan, Lynn and Dan Murtaugh, *Bloomberg*, "Shale oil boom could end in May after price collapse", 13 April 2015.

Doerner, Christiane, *Atlantic-Community.org*, "Colonialism reloaded: China is conquering Namibia", 9 January 2009.

Dugger, Celia W., *New York Times*, "Angola's New Constitution Consolidates President's Power", 21 January 2010.

Dyer, Geoff, *Financial Times*, "Beijing's elevated aspirations", 10 November 2010.

Dyer, Geoff, Jamil Anderlini and Henny Sender, *Financial Times*, "China's lending hits new heights", 17 January 2011.

Eccles, Louise, *The Daily Mail*, "Chinese buyers fuelling UK housing shortage: Far East speculators price Britons out of market across the country", 4 April 2014.

EIA, *Eurasia Review*, "Angola Energy Profile: Second largest oil producer in Sub-Saharan Africa behind Nigeria — Analysis", 4 January 2013.

England, Andrew, *Financial Times*, "Sata gives Chinese investors guarded welcome", 26 September 2011.

Farge, Emma, *Reuters*, "Sinopec's Addax loses court ruling on Gabon oil license-document", 13 September 2013.

Ferguson, Niall, *Empire: How Britain made the modern world*, Penguin Books, 2004.

Ferguson, Niall and Moritz Schularick, "'Chimerica' and the global asset market boom", *International Finance*, Volume 10, Issue 3, 2007.

Ferguson, Niall, *The Ascent of Money: A Financial History of the World*, Penguin Books, 2009.

Ferguson, Niall, *Colossus: The Rise and Fall of the American Empire*, 2009.

Ferguson, Niall and Moritz Schularick, Harvard Business School Working Paper, "The End of Chimerica", October 2009.

Fravel, M. Taylor, "China's Strategy in the South China Sea", *Contemporary Southeast Asia*, Volume 33 Issue 3, 1 December 2011.

Gallagher, Kevin P., *Berkeley Review of Latin American Studies*, "China discovers Latin America", Fall 2010.

Gallaher, Kevin P., Amos Irwin, Katherine Koleski, *Inter-Amerian Dialogue Paper*, "The New Banks in Town: Chinese Finance in Latin America", March 2012.

Gaouette, Nicole and Elise Labott, *CNN*, "South China Sea, North Korea tensions at issue in Kerry-Wang meeting", 24 February 2016, http://edition.cnn.com/2016/02/23/politics/u-s-china-kerry-wang/.

Gartzke, Erik and Yonatan Lupu, "Economic Interdependence and the First World War", draft paper, 5 February 2011.

Goodspeed, Peter, *National Post*, "Tenant protests expose Chinese corruption: millionaire developer probed over loans", 1 November 2003.

Heng Pheakday, *East Asia Forum*, "Chinese investment and aid in Cambodia a controversial affair", 16 July 2013.

Ho Binh Minh and Manuel Mogato, *Reuters*, "Vietnam mobs set fire to foreign factories in anti-China riots", 14 May 2014.

Hobsbawm, Eric, *Industry and Empire: The Birth of the Industrial Revolution*, The New Press, 1999.

Hong, Carrie, "China's offshore RMB endgame, Part II: China unbound", *Global Capital*, 24 April 2015.

Howe, Marc, "South African report highlights labor abuses in the Sub-Sahara", Mining.com, 9 November 2012.

Huang, Cary, *South China Morning Post*, "China-led Asian bank challenges US dominance of global economy", 11 April 2015.

IBISWorld Industry Report, "Global Footwear Manufacturing", 4 May 2010.

IMF, *World Economic Outlook*, "Tensions from the two-speed recovery: unemployment, commodities, and capital flows", April 2011.

Independent Online Zimbabwe, "Mugabe's former ally accuses him of foul play", 12 March 2005.

Ingram, Derek, "Commonwealth update", *The Round Table*, volume 367, page 585–611.

International Oil Daily, "Sinopec's Addax cuts deal in Gabon, ends dispute", 20 January 2014.

Ip, Saimond, "Hong Kong and Pearl River Delta: the Road Ahead", *ACCA Annual Conference*, March 2003.

Johnson, Tim, *McClatchy DC*, "Financing still a mystery as Nicaragua unveils details of giant canal", 9 July 2014.

Kennedy, Paul, *The Rise and Fall of the Great Powers*, Vintage, 1989.

KPMG *Quarterly China Report*, third quarter 2014.

Kristine Kwok and Zuraidah Ibrahim, *South China Morning Post*, "Beijing rejects Hanoi's legal challenge on Spratly, Paracel islands disputes", 13 December 2014.

Kwong, Phoenix, *South China Morning Post*, "China close to its goal of full yuan convertibility on its capital account", 21 June 2015.

Lahrichi, Kamilla, *Asia Sentinel*, "China's growing military sway in Latin America", 4 August 2014.

Lan Lan, *China Daily USA*, "China takes 10% of global rail market", 6 February 2015.

Lee, Bruce, *Artist of Life*, Tuttle Publishing, 1999.

Lee Kuan Yew, *From Third World to First: The Singapore Story: 1965–2000*, HarperCollins, 2000.

Legum, Colin, "The Soviet Union, China and the West in Southern Africa", *Foreign Affairs*, July 1976.

Lenin, Vi.I., *Imperialism: The Highest Stage of Capitalism*, Penguin Books, 2010.

Li Anshan, *A history of Overseas Chinese in Africa to 1911*, Diasporic Africa Press, 2012.

Li Xiaojun, "China as a trading superpower" in Nicholas Kitchen (editor), "China's Geoeconomic Stratecy", *LSE IDEAS Special Report*, 2012.

Lister, Gwen, *The Namibian 25th Anniversary Commemoration Magazine*, 27 August 2010.

Lister, Tim, *CNN*, "Sex and espionage: a long and sordid history", 18 April 2012, http://security.blogs.cnn.com/2012/04/18/sex-and-espionage-a-long-and-sordid-history/.

Marcella, Gabriel, "China's military activity in Latin America", *American Quarterly*, Winter 2012.

Miner, Sean, "China's current account in 2014", *Peterson Institute for International Economics*, 8 February 2015.

Mitchell, Tom and Shawn Donnan, *Financial Times*, "China currency is 'no longer undervalued', says IMF", 26 May 2015.

Morrison, Wayne, "China-US trade issues", Congressional Research Service, 17 March 2015.

Movement for Democratic Change report, "Stolen — How the elections were rigged", 12 April 2005.

Moyo, Rebecca, *The Zimbabwean*, "China and Zimbabwe trade doubled", 8 May 2012.

Muekalia, D.J., "Africa and China's strategic partnership", *African Security Review*, 13(1), pages 5–11, 2004.

Mukherjee, Andy, *Reuters*, "The lessons for China from Japan's lost decade", 3 September 2013.

Mutikani, Lucia, *Reuters*, "US current account deficit hits 14-year low", 19 March 2014.

Mwanangombe, Lewis, *Associated Press*, "China's footprint grows in Zambia", 1 November 2013.

Nathan Andrew and Robert S. Ross, *The Great Wall and the Empty Fortress: China's search for security*, W.W. Norton, 1998.

Ng, Joel, "Great Power Rivalry in Africa: Economic Engagement Holds Key", *Reliefweb*, 14 August 2012.

Office of the Historian, US Department of State, https://history.state.gov.

Parker, George and Jamil Anderlini, *Financial Times*, "Britain's red-carpet welcome for Xi baffles traditional allies", 18 October 2015.

Parks, Ken, *Wall Street Journal*, "Argentina-China deals reflect Asian country's growing influence", 20 July 2014.

People's Daily, "Children of the Master Voyager?", 3 November 2006.

People's Daily, "China ranks Zimbabwe's top investor: senior official", 24 April 2007.

Petty, Martin and Colin Packham, *Reuters*, "Vietnam protests China missile deployment, Australia, NZ urge restraint", 19 February 2016.

Prasad, Eswar, "The dollar is still king", *Project Syndicate*, 14 May 2014.

Quinn, Andrew and Chris Buckley, *Reuters*, "China warns US not to take sides in sea disputes as Clinton flies in", 4 September 2012.

Quinn, Frederick, *The French Overseas Empire*, Praeger, 2001.

Rabinovitch, Simon, *Financial Times*, "The debt dragon: Credit habit proves hard for China to kick", 26 August 2013.

Ramzy, Austin, *Time*, "A Step Back From the Brink in the South China Sea", 12 October 2011.

Rocha, Euan, *Reuters*, "CNOOC closes $15.1 billion acquisition of Canada's Nexen", 25 February 2013.

Rostoum, Elly, *Foreign Policy Association*, "China reaches the equivalent of peak US energy imports dependence", 14 July 2014.

Rothe, Andreas, *Media system and news selection in Namibia*, Lit. Verlag Munster, page 29 to 32, 2011.

Russell-Wood, A.J.R., *The Portuguese Empire 1415–1808: A World on the Move*, The Johns Hopkins University Press, 1998.

Slier, Hayley, *Channel NewsAsia* "Chinese firms making major investments in Israel", 14 July 2015.

Socialist Worker, "US violence for a century: Nicaragua: 1912–1933".

Stearns, Scott, *Voice of America*, "Clinton discusses investment, debt in Cambodia", 13 July 2012.

Stiglitz, Joseph, *MarketWatch*, "America's childish opposition to Asian infrastructure bank", 13 April 2015.

Tarling, Nicholas, *Anglo-Dutch Rivalry in the Malay World 1780–1824*, Cambridge University Press/University of Queensland Press, 1962.

Thayer, Carl, *The Diplomat*, "China and Vietnam Eschew Megaphone Diplomacy", 2 January 2015.

The Guardian, "Zambian miners kill Chinese supervisor and injure another in pay dispute", 5 August 2012.

The Hindu, "India, Myanmar to double bilateral trade to $3 billion", 27 September 2011.

The Nation, "South China Sea disputes: Clinton urges ASEAN to be united", 5 September 2012.

The New Paper, "S'pore China troops in first land war drill", 10 November 2014.

TNA: PRO FCO 15/1909, 18 June 1974, "Record of conversation between Mr Lee Kuan Yew Prime Minister of Singapore and the Minister of State and the Parliamentary Under Secretary of State at the Foreign and Commonwealth Office on 18 June at 10.15 am".

Toh Han Shih, *South China Morning Post*, "Sino-US trade marriage bound to end in tears", 21 March 2006.

Toh Han Shih, *South China Morning Post*, "Chinese loans go a long way in Africa", 20 July 2009.

Toh Han Shih, *South China Morning Post*, "China's massive rail building mirrors Britain's push", 2 January 2010.

Toh Han Shih, *South China Morning Post*, "Rail woes persist despite spending", 29 January 2010.

Toh Han Shih, *South China Morning Post*, "Costs and political sensitivities hit hopes of a pan-Asia rail link", 22 March 2010.

Toh Han Shih, *South China Morning Post*, "Ethiopia dam blot on China's record", 7 June 2010.

Toh Han Shih, *South China Morning Post*, "Africa looks to China as Western influence fades", 28 June 2010.

Toh Han Shih, *South China Morning Post*, "African conflicts pressure China's neutrality", 3 August 2010.

Toh Han Shih, *South China Morning Post*, "Joint pipeline with junta sparks rights debate", 9 August 2010.

Toh Han Shih, *South China Morning Post*, "Guangxi in major push for regional trade", 21 August 2010.

Toh Han Shih, *South China Morning Post*, "China's uphill battle to invest in Myanmar", 3 January 2011.

Toh Han Shih, *South China Morning Post*, "CRCC limits Mecca rail losses to 1.38 b yuan", 24 January 2011.

Toh Han Shih, *South China Morning Post*, "China's investment makes big imprint on Portuguese world", 31 January 2011.

Toh Han Shih, *South China Morning Post*, "Boom for contractors despite quality concerns", 13 July 2011.

Toh Han Shih, *South China Morning Post*, "Controversial Chinese projects in Cambodia bow to pressure", 3 September 2011.

Toh Han Shih, *South China Morning Post*, "China ties may be curse in disguise", 26 September 2011.

Toh Han Shih, *South China Morning Post*, "Dam postponement seen as rebuke to Beijing", 10 October 2011.

Toh Han Shih, *South China Morning Post*, "Yunnan, the new gateway", 19 November 2011.

Toh Han Shih, *South China Morning Post*, "China treads lightly to improve image in Africa", 28 January 2012.

Toh Han Shih and Jennifer Cheng, *South China Morning Post*, "China in Africa, no worse than others", 25 April 2012.

Toh Han Shih, *South China Morning Post*, "'Not everyone's a winner' in Africa's ties with China", 31 July 2012.

Toh Han Shih, *South China Morning Post*, "HK advisor 'gave US$100m to Mugabe secret police'", 5 August 2012.

Toh Han Shih, *South China Morning Post*, "Cambodian miner Khmer Resources plans to tap Hong Kong market", 18 January 2013.

Toh Han Shih, *South China Morning Post*, "China's formula to reduce poverty could help developing nations", 29 March 2013.

Toh Han Shih, *South China Morning Post*, "Rubbery numbers still add up to big role in Africa", 29 March 2013.

Toh Han Shih, *South China Morning Post*, "China Railway project in Venezuela hits snag", 11 April 2013.

Toh Han Shih, *South China Morning Post*, "US gets upper hand on crude oil", 18 April 2013.

Toh Han Shih, *South China Morning Post*, "China to remain influential in Myanmar even as Western firms arrive", 13 May 2013.

Toh Han Shih, *South China Morning Post*, "African leaders prefer China's hard cash to US overtures", 18 July 2013.

Toh Han Shih, *South China Morning Post*, "Vietnam shuns China's high-speed express", 19 July 2010.

Toh Han Shih, *South China Morning Post*, "Experts differ on China's 'soft power' in Africa", 22 July 2013.

Toh Han Shih, *South China Morning Post*, "Mexico offers China US$300b in infrastructure deals", 11 September 2013.

Toh Han Shih, *South China Morning Post*, "China faces tougher deals in Africa", 7 October 2013.

Toh Han Shih, *South China Morning Post*, "Three Gorges and EDP to pour US$2b into Africa", 15 November 2013.

Toh Han Shih, *South China Morning Post*, "China to provide Africa with US$1tr financing", 18 November 2013.

Toh Han Shih, *South China Morning Post*, "Chinese dam builders rush to Latin America", 6 January 2014.

Toh Han Shih, *South China Morning Post*, "South Sudan civil war still no deterrent to Chinese firms", 20 January 2014.

Toh Han Shih, *South China Morning Post*, "China's trade with Latin America set to outpace the EU within two years", 17 March 2014.

Toh Han Shih, *South China Morning Post*, "China's rivals catching up in investment race in Myanmar investment race", 21 July 2014.

Toh Han Shih, *South China Morning Post*, "China's surging investments in US heralds new multinational era", 4 August 2014.

Toh Han Shih, *South China Morning Post*, "Beijing seen as lifeline to Latin American economies", 20 November 2014.

Toh Han Shih, *South China Morning Post*, "Overseas investments raise key China questions", 17 December 2014.

Tomlinson, Peta, *South China Morning Post*, "More Asians buying into dream of owning property in France", 26 September 2012.

Torode, Greg, *South China Morning Post*, "US-China ties in troubled waters", 7 June 2010.

Torode, Greg, *South China Morning Post*, "US navy returns to Cam Ranh Bay", 27 August 2011.

Trotman, Andrew, *Daily Telegraph*, "Argentina files legal proceedings with UN against Obama government", 7 August 2014.

Verma, Sid, *Euromoney*, "China sows seeds for next global downturn", 16 October 2013.

Vu Truong-minh and Nguyen Thanh Trung, "A US-China Alliance or (still) a US-China-Vietnam Triangle?", *International Policy Digest*, 3 October 2014.

Vukelich, D., "A disaster foretold", *The Advocacy Project*.

Withnall, Adam, *Independent*, "No poor countries by 2035: Bill Gates annual letter says extreme poverty and child mortality could be virtually wiped out in next two decades", 21 January 2014.

Woodrow Wilson International Centre for Scholars, Institute of the Americas, Chinese Academy of Social Sciences, "China, Latin America and the United States: The New Triangle", January 2011.

Xinhua, "35,860 Chinese evacuated from unrest-torn Libya", 3 March 2011.

Xinhua, "Roundup, Cambodian PM's visit aims to enhance ties with China", 3 September 2012.

Yang Kaisheng, *Caixin*, "Do China's big banks enjoy a monopoly", 6 March 2014.

Yu Ning, Huang Kaixi, Yang Yanwen, *Caixin*, "Businessman linked to Sinopec's Angola deals said to face probe", 14 October 2015.

Zhang, Ed and Toh Han Shih, *South China Morning Post*, "China pays for risky African ventures", 25 January 2011.

Zhang Pinghui, *South China Morning Post*, "Trade with Africa will double by 2020, Li Keqiang tells Ethiopia conference", 6 May 2014.

Zhao Shengnan and Wang Chenyan, *China Daily*, "PLA diplomacy to ease tensions", 4 September 2012.

About the Author

Toh Han Shih (H.S. Toh) is a Singapore citizen who was born in Singapore. For most of his working career, he was a business journalist. In Singapore, he worked for a local newspaper, *The Business Times*, covering the dotcom boom and bust from 1995 to 2000. He has been living in Hong Kong since September 2003. In Hong Kong, he previously worked as a business reporter for the *South China Morning Post* for 10 years. It was during his stint at the *South China Morning Post*, reporting on Chinese overseas investments and trade, that the idea to write this book was conceived.

Printed in the United States
By Bookmasters